Date: 1/16/13

746.434 CHA
Chachula, Robyn,
Crochet stitches visual
encyclopedia /

Crochet Stitches

Stitches

VISUAL™

ENCYCLOPEDIA

In Memory of
David F. Kefauver

Crochet Stitches

VISUAL™ ENCYCLOPEDIA

300 Stitch Patterns, Edgings, and More

Robyn Chachula

WILEY

John Wiley & Sons, Inc.

Crochet Stitches VISUAL™ Encyclopedia

Copyright © 2011 by John Wiley & Sons, Inc., Hoboken, New Jersey. All rights reserved.

Published by John Wiley & Sons, Inc., Hoboken, New Jersey

No part of this publication may be reproduced, stored in a retrieval system or transmitted in any form or by any means, electronic, mechanical, photocopying, recording, scanning or otherwise, except as permitted under Sections 107 or 108 of the 1976 United States Copyright Act, without either the prior written permission of the Publisher, or authorization through payment of the appropriate per-copy fee to the Copyright Clearance Center, 222 Rosewood Drive, Danvers, MA 01923, (978) 750-8400, fax (978) 646-8600, or on the web at www.copyright.com. Requests to the Publisher for permission should be addressed to the Permissions Department, John Wiley & Sons, Inc., 111 River Street, Hoboken, NJ 07030, (201) 748-6011, fax (201) 748-6008, or online at http://www.wiley.com/go/permissions.

Wiley, the Wiley logo, Teach Yourself VISUALLY, and related trademarks are trademarks or registered trademarks of John Wiley & Sons, Inc. and/or its affiliates. All other trademarks are the property of their respective owners. John Wiley & Sons, Inc. is not associated with any product or vendor mentioned in this book.

The publisher and the author make no representations or warranties with respect to the accuracy or completeness of the contents of this work and specifically disclaim all warranties, including without limitation warranties of fitness for a particular purpose. No warranty may be created or extended by sales or promotional materials. The advice and strategies contained herein may not be suitable for every situation. This work is sold with the understanding that the publisher is not engaged in rendering legal, accounting, or other professional services. If professional assistance is required, the services of a competent professional person should be sought. Neither the publisher nor the author shall be liable for damages arising here from. The fact that an organization or Website is referred to in this work as a citation and/or a potential source of further information does not mean that the author or the publisher endorses the information the organization or Website may provide or recommendations it may make. Further, readers should be aware that Internet Websites listed in this work may have changed or disappeared between when this work was written and when it is read.

For general information on our other products and services or to obtain technical support please contact our Customer Care Department within the U.S. at (877) 762-2974, outside the U.S. at (317) 572-3993 or fax (317) 572-4002.

Wiley also publishes its books in a variety of electronic formats and by print-on-demand. Not all content that is available in standard print versions of this book may appear or be packaged in all book formats. If you have purchased a version of this book that did not include media that is referenced by or accompanies a standard print version, you may request this media by visiting http://booksupport.wiley.com. For more information about Wiley products, visit us www.wiley.com.

Library of Congress Control Number: 2011935817
ISBN: 978-1-118-03005-9 (cloth)
ISBN: 978-1-118-18317-5; 978-1-118-18316-8; 978-1-118-17165-3 (ebk)

Printed in the United States of America

10 9 8 7 6 5 4 3 2

Book production by John Wiley & Sons, Inc. Composition Services

Credits

Acquisitions Editor
Pam Mourouzis

Senior Project Editor
Donna Wright

Copy Editor
Marylouise Wiack

Technical Editor
Julie Holetz

Editorial Manager
Christina Stambaugh

Vice President and Publisher
Cindy Kitchel

Vice President and Executive Publisher
Kathy Nebenhaus

Interior Design
Jennifer Mayberry

Photography
Matt Bowen

Special Thanks...

The yarns used in the book were all graciously donated by the following yarn companies. Thank you so much for all your support and quick response to all my requests, I truly appreciate all that you have given me. They are

- Blue Sky Alpaca (Alpaca Silk)
- Cascade Yarns (Cascade 220 Sport and Pima Tencel)
- Lion Brand (Cottonease)
- Caron International (Country)
- Coats and Clark (Soft Yarn and Eco-ways).

Each yarn chosen highlights either the technique perfectly with amazing stitch definition or makes the color pop off the page with their wonderful color schemes.

About the Author

Robyn Chachula (Pittsburgh, PA) is a crochet designer with a background in structural engineering. Whether she is building a concrete building or a granny square blanket, her approach to designing them is the same: She takes a big project and breaks it down into little items that she can understand, then pieces them back together for the big picture. In her book *Blueprint Crochet: Modern Designs for the Visual Crocheter*, she used her engineering background and crochet symbols to bring crochet to new learners. Its follow-up, *Baby Blueprint Crochet*, marries more challenging stitch diagrams with a modern take on baby projects. Her patterns in *Mission Falls Goes Crochet* are for the whole family. Fans can catch her as one of the crochet experts on *Knit and Crochet Now* on PBS, or on her blog, Crochet by Faye (www.crochetbyfaye.blogspot.com).

Acknowledgments

This book gave me so much pleasure in diving into, researching, and testing all aspects of crochet; I want to thank all the creative designers who have come before me to inspire and challenge my own designs.

Crocheting all the swatches in the book was a pure joy, but I had to share the fun to get the book finished. I had the fantastic help from my wonderful friends and contract crocheters, Diane Halpern, Rebecca DeSensi, Megan Granholm, Virginia Boundy, Amy Maceyko, and Susan Jeffers.

Thank you to everyone at Wiley, especially Donna Wright, Pam Mourouzis, and Marylouise Wiack for making the ramblings of a sleep deprived mom sound intelligent. A special thank you to Julie Holetz, our technical crochet editor, for re-reading and counting every stitch in the book over and over with me.

Most importantly, I would like to thank my friends and family for all their love and support in every crazy challenge I take on. Your joy to jump in and help entertain the baby while I squirreled away on the book I cannot thank you enough. I would especially like to thank my husband, Mark, for his unwavering love. Without his encouragement and help, this book would not have been possible.

Lastly, I want to thank you. Thank you for enjoying what I love to do so much. Your enthusiasm of crochet is what keeps me energized to share my kooky designs, so thank you very much!

Table of Contents

CHAPTER 1 Simple Stitch Patterns 1

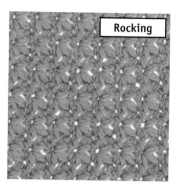

Rocking

Table of Contents

CHAPTER 2   Textured Stitch Patterns   18

Olivia Cable

CHAPTER 3   Lace Stitch Patterns   50

Iris Shell

CHAPTER 4 Unique Lace Stitch Patterns 88

Raya Clover

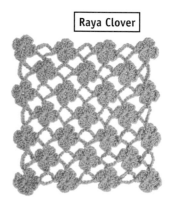

Table of Contents

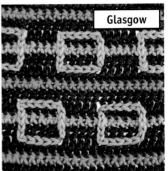

Glasgow

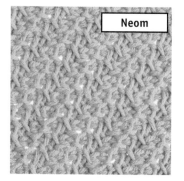

Neom

Sachem Blossom

Table of Contents

CHAPTER 8   Flower, Snowflake, and Joining Motifs   203

Lorena Motif

CHAPTER 9 Edgings 247

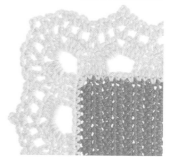

Mystic Edging

Appendix: Glossary 268

Introduction

As an art form and a craft, crochet spans centuries and countries around the world. In this book, I tried to pay homage to that fact. Inside you will find patterns that date from Victorian lacework, 1960s retro granny squares, and modern interpretations of crochet. The stitches span the globe from the United States to the Ukraine to Japan to South America and more. I wanted to compile and touch on as many forms of this unique craft as I could. You will find patterns that look deceptively like knitting, but in actuality are simply slip stitch crochet, and the patterns might look deceptively challenging—like the mosaic colorwork pattern—but in actuality are simply stripes of color. You will also find motifs that range from the classic granny square to gothic window inspired hexagons. In the Tunisian chapter, you can explore my favorite part of the technique, which is the woven-like fabric it can create.

Using my tips and tricks to make your work look sensational, I hope this book will jump-start your creativity in crochet. You can mix and match any of the edgings with any of the stitch patterns for unique scarves or blankets, or try new-to-you methods of joining motifs and granny squares for exceptional shawls and afghans. How about testing out complex cables as borders on your next cardigan?

Crochet Symbol Basics

Every stitch pattern in this book has a helpful diagram associated with it. With a few tips, these diagrams can become your best guide to successful crocheting. The key to understanding crochet symbols is that each symbol represents a crochet stitch. (For a list of crochet symbols, see page 270.) I like to think of them as little stick diagrams of the actual stitch because crochet symbols try to mimic the actual stitch as close as possible. The best thing about the symbols is they are used internationally. Once you master them, you can use the symbols in any crochet book from Russia to Japan.

Stitches

First let's look at the smallest stitch, the chain. The symbol is an oval. Why an oval? Well, think about making a chain stitch: It's a loop pulled through another loop that looks a lot like interlocking ovals. Next is the slip stitch, which is a filled dot. It is little and almost invisible, just like the actual stitch. The single crochet is a squat cross, again just like the stitch. The half double crochet is slightly taller than the single crochet. The double crochet is taller than the half double and has an extra cross in its middle. From the double crochet up, the little cross tells you how many yarn overs you have before you insert your hook. Go ahead, make a double crochet. Now look at your stitch: Do you see the little cross in the middle of the stitch? That's why the double crochet symbol has that bar in the middle of its post. The rest of the symbols fall in line with the same reasoning. If the stitch is short, the symbol will be short; if the stitch puffs out, the symbol will as well.

Diagrams

As previously mentioned, every pattern in the book has a stitch diagram alongside the written directions. This is to help guide you in the pattern and make it easier to see where the stitches will be created.

Granny Squares

To read granny square diagrams, you start in the center just as you would to crochet. Following the symbol key, crochet the stitches you see. The numbers on the diagram let you know where the beginning of each round is so you can keep track of where you are. Granny square diagrams feature each round in a new color so it's easy to keep track of what round you are on.

Stitch Pattern

Stitch pattern diagrams are not much different than granny square diagrams. The key difference is that instead of crocheting in the round, you crochet back and forth in turned rows. Therefore, when reading the diagram, you start at the bottom foundation chain. The diagrams in this book have a gray section that indicates the stitch pattern repeat. To start crocheting, make as many chains as the diagram shows. To do so, crochet a multiple of the number of chains in the gray highlighted area plus the ones not included in the shading. Then, following the symbol key, crochet the stitches you see for the first row. At the end of the row, turn, and continue crocheting the stitches you see for the following rows. The numbers on the diagram let you know where the beginning of each row is so you can keep track of where you are. Each diagram uses a new color for each row so it's easy to keep track of what row you are on.

CHAPTER 1

Simple Stitch Patterns

Slip Stitch

The smallest of all the stitches, this dense fabric makes great kitchen scrubbies with cotton yarn.

Ch any number of sts.

Row 1 (RS): Sl st in 1st ch from hk and ea ch across, turn.

Row 2: Sl st in ea sl st across, turn.

Rep row 2 to desired length.

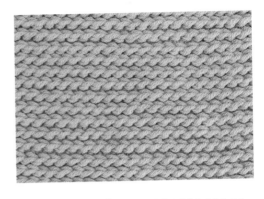

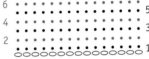

> **TIP**
>
> When crocheting slip stitch patterns, use a hook that is two to three times larger than recommended on the ball band of the yarn. Slip stitches tend to tighten up over time, so using a larger hook helps to guarantee that your swatch does not become smaller as you work.

Front Loop Slip Stitch

This simple pattern makes a thin fabric that is great for hats.

Ch any number of sts.

Row 1 (RS): Sl st in 1st ch from hk and ea ch across, turn.

Row 2: Sl st flp in ea sl st across, turn.

Rep row 2 to desired length.

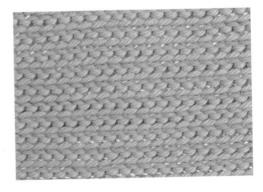

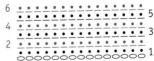

Back Loop Slip Stitch

Looking for a ribbing that very closely matches knitting? This pattern is for you.

Ch any number of sts.

Row 1 (RS): Sl st in 1st ch from hk and ea ch across, turn.

Row 2: Sl st blp in ea sl st across, turn.

Rep row 2 to desired length.

Purl Slip Stitch

This pattern can easily pass for purl stitches in knitting.

Ch any number of sts.

Row 1 (RS): Sl st in 1st ch from hk and ea ch across, turn.

Row 2: Sl st blp in ea sl st across, turn.

Row 3: Sl st flp in ea sl st across, turn.

Rep rows 2 and 3 to desired length.

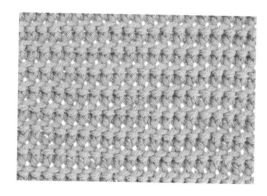

Single Crochet

The fattest of all the stitches, single crochet comes in handy for any project, from sweaters to toys.

Ch any number of sts.

Row 1 (RS): Sc in 2nd ch from hk and ea ch across, turn.

Row 2: Ch 1, sc in ea sc across, turn.

Rep row 2 to desired length.

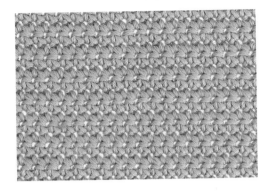

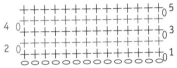

Foundation Single Crochet

This is a great way to start projects if your crochet chains are always too tight. It creates the chain and first row of single crochet at the same time.

Ch 2, insert hk in 2nd ch from hk, pull up lp, yo, draw through 1 lp (the "ch"), yo, draw through 2 lps (the "sc"), *insert hk under 2 lps of the "ch" st of last st and pull up lp, yo, and draw through 1 lp, yo and draw through 2 lps; rep from * for length of foundation.

Single Crochet Ribbing

This ribbing is faster to crochet than slip stitch ribbing, with the same amount of elasticity.

Ch any number of sts.

Row 1 (RS): Sc in 2nd ch from hk and ea ch across, turn.

Row 2: Ch 1, sc blp in ea sc across, turn.

Rep row 2 to desired length.

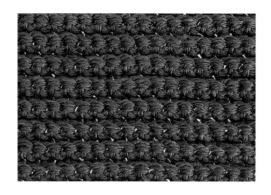

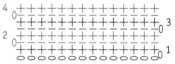

To join the ribbing to sweater cuffs or a collar, join the yarn to the edge of the sweater with a slip stitch. Crochet the desired number of chains and complete row 1. At the end of the row, slip stitch twice to the edge of the sweater—once to join the ribbing to the sweater, and a second time as a turning chain. Do not chain 1 and complete row 2. Continue around the sweater with slip stitch to the sweater edge every other row.

Alternating Single Crochet Spike

This fabric makes very warm vests for men and kids.

Single Crochet Spike (sc spike): Insert hk into st 1 row below, pull up lp, yo, and pull through all lps on hk.

Ch an even number of sts.

Row 1 (RS): Sc in 2nd ch from hk and ea ch across, turn.

Row 2: Ch 1, sc in 1st sc, *sc spike over next sc into ch below, sc in next sc; rep from * across, turn.

Row 3: Ch 1, sc in 1st 2 sc, *sc spike over next sc, sc in next sc; rep from * across to last sc, sc in last sc, turn.

Row 4: Ch 1, sc in 1st sc, *sc spike over next sc, sc in next sc; rep from * across, turn.

Rep rows 3 and 4 to desired length.

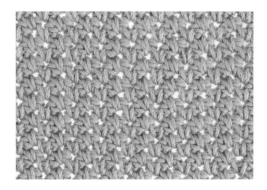

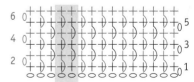

Tweed

This simple stitch pattern can transform itself into tweed when you crochet each row in a different color.

Ch an even number of sts.

Row 1 (RS): Sc in 2nd ch from hk, *ch 1, sk next ch, sc in next ch; rep from * across, turn.

Row 2: Ch 1, sc in 1st sc, sc in next ch-1 sp, *ch 1, sk next sc, sc in next ch-1 sp; rep from * across to last sc, sc in last sc, turn.

Row 3: Ch 1, sc in 1st sc, *ch 1, sk next sc, sc in next ch-1 sp; rep from * across to last 2 sts, ch 1, sk next sc, sc in last sc, turn.

Rep rows 2 and 3 to desired length.

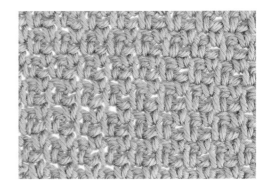

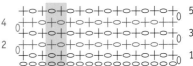

Angled

This lightweight pattern is perfect for cardigans and skirts that need to move.

Ch a multiple of 3 sts.

Row 1 (RS): Sc in 2nd ch from hk, ch 3, sc in next ch, sk next ch, *sc in next ch, ch 3, sc in next ch, sk next ch; rep from * across, turn.

Row 2: Ch 1, (sc, ch 3, sc) in ea ch-3 sp across, turn.

Rep row 2 to desired length.

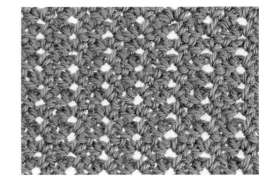

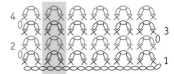

Rocking

A mix of lace and texture makes this simple pattern great for baby blankets.

Ch an even number of sts.

Row 1 (RS): Sc2tog over 2nd and 3rd ch from hk, *ch 1, sc3tog over prev ch and next 2 ch; rep from * across to last 2 ch, ch 1, sc2tog over prev ch and last ch, turn.

Row 2: Ch 1, sc2tog over 1st sc and next ch-1 sp, *ch 1, sc3tog over prev ch-1 sp and next sc and ch-1 sp; rep from * across to last ch-1 sp, ch 1, sc2tog over prev ch-1 sp and last sc, turn.

Rep row 2 to desired length.

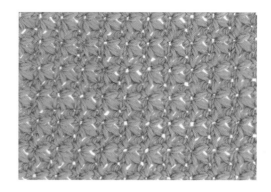

Extended Single Crochet

This very thin fabric works well for all types of projects, from socks to gloves.

Extended single crochet (esc): Insert hk into next st, yo and pull up a lp, yo, draw through 1 lp on hk, yo, and draw through rem 2 lps on hk.

Ch any number of sts.

Row 1 (RS): Esc in 3rd ch from hk (sk ch counts as esc) and ea ch across, turn.

Row 2: Ch 2 (counts as esc), esc in ea esc across to t-ch, esc in top of t-ch, turn.

Rep row 2 to desired length.

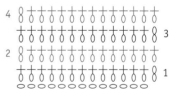

Extended Mesh

Extended stitch sits slightly angled, and when combined with classic mesh, it makes a drapey fabric that is great for lots of projects.

Ch an odd number of sts.

Row 1 (RS): Esc in 5th ch from hk (counts as esc, ch-1 sp), *ch 1, sk 1 ch, esc in next ch; rep from * across, turn.

Row 2: Ch 3 (counts as esc, ch-1 sp), *sk next ch-1 sp, esc in next esc, ch 1; rep from * across to t-ch, esc in top of t-ch, turn.

Rep row 2 to desired length.

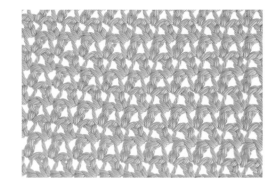

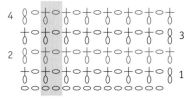

HALF DOUBLE CROCHET PATTERNS

Half Double Crochet

Being short and thick, half double crochet stitches can be the black sheep of the crochet family, but they are unique in the way they wrap yarn overs around the post. They form the basis for a number of amazing stitch patterns.

Ch any number of sts.

Row 1 (RS): Hdc in 3rd ch from hk (sk ch counts as hdc), hdc in ea ch across, turn.

Row 2: Ch 2 (counts as hdc), hdc in ea hdc across, turn.

Rep row 2 to desired length.

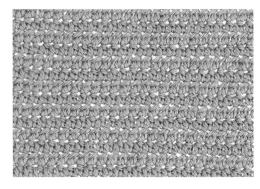

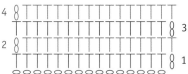

Waffle Rib

A very textured stitch pattern makes for a great fabric for warm, snuggly sweaters.

Ch an even number of sts.

Row 1 (RS): Hdc in 3rd ch from hk (sk ch counts as hdc), hdc in ea ch across, turn.

Row 2: Ch 2 (counts as hdc), *hdc blp in next hdc, hdc flp in next hdc; rep from * across to last 2 sts, hdc blp in next hdc, hdc in top of t-ch, turn.

Rep row 2 to desired length.

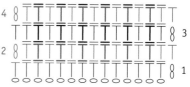

Middle Bar Half Double Crochet

Crocheting in the middle bar makes a great fabric with a defined horizontal line.

Middle Bar: Insert hk into middle of wrong side of the hdc st that is formed by the yo in the hdc st. The middle bar is below the top 2 lps.

Ch any number of sts.

Row 1 (RS): Hdc in 3rd ch from hk (sk ch counts as hdc), hdc in ea ch across, turn.

Row 2: Ch 2 (counts as hdc), hdc in middle bar of ea hdc across to t-ch, hdc in top of t-ch, turn.

Row 3: Ch 2 (counts as hdc), hdc in ea hdc across to last t-ch, hdc in top of t-ch, turn.

Rep rows 2 and 3 to desired length.

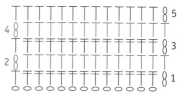

You can crochet in the middle bar of any stitch taller than half double crochet. A nice variation of this pattern is to single crochet in the middle bar of the half double crochet in row 2. Doing so shortens the distance between the horizontal lines.

Forked Half Double Crochet

Crocheting in the middle bar makes a great fabric with a defined horizontal line.

Forked Half Double Crochet (fk hdc): Yo hk, insert hk into next st indicated, pull up lp, yo hk, insert hk into next st indicated, pull up lp, yo hk, pull through 3 lps on hk, yo hk, pull through last 3 lps on hk.

Ch any number of sts.

Row 1 (RS): Fk hdc in 3rd and 4th ch from hk (sk ch counts as dc), fk hdc in prev and next ch across to last ch, dc in last ch, turn.

Row 2: Ch 3 (counts as dc), fk hdc in 3rd ch and next hdc, fk hdc in prev and next hdc across to t-ch, dc in top of t-ch, turn.

Rep row 2 to desired length.

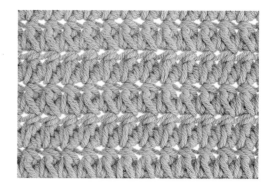

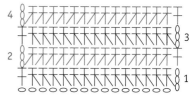

DOUBLE CROCHET PATTERNS

Double Crochet

The double crochet is the most useful stitch in a crocheter's toolbox. It can make thin fabric and when combined with other stitches can form an infinite number of patterns.

Ch any number of sts.

Row 1 (RS): Dc in 4th ch from hk (sk ch counts as dc), dc in ea ch across, turn.

Row 2: Ch 3 (counts as dc), dc in ea dc across to t-ch, dc in top of t-ch, turn.

Rep row 2 to desired length.

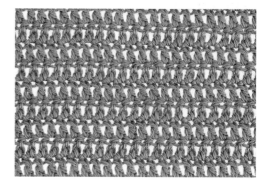

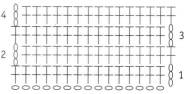

Foundation Double Crochet

Foundation double crochet is perfect to use when your project needs an elastic foundation.

Ch 4 sts.

Yo, insert hk into 4th ch from hk, pull up lp, yo, draw through 1 lp (the "ch"), [yo, draw through 2 lps] twice (the "dc").

Yo, insert hk under 2 lps of the "ch" portion of last st and pull up lp, yo, and draw through 1 lp, [yo and draw through 2 lps] twice.

Rep for desired length.

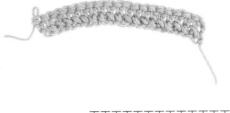

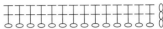

Herringbone Double Crochet

This is a fun stitch that puts a new twist on a classic just by slightly changing how you pull off the loops.

Herringbone Double Crochet (herr dc): Yo hk, insert hk into next st indicated, yo, pull through st and 1st lp on hk, yo, pull through 1 lp on hk, yo, pull through last 2 lps on hk.

Ch any number of sts.

Row 1: Herr dc in 4th ch from hk and ea ch across, turn.

Row 2: Ch 3 (counts as herr dc), herr dc in ea dc across, turn.

Rep row 2 for desired length.

Double Crochet Group

By grouping double crochet stitches, you end up with an interesting vertical stitch pattern that looks more than just simple.

Ch an odd number of sts.

Row 1 (RS): Dc in 5th ch from hk (sk ch counts as dc), dc in same ch, *sk 1 ch, 2 dc in next ch; rep from * across to last 2 ch, sk 1 ch, dc in last ch, turn.

Row 2: Ch 3 (counts as dc), 2 dc btw next 2 dc group across, dc in top of t-ch, turn.

Rep row 2 to desired length.

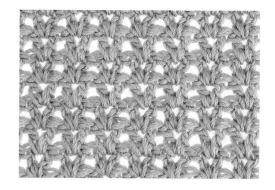

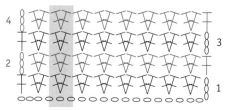

Diamond Tweed

This tweed stitch pattern forms tiny little diamonds all over the fabric for a lacy effect.

Ch an odd number of sts.

Row 1 (RS): Dc in 4th ch from hk (sk ch counts as dc2tog), ch 1, *dc2tog in prev ch and ch 2 away (skipping 1 ch), ch 1; rep from * across to last ch, dc2tog in prev and last ch, turn.

Row 2: Ch 3 (counts as dc), *dc2tog in prev and next dc2tog (sk ch-sp), ch 1; rep from * across to t-ch, dc2tog in prev dc2tog and top of t-ch, dc in top of t-ch, turn.

Row 3: Ch 2, dc in 1st dc2tog, *ch 1, dc2tog in prev and next dc2tog (sk ch-sp); rep from * across to t-ch, ch 1, dc2tog in prev dc2tog and top of t-ch, turn.

Rep rows 2 and 3 to desired length.

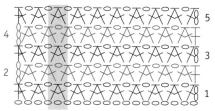

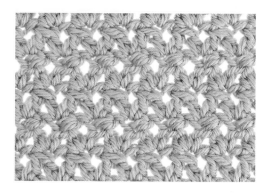

Wrapped Double Crochet

Wrapped stitches spice up an otherwise boring stitch pattern by changing the direction of the stitch from vertical to horizontal. Use them anytime you want to add a little pop of texture.

Wrapped Double Crochet Two Together (wdc2tog): *Yo, insert hk from front of fabric around posts of prev 2 dc, yo, pull up lp, yo, pull through 2 lps on hk; rep from * once around same 2 dc, yo, pull through rem lps on hk.

V-Stitch (v-st): [Dc, ch 1, dc] in st indicated.

Ch a multiple of 6 sts plus 3.

Row 1 (RS): Dc in 4th ch from hk (counts as dc), *sk next ch, v-st in next ch, sk next ch, dc in next 3 ch; rep from * across to last 5 ch, sk next ch, v-st in next ch, sk next ch, dc in last 2 ch, turn.

Row 2: Ch 3 (counts as dc), dc in next dc, v-st in next ch-1 sp, *dc in next 2 dc, wdc2tog around prev 2 dc, v-st in next ch-1 sp; rep from * across to last 2 dc, dc in next dc, dc in top of t-ch, turn.

Row 3: Ch 3 (counts as dc), dc in next dc, v-st in next ch-1 sp, *dc in next 3 dc, v-st in next ch-1 sp; rep from * across to last 2 dc, dc in next dc, dc in top of t-ch, turn.

Rep rows 2 and 3 to desired length.

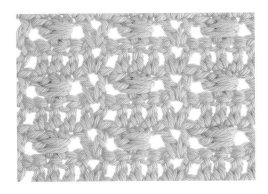

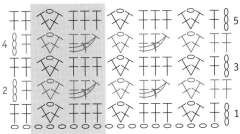

TREBLE CROCHET PATTERNS

Treble Crochet

The treble crochet and taller stitches (like double treble and triple treble) make a lacy fabric just by the natural height of their stitch.

Ch any number of sts.

Row 1 (RS): Tr in 5th ch from hk (sk ch counts as tr), tr in ea ch across, turn.

Row 2: Ch 4 (counts as tr), tr in ea st across, turn.

Rep row 2 to desired length.

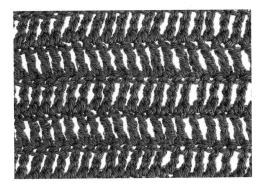

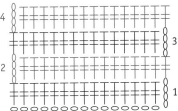

Linked Treble Crochet

This unique stitch makes a fantastic solid fabric without adding weight to your project. The horizontal lines also make a great chart to embroider on later.

Linked Treble Crochet (ltr): Description is below.

Setup Stitch: Ch 4, insert hk into 2nd ch from hk, yo, pull up lp, insert hk into 3rd ch from hk, yo, pull up lp, insert hk into next st, yo, pull up lp (4 lps on hk), yo, draw through 2 lps on hk, yo, draw through next 2 lps, yo, draw through last 2 lps (1st st made).

Next Stitches: Insert hk into upper horiz bar of prev st from top to bottom (the 1st bar is found below the sts' top 2 lps), yo, pull up lp, insert hk into lower horiz bar, yo, pull up lp, insert hk into next st, yo, pull up lp (4 lps on hk), yo, draw through 2 lps on hk, yo, draw through next 2 lps, yo, draw through last 2 lps.

Ch any number of sts.

Row 1 (RS): Complete 1st ltr in 2nd, 3rd, and 5th ch from hk, ltr in ea ch across, turn.

Row 2: Ch 4 (does not count as a tr), ltr in 2nd ch, 3rd ch, and next st, ltr in ea st across, turn.

Rep row 2 to desired length.

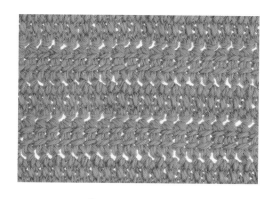

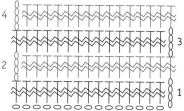

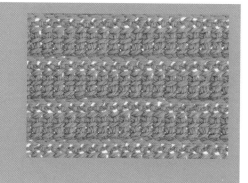

TIP

You can link any stitch above a double crochet in height. You will use as many middle bars as there are yarn overs needed to complete the stitch. For example, a linked double crochet goes into one middle bar before completing the stitch. Also, to get continuous "railroad tracks" across the front of your fabric, you need to complete the first row as above. On the second row, single crochet in the front loop across. On the next row, crochet the linked stitches in the back loop across. Alternate between the single crochet through the front loop and linked treble crochet through the back loop to your desired length. The right side of your fabric will have these great horizontal lines running continuously up your project.

Brick

This stitch pattern is another unique combination of uncomplicated texture without weight. It makes a great fabric for coats or afghans.

Ch a multiple of 4 sts plus 2.

Row 1 (WS): Sc in 2nd ch from hk, *ch 3, sk 3 ch, sc in next ch; rep from * across to end, turn.

Row 2: Ch 3 (counts as dc), 3 dc in ea ch-3 sp across, dc in last sc, turn.

Row 3: Ch 1, sc in 1st dc, ch 3, sk 3 dc, *sc btw prev and next dc, ch 3, sk 3 dc; rep from * across to t-ch, sc in top of t-ch, turn.

Rep rows 2 and 3 to desired length.

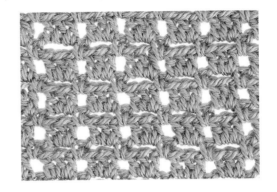

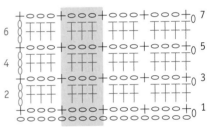

Block

Similar to the brick stitch pattern, this one steps up the texture a notch with post stitches.

Ch a multiple of 3 sts plus 2.

Row 1 (WS): Sc in 2nd ch from hk, *ch 2, sk 2 ch, sc in next ch; rep from * across, turn.

Row 2: Ch 3 (counts as dc), *2 dc in next ch-2 sp, FPdc around next sc; rep from * across to last ch-2 sp, 2 dc in last ch-2 sp, dc in last sc, turn.

Row 3: Ch 1, sc in 1st dc, *ch 2, sk 2 dc, sc in next dc; rep from * across to last FPdc, ch 2, sk 2 dc, sc in top of t-ch, turn.

Rep rows 2 and 3 to desired length.

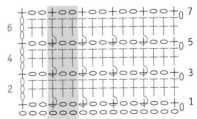

Aligned

This unassuming stitch pattern makes a lovely fabric for garments with its mixture of double and single crochet stitches.

Ch an odd number of sts.

Row 1 (RS): 2 dc in 5th ch from hk (sk ch counts as dc), *sk 1 ch, 2 dc (dc group made) in next ch; rep from * across to last 2 ch, sk 1 ch, dc in last ch, turn.

Row 2: Ch 1, sc in 1st dc, *ch 1, sc in sp btw next 2 dc (center of dc group); rep from * across to t-ch, ch 1, sc in top of t-ch, turn.

Row 3: Ch 3 (counts as dc), 2 dc in ea sc across to last sc, dc in last sc, turn.

Rep rows 2 and 3 to desired length.

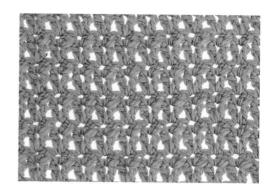

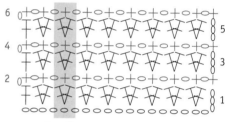

Jacquard

When alternating colors in this stitch pattern, you get a great jacquard-like tweed. Because the stitch pattern is a combination of double and single crochet, it is light enough even for garments.

Ch an odd number of sts.

Row 1 (RS): Dc in 4th ch from hk, *ch 1, dc2tog in same ch and 2 ch away (sk 1 ch); rep from * across to last 2 ch, ch 1, dc2tog in last 2 ch, turn.

Row 2: Ch 1, sc in dc2tog, *sc in ch-1 sp, ch 1, sk dc2tog; rep from * across to last ch-1 sp, sc in last ch-1 sp, sc in dc, turn.

Row 3: Ch 3 (counts as dc), dc2tog in 1st sc and ch-1 sp, *ch 1, dc2tog in same ch-1 sp and next ch-1 sp; rep from * across to last ch-1 sp, ch 1, dc2tog in last ch-1 sp and last sc, dc in last sc, turn.

Row 4: Ch 1, sc in dc, *ch 1, sk dc2tog, sc in ch-1 sp; rep from * across to last ch-1 sp, sc in last ch-sp, ch 1, sk dc2tog, sc in top of t-ch, turn.

Row 5: Ch 2, dc in ch-1 sp, *ch 1, dc2tog in same ch-1 sp and next ch-1 sp; rep from * across to last ch-1 sp, ch 1, dc2tog in last ch-1 sp and last sc, turn.

Rep rows 2–5 to desired length.

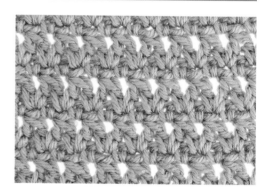

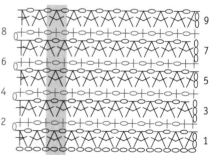

Chicken Foot

Half double crochet takes a starring role in this stitch pattern by leaving little, diagonal star-like lines in the fabric.

Ch an even number of sts.

Row 1 (WS): Sc in 2nd ch from hk, *ch 1, sk 1 ch, sc in next ch; rep from * across, turn.

Row 2: Ch 3 (counts as hdc, ch 1), *hdc2tog in next ch-1 sp and sc, ch 1; rep from * across to last ch-1 sp and sc, hdc2tog in last ch-1 sp and sc, turn.

Row 3: Ch 1, sc in hdc2tog, sc in ch-1 sp, *ch 1, sk next hdc2tog, sc in next ch-1 sp; rep from * across to t-ch, sc in 2nd ch on t-ch, turn.

Row 4: Ch 2 (counts as hdc), hdc2tog in 1st 2 sc, ch 1, *hdc2tog in next ch-1 sp and sc, ch 1; rep from * across to last ch-1 sp, hdc2tog in last ch-1 sp and next sc, hdc in last sc, turn.

Row 5: Ch 1, sc in hdc, *ch 1, sk next hdc2tog, sc in next ch-1 sp; rep from * across to t-ch, ch 1, sk hdc2tog, sc in top of t-ch, turn.

Rep rows 2–5 to desired length.

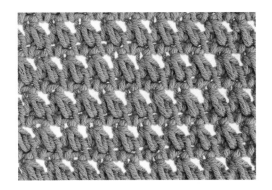

CHAPTER 2

Textured Stitch Patterns

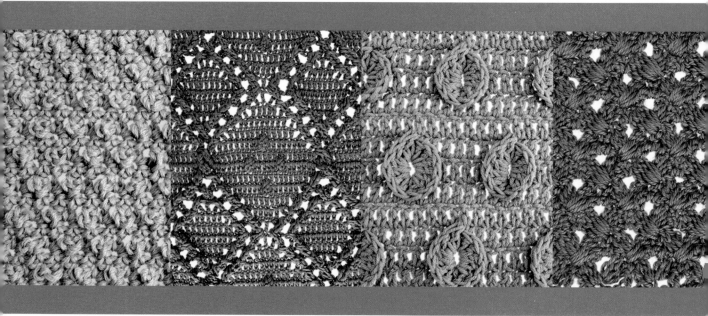

Crunchy Stitch

This fabric makes very bold, diagonal lines, which can be great for highlighting parts of your project where you want a strong fabric.

Ch an even number of sts.

Row 1 (RS): Sl st in 2nd ch from hk, *hdc in next ch, sl st in next ch; rep from * across, turn.

Row 2: Ch 2, *sl st in next hdc, hdc in next sl st; rep from * across, turn.

Row 3: *Sl st in hdc, hdc in next sl st; rep from * across to t-ch, sl st in top of t-ch, turn.

Rep rows 2 and 3 to desired length.

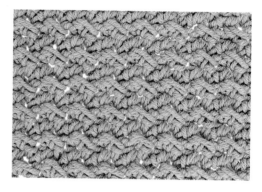

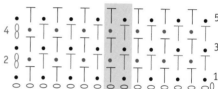

TIP

Fiber Counts

Textured stitch patterns are unique in their three-dimensional look, but different fiber contents in your yarn can produce wildly different results. Silk and bamboo have natural drape in them, while making a flowing fabric will hide your stitch pattern unless you drop your hook size significantly. Cotton has great stitch definition and your cables will want to jump off of your fabric, but be careful, as it can also make a stiff fabric. Superwash wool has always been my favorite for both stitch definition and lightweight fabric.

Kuranchi Stitch

This simple variation of the crunchy stitch highlights the popping double crochet lines while still making a fabric gentle enough for sweaters.

Ch an odd number of sts.

Row 1 (RS): Dc in 4th ch from hk and ea ch across, turn.

Row 2: Sl st in 1st dc, *dc in next dc, sl st in next dc; rep from * across, ending sl st in top of t-ch, turn.

Row 3: Ch 3 (counts as dc), dc in ea st across, turn.

Rep rows 2 and 3 to desired length.

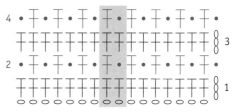

Kroller Stitch

This stitch pattern is my hands-down favorite for baby projects in that it makes a gentle texture that babies love to pet.

Ch a multiple of 3 sts plus 1.

Row 1 (RS): [Sc, hdc, dc] in 4th ch from hk, *sk 2 ch, [sc, hdc, dc] in next ch; rep from * across to last ch, hdc in last ch, turn.

Row 2: Ch 2 (counts as hdc), [sc, hdc, dc] in next dc and ea dc across, hdc in top of t-ch, turn.

Rep row 2 to desired length.

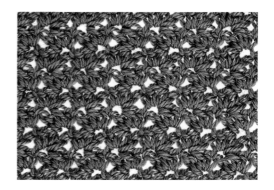

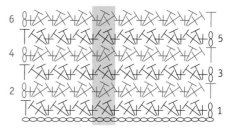

Bloque Stitch

The dropped double crochet puffs out, creating a thick, yet soft, woven-like fabric.

Ch a multiple of 4 sts plus 2.

Row 1 (RS): Dc in 4th ch from hk (sk sts count as dc), dc in next ch, *ch 2, sk 2 ch, dc in next 2 ch; rep from * across to last ch, dc in last ch, turn.

Row 2: Ch 4 (counts as hdc, ch 2), *sk next 2 dc, dc in next 2 ch on foundation ch (working over ch-2 sp), ch 2; rep from * across, hdc in t-ch, turn.

Row 3: Ch 2 (counts as hdc), *dc in next 2 dc 2 rows below (working over ch-2 sp), ch 2, sk next 2 dc; rep from * across, dc in next 2 dc 2 rows below, hdc in t-ch, turn.

Row 4: Ch 4 (counts as hdc, ch 2), *sk next 2 dc, dc in next 2 dc 2 rows below (working over ch-2 sp), ch 2; rep from * across, hdc in t-ch, turn.

Rep rows 3 and 4 to desired length.

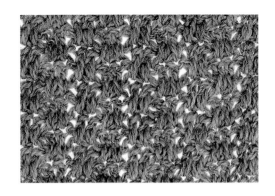

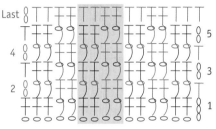

Kabeli Corded Stitch

Reverse single crochet stitches create a bold line in this pattern, which can be great for cleaning pads or for showing off tiny waistlines.

Reverse Single Crochet (rev sc): Insert hk back into prev st (to the right in the clockwise direction), yo, pull up lp twisting hk around to face upwards, yo, pull through sts on hk.

Ch any number of sts.

Row 1 (RS): Dc in 4th ch from hk and ea ch across, do not turn.

Row 2: Working from left to right, ch 1, rev sc in flp of ea dc across, sl st to top of t-ch, do not turn.

Row 3: Ch 3, dc blp in ea dc 2 rows below (working in rem lp behind rev sc), do not turn.

Rep rows 2 and 3 to desired length.

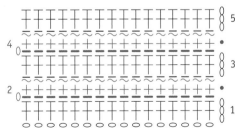

Arruga Stitch

Post stitches in this pattern pop out the double crochet in a rhythm that mimics a woven fabric.

Ch an even number of sts.

Row 1 (RS): Dc in 4th ch from hk and ea ch across, turn.

Row 2: Ch 1, sc in 1st dc, *BPsc in next sc, FPsc in next sc; rep from * across, sc in top of t-ch, turn.

Row 3: Ch 3 (counts as dc), dc in ea sc across, turn.

Row 4: Ch 1, sc in 1st dc, *FPsc in next sc, BPsc in next sc; rep from * across, sc in top of t-ch, turn.

Row 5: Ch 3 (counts as dc), dc in ea sc across, turn.

Rep rows 2–5 to desired length.

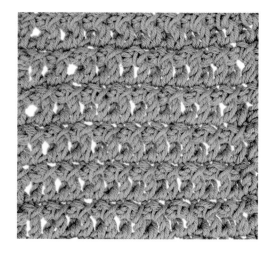

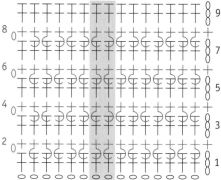

Woven Shell Stitch

By crossing the double crochet groups in the shell, you make a thatched roof look. Using thin or silky yarn makes a drapable fabric.

Shell (sh): Sk 5 dc, 3 dc in next dc, ch 3, 3 dc in 2nd skipped dc (in front of dc just made).

Ch a multiple of 6 sts plus 3.

Row 1 (RS): 3 dc in 7th ch from hk, ch 3, 3 dc in 5th skipped ch (in front dc just made), *sk 1 ch, dc in next ch, sk 3 ch, 3 dc in next ch, ch 3, 3 dc in 2nd skipped ch (in front of dc just made); rep from * to last 2 ch, sk 1 ch, dc in last ch, turn.

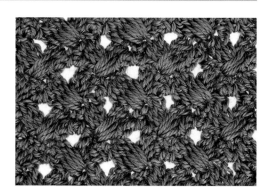

Row 2: Ch 3 (counts as dc), 3 dc in 1st dc, *sc in next ch-3 sp, sh over next 6 dc; rep from * across to last ch-3 sp, sc in last ch-3 sp, 4 dc in top of t-ch, turn.

Row 3: Ch 3 (counts as dc), *sh over next 6 dc, sc in next ch-3 sp; rep from * across to t-ch, dc in top of t-ch, turn.

Rep rows 2 and 3 to desired length.

Romeo Cluster Stitch

This simple fabric pattern staggers little dots of texture throughout, making it a great pattern for kids' clothes.

Ch a multiple of 6 sts plus 3.

Row 1 (RS): Dc in 4th ch from hk and ea ch across, turn.

Row 2: Ch 1, sc in ea dc across to t-ch, sc in top of t-ch, turn.

Row 3: Ch 3 (counts as dc), dc in next 2 sc, *sk next sc, 2 dc-cl in next sc, 2 dc-cl in skipped sc (behind prev 2 dc-cl), dc in next 4 dc; rep from * across to last 4 sc, sk next sc, 2 dc-cl in next sc, 2 dc-cl in skipped sc, dc in last 2 dc, turn.

Row 4: Ch 1, sc in ea st across to t-ch, sc on top of t-ch, turn.

Row 5: Ch 3 (counts as dc), dc in ea sc across, turn.

Row 6: Rep row 2 once.

Row 7: Ch 3 (counts as dc), dc in next 5 sc, *sk next sc, 2 dc-cl in next sc, 2 dc-cl in skipped sc, dc in next 4 dc; rep from * across to last 7 sc, sk next sc, 2 dc-cl in next sc, 2 dc-cl in skipped sc, dc in last 5 dc, turn.

Rows 8 and 9: Rep rows 4 and 5.

Rep rows 2–9 to desired length.

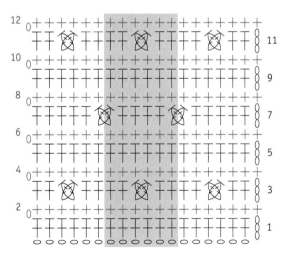

Kyla Shell Stitch

Half double crochet clusters make the shells come alive in this pattern, perfect for afghans.

Shell (sh): [(3 hdc-cl, ch 2) twice, 3 hdc-cl] in st indicated.

Ch a multiple of 8 sts plus 2.

Row 1 (RS): Sc in 2nd ch from hk, *sk 3 ch, sh in next ch, ch 1, sk 3 ch, sc in next ch; rep from * across, turn.

Row 2: Ch 3 (counts as dc), dc in 1st sc, *ch 2, sk 1 hdc-cl, sc in next hdc-cl, ch 2, 3 dc in next sc; rep from * across to last sc, 2 dc in last sc, turn.

Row 3: Ch 2, [hdc, ch 2, 3 hdc-cl] in 1st dc, ch 1, *sc in next sc, sk 1 dc, sh in next dc, ch 1; rep from * to last sc, sc in last sc, [3 hdc-cl, ch 2, 2 hdc-cl] in top of t-ch, turn.

Row 4: Ch 1, sc in hdc-cl, *ch 2, 3 dc in next sc, ch 2, sk hdc-cl, sc in next hdc-cl; rep from * across, turn.

Row 5: Ch 1, sc in 1st sc, *sk 1 dc, sh in next dc, ch 1, sc in next sc; rep from * across, turn.

Rep rows 2–5 to desired length.

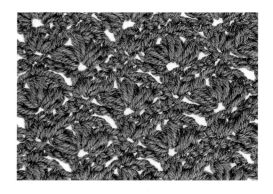

Marguerite Stitch

The half double stitches make the yarn strands star in this fabric.

Half Double Crochet Five Together (hdc5tog): Yo, insert hk in top of hdctog just made and pull up a lp, yo, insert hk around post of hdctog just made and pull up a lp, yo, insert hk into prev sc and pull up a lp, [yo, insert hk into next sc and pull up a lp] twice, yo, pull through all lps on hk.

Ch an even number of sts.

Row 1 (RS): Sc in 2nd ch from hk and ea ch across, turn.

Row 2: Ch 3, hdc5tog over [2nd ch, 3rd ch, next 3 sc], *ch 1, hdc-5tog; rep from * across to end, turn.

Row 3: Ch 1, *sc in hdctog, sc in ch-1 sp; rep from * across to t-ch, sc in 1st ch of t-ch, sc in 2nd ch of t-ch, turn.

Rep rows 2 and 3 to desired length.

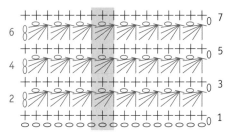

Bobblet Stitch

The extended stitches in the fabric are a great substitute for classic bobbles, making this fabric gentle enough for wearable projects.

Extra Extended Single Crochet (eesc): Insert hk into st indicated and pull up a lp, [yo and pull through 1 lp on hk] twice, yo and pull through all lps on hk.

Ch an even number of sts.

Row 1 (WS): Sc in 2nd ch from hk and ea ch across, turn.

Row 2: Ch 1, sc in 1st sc, *eesc in next sc, sc in next sc; rep from * across, turn.

Row 3: Ch 1, sc in ea st across, turn.

Row 4: Ch 1, sc in 1st 2 sc, *eesc in next sc, sc in next sc; rep from * across to last sc, sc in last sc, turn.

Row 5: Ch 1, sc in ea st across, turn.

Rep rows 2–5 to desired length.

TIP

Bobbles are the perfect stitch patterns for color. To rev up your fabric, try switching colors on all the bobbles or cables in the pattern. You need to strand the color in most cases to make this work, but it is definitely worth the effort.

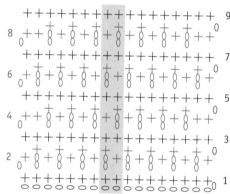

Diagonal Bob Stitch

By moving the extended stitches over one stitch every other row, you create diagonal bobble lines in a soft fabric.

Extra Extended Single Crochet (eesc): Insert hk into st indicated and pull up a lp, [yo and pull through 1 lp on hk] twice, yo and pull through all lps on hk.

Ch a multiple of 6 sts.

Row 1 (WS): Sc in 2nd ch from hk and ea ch across, turn.

Row 2: Ch 1, sc in 1st sc, *eesc in next sc, sc in next sc, eesc in next sc, sc in next 3 sc; rep from * to last 4 sc, [eesc in next sc, sc in next sc] twice, turn.

Row 3: Ch 1, sc in ea st across, turn.

Row 4: Ch 1, sc in 1st 2 sc, *eesc in next sc, sc in next sc, eesc in next sc, sc in next 3 sc; rep from * to last 3 sc, eesc in next sc, sc in last 2 sc, turn.

Row 5: Ch 1, sc in ea st across, turn.

Row 6: Ch 1, sc in 1st 3 sc, *eesc in next sc, sc in next sc, eesc in next sc, sc in next 3 sc; rep from * to last 2 sc, eesc in next sc, sc in last sc, turn.

Row 7: Ch 1, sc in ea st across, turn.

Row 8: Ch 1, sc in 1st 4 sc, *eesc in next sc, sc in next sc, eesc in next sc, sc in next 3 sc; rep from * to last sc, sc in last sc, turn.

Row 9: Ch 1, sc in ea st across, turn.

Row 10: Ch 1, sc in 1st sc, eesc in next sc, sc in next 3 sc, *eesc in next sc, sc in next sc, eesc in next sc, sc in next 3 sc; rep from * to end, turn.

Row 11: Ch 1, sc in ea st across, turn.

Row 12: Ch 1, sc in 1st 2 sc, eesc in next sc, *sc in next 3 sc, eesc in next sc, sc in next sc, eesc in next sc; rep from * to last 2 sc, sc in last 2 sc, turn.

Row 13: Ch 1, sc in ea st across, turn.

Rep rows 2–13 to desired length.

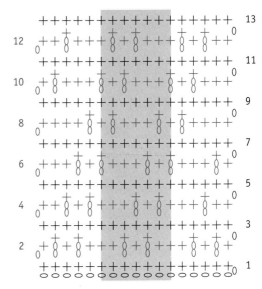

Filet Bobbles Stitch

Half double clusters transform the classic filet stitch pattern to a sculptural fabric.

Ch a multiple of 8 sts.

Row 1 (WS): Sc in 2nd ch from hk and ea ch across, turn.

Row 2: Ch 4 (counts as dc, ch 1), sk 1st 2 sc, *dc in next sc, ch 1, sk next sc; rep from * across to last sc, dc in last sc, turn.

Row 3: Ch 1, *sc in dc, sc in ch-1 sp; rep from * across to t-ch, sc in 4th ch of t-ch, sc in 3rd ch of t-ch, turn.

Row 4: Ch 4 (counts as dc, ch 1), sk 1st 2 sc, *dc in next sc, 4 hdc-cl in next sc, [dc in next sc, ch 1, sk next sc] 3 times; rep from * across to last 5 sc, dc in next sc, 4 hdc-cl in next sc, dc in next sc, ch 1, dc in last sc, turn.

Row 5: Ch 1, sc in ea st across, turn.

Rows 6 and 7: Rep rows 2 and 3 once.

Row 8: Ch 4 (counts as dc, ch 1), sk 1st 2 sc, [dc in next sc, ch 1, sk next sc] twice, *dc in next sc, 4 hdc-cl in next sc, [dc in next sc, ch 1, sk next sc] 3 times; rep from * across to last sc, dc in last sc, turn.

Row 9: Rep row 5.

Rep rows 2–9 to desired length.

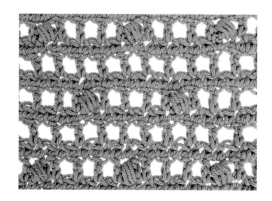

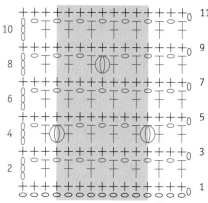

Diamante Bobble Stitch

Alternating bobbles create columns of diamonds that are still lacy enough for garment projects as well.

Ch a multiple of 8 sts plus 2.

Row 1 (WS): Sc in 2nd ch from hk and ea ch across, turn.

Row 2: Ch 2 (counts as hdc), hdc in next 2 sc, *ch 1, sk next sc, 3 hdc-cl in next sc, ch 1, sk next sc, hdc in next 5 sc; rep from * across to last 6 sc, ch 1, sk next sc, 3 hdc-cl in next sc, ch 1, sk next sc, hdc in last 3 sc, turn.

Row 3: Ch 1, sc in ea hdc and ch-1 sp across, turn.

Row 4: Ch 2 (counts as hdc), hdc in next 2 sc, *3 hdc-cl in next sc, ch 1, sk next sc, 3 hdc-cl in next sc, hdc in next 5 sc; rep from * across to last 6 sc, 3 hdc-cl in next sc, ch 1, sk next sc, 3 hdc-cl in next sc, hdc in last 3 sc, turn.

Row 5: Ch 1, sc in ea hdc and ch-1 sp across, turn.

Rep rows 2–5 to desired length.

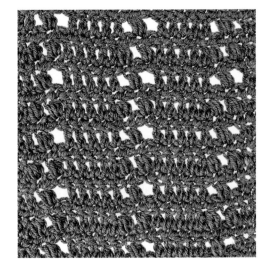

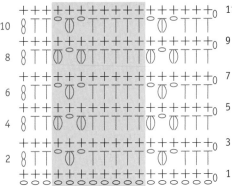

Popcorn Line Stitch

Popcorn all lined up in neat rows makes this pattern great for geometric and symmetric projects, as in a block in an afghan.

Popcorn (pop): 5 dc in st indicated, remove hk, insert hk into 1st dc (from front to back), place free lp back on hk and pull through 1st dc.

Ch a multiple of 4 sts plus 2.

Row 1 (RS): [Sc, ch 3, pop] in 2nd ch from hk, *sk 3 ch, [sc, ch 3, pop] in next ch; rep from * across to last 4 ch, sk 3 ch, sc in last sc, turn.

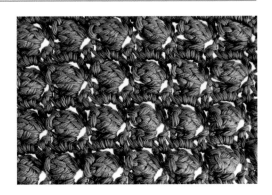

Row 2: Ch 3 (counts as dc), *[2 sc, hdc] in next ch-3 sp, dc in next sc; rep from * across, turn.

Row 3: Ch 1, *[sc, ch 3, pop] in dc, sk 3 sts; rep from * across to t-ch, sc in top of t-ch, turn.

Rep rows 2 and 3 to desired length.

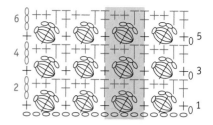

Balloon Stitch

Clusters pop from the fabric, making this stitch pattern great for fun projects like hats and mittens.

Ch a multiple of 6 sts plus 1.

Row 1 (RS): Dc in 4th ch from hk and ea ch across, turn.

Row 2: Ch 1, sc in 1st 2 dc, *5 dc-cl in next dc, sc in next 5 dc; rep from * across to last 3 sts, 5 dc-cl in next sc, sc in last dc, sc in top of t-ch, turn.

Row 3: Ch 3 (counts as dc), dc in ea st across, turn.

Row 4: Ch 1, sc in 1st 5 dc, *5 dc-cl in next dc, sc in next 5 dc; rep from * across, turn.

Row 5: Ch 3 (counts as dc), dc in ea st across, turn.

Rep rows 2–5 to desired length.

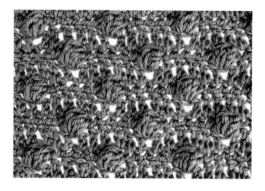

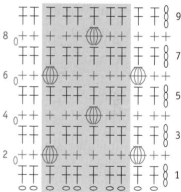

Judith Bobble Stitch

This beautifully classic cable fabric looks equally great in projects from sweaters to afghans.

Ch a multiple of 12 sts plus 8.

Row 1 (RS): Sc in 2nd ch from hk and ea ch across, turn.

Row 2: Ch 1, sc in ea st across, turn.

Row 3: Ch 1, sc in 1st 2 sc, *FPdc around next st 2 rows below, sc in next sc, FPdc around next st 2 rows below, sc in next 4 sc, 4 hdc-cl in next sc, sc in next 4 sc; rep from * across to last 5 sts, FPdc around next st 2 rows below, sc in next sc, FPdc around next st 2 rows below, sc in last 2 sc, turn.

Row 4: Rep row 2.

Row 5: Ch 1, sc in 1st 2 sc, *FPdc around next st 2 rows below, sc in next sc, FPdc around next st 2 rows below, sc in next 2 sc, 4 hdc-cl in next sc, sc in next 3 sc, 4 hdc-cl in next sc, sc in next 2 sc; rep from * across to last 5 sts, FPdc around next st 2 rows below, sc in next sc, FPdc around next st 2 rows below, sc in last 2 sc, turn.

Rows 6 and 7: Rep rows 2 and 3.

Row 8: Rep row 2.

Row 9: Ch 1, sc in 1st 2 sc, *FPdc around next st 2 rows below, sc in next sc, FPdc around next st 2 rows below, sc in next 9 sc; rep from * across to last 5 sts, FPdc around next st 2 rows below, sc in next sc, FPdc around next st 2 rows below, sc in last 2 sc, turn.

Rep rows 2–9 to desired length.

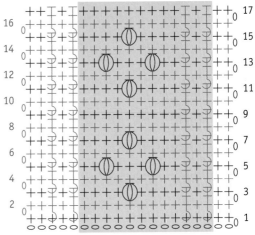

Popping Cable Stitch

The cables in this pattern literally jump off the fabric surface, making this stitch great for accessories that can handle the three-dimensional nature of this fabric.

Cable: Ch 4, sl st around post of next sc 3 rows below, turn, 4 sc in ch-4 sp, turn.

Ch a multiple of 6 sts.

Row 1 (RS): Sc in 2nd ch from hk and ea ch across, turn.

Rows 2–4: Ch 1, sc in ea sc across, turn.

Row 5: Ch 1, sc in 1st 2 sc, *cable in next sc 3 rows below, sk next sc on current row, sc in next 5 sc; rep from * to last 3 sc, cable in next sc 3 rows below, sc in last 2 sc, turn.

Row 6: Ch 1, sc in ea st across, turn.

Row 7: Ch 1, sc in 1st 2 sc, *cable in next sc 3 rows below (behind prev cable), sk next sc on row, sc in next 5 sc; rep from * to last 3 sc, cable in next sc 3 rows below, sc in last 2 sc, turn.

Rep rows 6–7 to desired length.

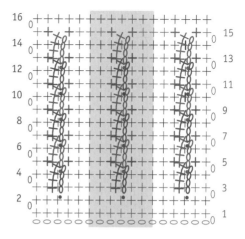

Popping Circle Stitch

Bursting from the fabric are sculptural circles that you can highlight even more with a color change.

Circle: 6 dc around post of next dc, turn work 180 degrees, 6 dc around post of prev dc (circle made).

Ch a multiple of 8 sts plus 2.

Row 1 (RS): Dc in 4th ch from hk and ea ch across, turn.

Row 2: Ch 3 (counts as dc), dc in ea dc across, dc in top of t-ch, turn.

Row 3: Ch 3 (counts as dc), dc in next 3 dc, *circle around post of next and prev dc, dc in top of same dc (behind circle), dc in next 7 dc; rep from * across to last 4 dc, circle in around post of next and prev dc, dc in top of same dc (behind circle), dc in next 2 dc, dc in top of t-ch, turn.

Rows 4–6: Ch 3 (counts as dc), dc in ea dc across, turn.

Row 7: Ch 3 (counts as dc), dc in next 7 dc, *circle around post of next and prev dc, dc in top of same dc (behind circle), dc in next 7 dc; rep from * across, turn.

Rows 8–10: Ch 3 (counts as dc), dc in ea dc across, turn.

Rep rows 3–10 to desired length.

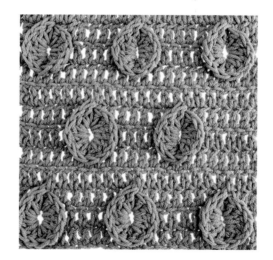

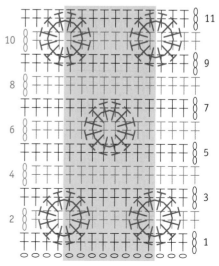

Popping Flower Stitch

By adding a few chains, you can turn the circles in the Popping Circle Stitch into flowers. This fabric is great for playmats for babies or for statement scarves.

Flower: [(Dc, ch 3) 6 times] around post of next dc, turn work 180 degrees, [(dc, ch 3) 5 times, dc] around post of prev dc.

Ch a multiple of 12 sts.

Row 1 (RS): Dc in 4th ch from hk and ea ch across, turn.

Rows 2–4: Ch 3 (counts as dc), dc in ea dc across, dc in top of t-ch, turn.

Row 5: Ch 3 (counts as dc), dc in next 4 dc, *flower around post of next and prev dc, dc in top of same dc (behind flower), dc in next 11 dc; rep from * across to last 5 dc, flower around post of next and prev dc, dc in top of same dc (behind circle), dc in next 3 dc, dc in top of t-ch, turn.

Rows 6–8: Ch 3 (counts as dc), dc in ea dc across, turn.

Row 9: Ch 3 (counts as dc), dc in next 4 dc, *dc in next 6 dc, flower around post of next and prev dc, dc in top of same dc (behind flower), dc in next 5 dc; rep from * across to last 5 dc, dc in next 4 dc, dc in top of t-ch, turn.

Rep rows 2–9 to desired length.

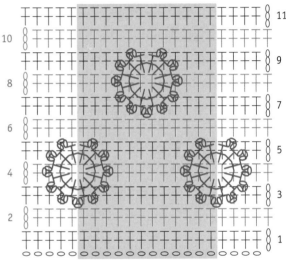

CABLE STITCH PATTERNS

Single Rib

The start of every good cable comes down to just a simple post stitch. This pattern highlights the beauty in the simplicity.

Ch an even number of sts.

Row 1 (RS): Dc in 4th ch from hk and ea ch across, turn.

Row 2: Ch 3 (counts as dc), *FPdc in next dc, BPdc in next dc; rep from * across to t-ch, dc in top of t-ch, turn.

Rep row 2 to desired length.

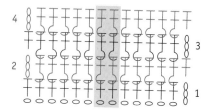

TIP

Cables are one technique that does take some time to master. The key to mastering them is the post stitches. If you are a tight crocheter, they can be really difficult to do since you usually need to cross over other stitches. Try going up a few hook sizes to force yourself to make a looser gauge. Try exaggerating the yarn overs by pulling your loops all the way to the top of the row to give you just a bit of extra yarn to do those crosses.

Basketweave Stitch

This classic stitch works great for home projects from blankets to pillows.

Ch a multiple of 8 sts plus 4.

Row 1 (RS): Dc in 4th ch from hk and ea ch across, turn.

Row 2: Ch 3 (counts as dc), *FPdc in next 4 dc, BPdc in next 4 dc; rep from * across to t-ch, dc in top of t-ch, turn.

Row 3: Ch 3 (counts as dc), *BPdc in next 4 dc, FPdc in next 4 dc; rep from * across to t-ch, dc in top of t-ch, turn.

Rows 4 and 5: Rep rows 2 and 3 once.

Row 6: Ch 3 (counts as dc), *BPdc in next 4 dc, FPdc in next 4 dc; rep from * across to t-ch, dc in top of t-ch, turn.

Row 7: Ch 3 (counts as dc), *FPdc in next 4 dc, BPdc in next 4 dc; rep from * across to t-ch, dc in top of t-ch, turn.

Rows 8 and 9: Rep rows 6 and 7 once.

Rep rows 2–9 to desired length.

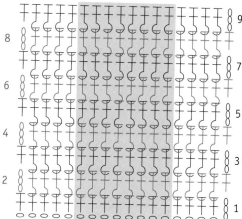

Woven Stitch

Alternating post stitches creates a woven-like fabric that is thick and soft. This makes great hats and slippers.

Ch an even number of sts.

Row 1 (RS): Dc in 4th ch from hk and ea ch across, turn.

Row 2: Ch 3 (counts as dc), *FPdc in next dc, BPdc in next dc; rep from * across to t-ch, dc in top of t-ch, turn.

Row 3: Ch 3 (counts as dc), *BPdc in next dc, FPdc in next dc; rep from * across to t-ch, dc in top of t-ch, turn.

Rep rows 2 and 3 to desired length.

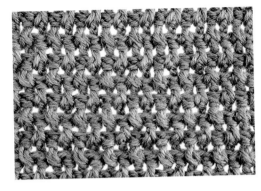

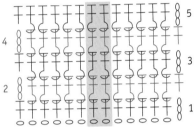

Twisted Columns

Gentle columns of twists make a great pattern for bags and other accessories where you want to add vertical lines.

Ch a multiple of 6 sts plus 2.

Row 1 (RS): Sc in 2nd ch from hk and ea ch across, turn.

Row 2: Ch 1, sc in ea st across, turn.

Row 3: Ch 1, sc in 1st 2 sc, *sk next 2 sc, FPdc in next sc 2 rows below, sc in 2nd skipped sc, FPdc in 1st skipped sc 2 rows below behind prev post st, sc in next 3 sc; rep from * across, ending sc in last 2 sc, turn.

Row 4: Rep row 2.

Row 5: Ch 1, sc in 1st 2 sc, *sk next 2 sc, FPdc in next FPdc 2 rows below, sc in 2nd skipped sc, FPdc in prev FPdc 2 rows below behind prev post st, sc in next 3 sc; rep from * across, ending sc in last 2 sc, turn.

Rep rows 4 and 5 to desired length.

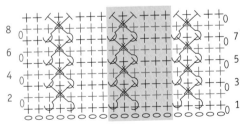

Cable Towers

The taller stitches in these classic cables give you a slight extra drape that makes this pattern great for afghans.

Ch a multiple of 8 sts plus 3.

Row 1 (RS): Hdc in 3rd ch from hk and ea ch across, turn.

Row 2: Ch 2 (counts as hdc), hdc in ea st across, hdc in top of t-ch, turn.

Row 3: Ch 2 (counts as hdc), hdc in next 2 hdc, *FPtr in next 4 sts 2 rows below, hdc in next 4 hdc; rep from * across, ending hdc in last 3 sts, turn.

Row 4: Rep row 2.

Row 5: Ch 2 (counts as hdc), hdc in next 2 hdc, *sk 2 sts, FPtr in next 2 sts 2 rows below, FPtr in skipped 2 sts 2 rows below, hdc in next 4 sts; rep from * across, ending hdc in last 3 sts, turn.

Rows 6 and 7: Rep rows 2 and 3.

Rep rows 2–7 to desired length.

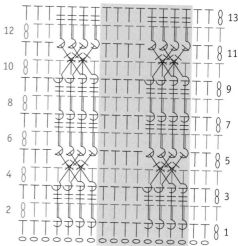

Petal Link Stitch

The mix of lace and post stitches makes the clusters in this pattern pop in and out of the fabric, allowing you to make fantastic garments.

Shell (sh): [Dc2tog, ch 2, dc2tog] in stitch indicated.

Ch a multiple of 6 sts plus 3.

Row 1 (RS): Sh in 6th ch from hk, *sk 2 ch, dc in next ch, sk 2 ch, sh in next ch; rep from * across to last 3 ch, sk 2 ch, dc in last ch, turn.

Row 2: Ch 3 (counts as dc), *sh in ch-2 sp of next sh, BPdc around next dc; rep from * across to t-ch, dc in top of t-ch, turn.

Row 3: Ch 4 (counts as dc, ch-1 sp), 2 dc-cl in 1st dc, *dc in ch-2 sp of next sh, sh in next dc; rep from * across to last sh, dc in ch-2 sp of last sh, [2 dc-cl, ch 1, dc] in top of t-ch, turn.

Row 4: Ch 4 (counts as dc, ch-1 sp), 2 dc-cl in 1st dc, *BPdc around next dc, sh in ch-2 sp of next sh; rep from * across to last sh, BPdc around next dc, [2 dc-cl, ch 1, dc] in 3rd ch of t-ch, turn.

Row 5: Ch 3 (counts as dc), *sh in next dc, dc in ch-2 sp of next sh; rep from * across to last sh, sh in next dc, dc in 3rd ch of t-ch, turn.

Row 6: Ch 3 (counts as dc), *sh in ch-2 sp of next sh, BPdc around next dc; rep from * across to t-ch, dc in top of t-ch, turn.

Rep rows 3–6 to desired length.

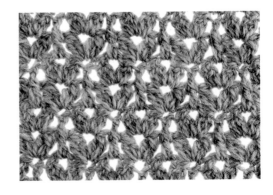

Greene Lace

Sometimes opposites do attract, especially in this fabric of lace and cables; both make the other look even more impressive.

Shell (sh): [(Dc, ch 1) 3 times, dc] in st indicated.

Ch a multiple of 14 sts plus 4.

Row 1 (RS): Sh in 6th ch from hk, sk next 2 ch, *dc in next 4 ch, sk 2 ch, sh in next ch, sk 4 ch, sh in next ch, sk 2 ch; rep from * across to last 10 ch, dc in next 4 ch, sk 2 ch, sh in next ch, dc in last ch, turn.

Row 2: Ch 3 (counts as dc), sh in center ch-1 sp of next sh, sk [dc, ch 1, dc], *BPtr in next 4 sts, [sh in center ch-1 sp of next sh] twice, sk [dc, ch1, dc]; rep from * across to last sh, sh in center ch-1 sp of last sh, dc in top of t-ch, turn.

Row 3: Ch 3 (counts as dc), sh in center ch-1 sp of next sh, *FPtr in next tr, sk next tr, FPtr in next tr, FPtr in skipped tr (crossing in front of prev st), FPtr in next tr, [sh in center ch-1 sp of next sh] twice; rep from * across to last 4 tr, FPtr in next tr, sk 1 tr, FPtr in next tr, FPtr in skipped tr (in front of prev st), FPtr in next tr, sh in center ch-1 sp of last sh, dc in top of t-ch, turn.

Rep rows 2 and 3 to desired length.

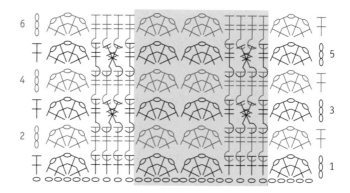

Ginger Stitch

Post stitches in this lace pattern help pop the pattern into your vision. This fabric is equally great for garments or blankets.

Shell (sh): [2 dc, ch 1, 2 dc] in st indicated.

V-Stitch (v-st): [Dc, ch 1, dc] in st indicated.

Ch a multiple of 8 sts plus 4.

Row 1 (RS): 2 dc in 4th ch from hk (counts as half sh), *sk 3 ch, v-st in next ch, sk 3 ch, sh in next ch; rep from * across to last 8 ch, sk 3 ch, v-st in next ch, sk 3 ch, 3 dc in last ch, turn.

Row 2: Ch 3 (counts as dc), 2 dc in 1st dc (counts as half sh), *sk 2 dc, BPdc around next dc, ch 1, BPdc around next dc, sh in ch-1 sp of next sh; rep from * across to last 5 dc, BPdc around next dc, ch 1, BPdc around next dc, 3 dc in top of t-ch, turn.

Row 3: Ch 3 (counts as dc), 2 dc in 1st dc, *sk 2 dc, FPdc around next dc, ch 1, FPdc around next dc, sh in ch-1 of next sh; rep from * across to last 5 dc, FPdc around next dc, ch 1, FPdc around next dc, 3 dc in top of t-ch, turn.

Row 4: Ch 3 (counts as dc), dc in 1st dc, *sh in next ch-1 sp, v-st in ch-1 sp of next sh; rep from * across to last ch-1 sp, sh in last ch-1 sp, 2 dc in top of t-ch, turn.

Row 5: Ch 3 (counts as dc), dc in next dc, *sh in ch-1 sp of next sh, sk 2 dc, FPdc around next dc, ch 1, FPdc around next dc; rep from * across to last ch-1 sp, sh in last ch-1 sp, 2 dc in top of t-ch, turn.

Row 6: Ch 3 (counts as dc), dc in next dc, *sh in ch-1 sp of next sh, sk 2 dc, BPdc around next dc, ch 1, BPdc around next dc; rep from * across to last ch-1 sp, sh in last ch-1 sp, 2 dc in top of t-ch, turn.

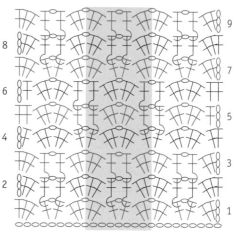

Row 7: Ch 3 (counts as dc), 2dc in 1st dc, *v-st in ch-1 sp of next sh, sh in next ch-1 sp; rep from * across to last ch-1 sp, v-st in last ch-1 sp, 3 dc in top of t-ch, turn.

Rep rows 2–7 to desired length.

Ripple Lace

Simple diagonal lines of post stitches make a unique fabric that looks amazing in scarves and shawls.

Ch a multiple of 3 sts.

Row 1 (WS): Sc in 2nd ch from hk and ea ch across, turn.

Row 2: Ch 3 (counts as dc), sk 1st sc, *sk next 2 sc, dc in next sc, ch 1, dc in 1st sk sc; rep from * to last sc, dc in last sc, turn.

Row 3: Ch 1, sc in ea st and ch-sp across, turn.

Row 4: Ch 3 (counts as dc), sk 1st sc, *sk next 2 sc, FPtr in next dc 2 rows below, ch 1, dc in 1st sk sc; rep from * to last sc, dc in last sc, turn.

Rep rows 3 and 4 to desired length.

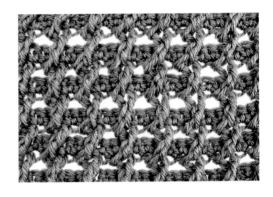

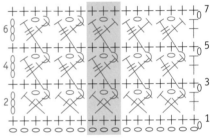

Jeobneun Stitch

Dropping post stitches a few rows below, results in a pattern of embedded Vs.

Right Post Stitch (rt post st): Yo, insert hk in next sc and pull up a lp, yo and pull through 2 lps on hk, yo twice, sk next sc, insert hk around post of next dc 2 rows below, from front to back to front, and pull up a lp, [yo and pull through 2 lps on hk] twice, yo and pull through all lps on hk.

Left Post Stitch (lf post st): Yo twice, insert hk around post of same st as rt post st 2 rows below from front to back to front, and pull up a lp, [yo and pull through 2 lps on hk] twice, yo, insert hk in next sc and pull up a lp, yo and pull through 2 lps on hk, yo and pull through all lps on hk.

Ch a multiple of 6 sts plus 3.

Row 1 (RS): Dc in 4th ch from hk, dc in next 4 ch, *ch 1, sk 1 ch, dc in next 5 ch; rep from * to last ch, dc in last ch, turn.

Row 2: Ch 1, sc in 1st 6 dc, *ch 1, sk ch-sp, sc in next 5 dc; rep from * to t-ch, sc in top of t-ch, turn.

Row 3: Ch 3 (counts as dc), *rt post st in next sc, dc in next 3 sc, lf post st in next sc, ch 1, sk ch-sp; rep from * to last 6 sc, rt post st in next sc, dc in next 3 sc, lf post st in next sc, dc in last sc.

Rep rows 2 and 3 to desired length.

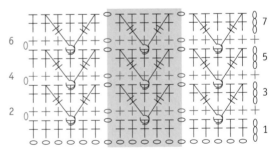

Pine Tree Stitch

Post stitches combined with crocheting into previous stitches create a forest of trees in this stitch pattern.

Pine Tree Stitch (tree): [Ch 1, ttr, ch 1, dtr in 4th horiz bar of prev ttr, ch 1, tr in 3rd horiz bar of prev dtr, ch 1, dc in 2nd horiz bar of prev tr, ch 2, hdc in horiz bar of prev dc, ch 1, dc in 2nd horiz bar of prev tr, ch 1, tr in 3rd horiz bar of prev dtr, ch 1, dtr in 4th horiz bar of prev ttr, ch 1] in st indicated.

Back Post Treble Four Together (BPtr4tog): *Sk next ch-sp, yo twice, insert hk around post of next st, from back to front to back, and pull up a lp, [yo and pull through 2 lps] twice; rep from * 3 more times.

Back Post Treble Eight Together (BPtr8tog): *Yo twice, insert hk around post of next st, from back to front to back, and pull up a lp, [yo and pull through 2 lps] twice, sk ch-sp; rep from * 3 more times, sk next (ch-1, sc, ch-1); rep from * 4 times.

Left Decrease (left dec): *Yo twice, insert hk around post of next st from back to front to back and pull up a lp, [yo and pull through 2 lps] twice; rep from * 3 more times, yo 3 times, insert hk in last sc and pull up a lp, [yo and pull through 2 lps] 3 times, yo and pull through all lps on hk.

Right Decrease (right dec): *Yo twice, insert hk around post of next st from front to back to front and pull up a lp, [yo and pull through 2 lps] twice; rep from * 3 more times, yo 3 times, insert hk in last sc and pull up a lp, [yo and pull through 2 lps] 3 times, yo and pull through all lps on hk.

Front Post Treble Four Together (FPtr4tog): Work as for BPtr4tog except insert hk from front to back to front around post of indicated st.

Front Post Treble Eight Together (FPtr8tog): Work as for BPtr8tog except insert hk from front to back to front around post of indicated st.

Ch a multiple of 10 sts plus 4.

Row 1 (RS): 3 dc in 4th ch from hk, sk 4 ch, sc in next ch, *sk 4 ch, 7 dc in next ch, sk 4 ch, sc in next ch; rep from * to last 5 ch, sk 4 ch, 4 dc in last ch, turn.

Row 2: Ch 1, sc in 1st dc, *tree in next sc, sk 3 dc, sc in next dc; rep from * across to t-ch, sc in top of t-ch, turn.

Row 3: Ch 5, BPtr4tog over next 4 sts, ch 4, *sc in next ch-2 sp, ch 4, BPtr8tog over next 8 sts, ch 4; rep from * across to last ch-2 sp, sc in last ch-2 sp, ch 4, left dec over last 5 sts (skipping ch-sps), turn.

Row 4: Ch 3 (counts as dc), 3 dc in 1st st, *sc in next sc, sk ch-4 sp, 7 dc in next st; rep from * to last sc, sc in last sc, 4 dc in last st, turn.

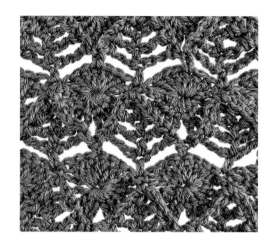

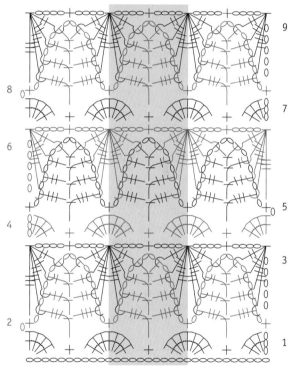

Row 5: Rep row 2.

Row 6: Ch 5, FPtr4tog over next 4 sts, ch 4, *sc in next ch-2 sp, ch 4, FPtr8tog over next 8 sts, ch 4; rep from * across to last ch-2 sp, sc in last ch-2 sp, ch 4, right dec over last 5 sts (skipping ch-sps), turn.

Row 7: Rep row 4.

Rep rows 2–7 to desired length.

Cable Lattice Stitch

Post stitches in this lace pattern mimic a lattice fabric that you can use for anything from shawls to sweaters.

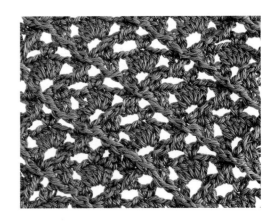

Left Decrease (left dec): Yo, insert hk around st from front to back to front and pull up a lp, yo and pull through 2 lps on hk, yo, insert hk into next st and pull up a lp, yo and pull through 2 lps on hk, yo and pull through all lps on hk.

Shell (sh): 5 dc in same sp.

Ch a multiple of 12 sts plus 11.

Row 1 (WS): Sc in 2nd ch from hk, sc in next 9 sc, *ch 4, sk 2 ch, sc in next 10 sc; rep from * across, sc in last ch, turn.

Row 2: Ch 5 (counts as tr, ch-1 sp), *sk 3 sc, dc in next 2 sc, tr in 2nd sk sc (in front of prev sts), sk 3 sc, tr in next sc, dc in 1st and 2nd sk sc (behind tr), ch 1, sh in ch-4 sp, ch 1; rep from * across to last ch-sp, sk 3 sc, dc in next 2 sc, tr in 2nd sk sc (in front of prev sts), sk 3 sc, tr in next sc, dc in 1st and 2nd sk sc (behind tr), ch 1, tr in last sc, turn.

Row 3: Ch 3 (counts as hdc, ch 1),sk 1st tr, sk ch-1 sp, sk 2 dc, *sk 1 tr, BPtr around next tr, dc in next 2 dc (behind tr), ch 2, dc in next 2 dc, tr in sk tr (behind tr, in front of dc), ch 2, 2 sc in center st of next sh, ch 2; rep from * across to last 2 tr, sk 1 tr, BPtr around next tr, dc in next 2 dc (behind tr), ch 2, dc in next 2 dc, tr in sk tr (behind tr, in front of dc), ch 1, hdc in 4th ch of t-ch, turn.

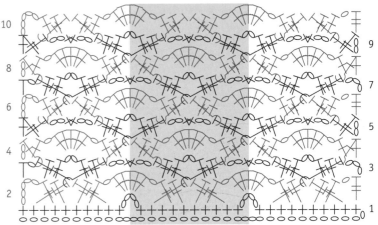

Row 4: Ch 2, FPdc around next tr, dc in sk ch-1 sp (behind tr), *ch 1, sh in ch-4 sp, ch 1, 2 dc in next ch-2 sp, FPtr in sk tr (in front of prev dc), FPtr in next tr, 2 dc in sk ch-2 sp (behind tr); rep from * across to last ch-2 sp, ch 1, sh in next ch-4 sp, ch 1, dc in t-ch, left dec in last tr and t-ch, turn.

Row 5: Ch 2, sk 1st st, dc in next dc, dc in 1st st (in front of prev dc), *ch 2, 2 sc in center st of sh, ch 2, sk 1 tr, BPtr around next tr, dc in next 2 dc (behind tr), ch 2, dc in next 2 dc, tr in sk tr (behind tr, in front of dc); rep from * across to last 7 dc, ch 2, 2 sc in center st of sh, 2 sc in next dc, ch 2, dc in last st, dc2tog in sk dc and last dc (behind prev dc), turn.

Row 6: Ch 5 (counts as tr, ch 1), 2 dc in next ch-2 sp, FPtr in sk tr (in front of prev sts), FPtr in next tr, 2dc in sk ch-2 sp (behind tr), *ch 1, sh in next ch-4 sp, ch 1, 2 dc in next ch-2 sp, FPtr in sk tr (in front of prev sts), FPtr in next tr, 2 dc in sk ch-2 sp (behind tr); rep from * across to last ch-2 sp, ch 1, tr in last st, turn.

Rep rows 3–6 to desired length.

Diamond Stitch

This subtle diamond pattern makes a great overall fabric that is versatile enough for projects from hats to bags.

Front Post Double Crochet Two Together (FPdc2tog): Dc2tog around the post of the sts indicated, inserting hk from front to back to front.

Back Post Double Crochet Two Together (BPdc2tog): Dc2tog around the post of the sts indicated, inserting hk from back to front to back.

Front Post or Back Post Double Crochet Three Together (FP or BPdc3tog): Dc3tog around the post of the sts indicated, inserting hk from back to front to back for "BP" and from front to back to front for "FP".

Ch a multiple of 10 sts plus 5.

Row 1 (WS): Dc in 4th ch from hk, dc in next 4 ch, *ch 1, sk 1 ch, dc in next 9 ch; rep from * across to last 7 ch, ch 1, sk 1 ch, dc in last 6 ch, turn.

Row 2: Ch 3 (counts as dc), dc in next 3 dc, FPdc2tog over next 2 dc, *ch 1, dc in next ch-1 sp, ch 1, FPdc2tog over next 2 dc, dc in next 5 dc, FPdc2tog over next 2 dc; rep from * across to last ch-sp, ch 1, dc in last ch-1 sp, ch 1, FPdc2tog in over next 2 dc, dc in next 3 dc, dc in top of t-ch, turn.

Row 3: Ch 3 (counts as dc), dc in next 2 dc, BPdc2tog over next 2 dc, *ch 1, dc in ch-1 sp, dc in dc, dc in ch-1 sp, ch 1, BPdc2tog over next 2 dc, dc in next 3 dc, BPdc2tog over next 2 dc; rep from * across to last 2 ch-sps, ch 1, dc in ch-1 sp, dc in dc, dc in ch-1 sp, ch 1, BPdc2tog over next 2 dc, dc in next 2 dc, dc in top of t-ch, turn.

Row 4: Ch 3 (counts as dc), dc in next dc, *FPdc2tog over next 2 dc, ch 1, dc in next ch-1 sp, dc in next 3 dc, dc in ch-1 sp, ch 1, FPdc2tog over next 2 dc, dc in next dc; rep from * across to t-ch, dc in top of t-ch, turn.

Row 5: Ch 3 (counts as dc), BPdc2tog over next 2 dc, *ch 1, dc in ch-1 sp, dc in next 5 dc, dc in ch-1 sp, ch 1, BPdc3tog over next 3 dc; rep from * across to last 3 dc, BPdc2tog over next 2 dc, dc in top of t-ch, turn.

Row 6: Ch 4 (counts as dc, ch 1), *dc in ch-1 sp, dc in next 7 dc, dc in next ch-1 sp, ch 1, sk 1 st; rep from * across to t-ch, dc in top of t-ch, turn.

Row 7: Ch 3 (counts as dc), *dc in ch-1 sp, ch 1, BPdc2tog over next 2 dc, dc in next 5 dc, BPdc2tog over next 2 dc, ch 1; rep from * across to last ch-1 sp, dc last ch-1 sp, dc in 3rd ch of t-ch, turn.

Row 8: Ch 3 (counts as dc), dc in next dc, *dc in ch-1 sp, ch 1, FPdc2tog over next 2 dc, dc in next 3 dc, FPdc2tog

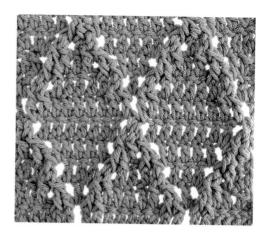

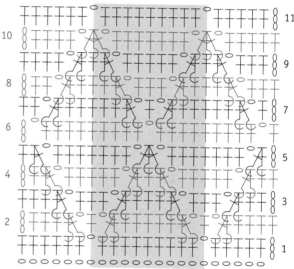

over next 2 dc, ch 1, dc in ch-1 sp, dc in next dc; rep from * across, dc in top of t-ch, turn.

Row 9: Ch 3 (counts as dc), dc in next 2 dc, *dc in ch-1 sp, ch 1, BPdc2tog over next 2 dc, dc in next dc, BPdc2tog over next 2 dc, ch 1, dc in ch-1 sp, dc in next 3 dc; rep from * across, turn.

Row 10: Ch 3 (counts as dc), *dc in next 3 dc, dc in ch-1 sp, ch 1, FPdc3tog over next 3 dc, ch 1, dc in ch-1 sp, dc in next 2 dc; rep from * across to last 2 dc, dc in next dc, dc in top of t-ch, turn.

Row 11: Ch 3 (counts as dc), dc in next 4 dc, dc in next ch-1 sp, ch 1, sk next st, *dc in ch-1 sp, dc in next 7 dc, dc in next ch-1 sp, ch 1, sk 1 st; rep from * across to last ch-sp, dc in ch-sp, dc in next 4 dc, dc in top of t-ch, turn.

Rep rows 2–11 to desired length.

Stella Cable

You can add this modest cable band to any project, like a bag, to take it to the next level.

Ch 15 sts.

Row 1 (WS): Sc in 2nd ch from hk and ea ch across, turn—14 sc.

Row 2: Ch 1, sc in 1st 3 sc, FPdc in next 2 sc, sc in next 4 sc, FPdc in next 2 sc, sc in next 3 sc, turn.

Row 3: Ch 1, sc in ea st across, turn.

Row 4: Ch 1, sc in 1st 4 sc, FPdc in next 2 dc 2 rows below, sk 2 sc, sc in next 2 sc, FPdc in next 2 dc 2 rows below, sc in last 4 sc, turn.

Rep row 3 for all odd rows.

Row 6: Ch 1, sc in 1st 5 sc, FPdc in next 4 dc 2 rows below, sk 4 sc, sc in last 5 sc, turn.

Row 8: Rep row 6.

Row 10: Rep row 4.

Row 12: Ch 1, sc in 1st 3 sc, FPdc in next 2 dc 2 rows below, sk 2 sc, sc in next 4 sc, FPdc in next 2 dc 2 rows below, sc in last 3 sc, turn.

Row 14: Ch 1, sc in 1st 2 sc, FPdc in next 2 dc 2 rows below, sk 2 sc, sc in next 6 sc, FPdc in next 2 dc 2 rows below, sc in last 2 sc, turn.

Row 16: Rep row 12.

Rep rows 3–16 to desired length.

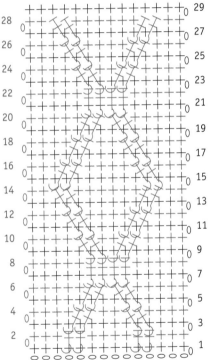

Arabel Cable

This thick cable makes quite the statement on the border of any project.

Ch 19 sts.

Row 1 (RS): Dc in 4th ch from hk and ea ch across, turn—17 dc.

Row 2: Ch 3 (counts as dc), dc in next 3 dc, sk 3 dc, FPtr in next 3 dc, FPtr in 3 sk dc, FPdc in next 3 dc, dc in next 3 dc, dc in top of t-ch, turn.

Row 3: Ch 2 (counts as hdc), hdc in next 3 dc, BPdc in next 9 sts, hdc in next 3 dc, hdc in top of t-ch, turn.

Row 4: Ch 3 (counts as dc), dc in next 3 dc, FPdc in next 3 dc, sk 3 dc, FPtr in next 3 dc, FPtr in 3 sk dc, dc in next 3 dc, dc in top of t-ch, turn.

Row 5: Rep row 3.

Rep rows 2–5 to desired length.

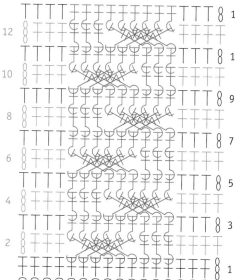

Olivia Cable

You can add this charming cable to any sweater by using a hook size that is large enough to ensure the cable is not too stiff.

Ch 17 sts.

Row 1 (WS): Sc in 2nd ch from hk and ea ch across, turn—16sc.

Row 2: Ch 1, sc in 1st 2 sc, FPdc in next 2 sc, sc in next 2 sc, FPdc in next 4 sc, sc in next 2 sc, FPdc in next 2 sc, sc in last 2 sc, turn.

Row 3: Ch 1, sc in ea st across, turn.

Row 4: Ch 1, sc in 1st 2 sc, FPdc in next 2 dc 2 rows below, sk 2 sc, sc in next 2 sc, sk 2 sc, FPdc in next 2 dc 2 rows below, FPdc in 2 sk dc 2 rows below (behind prev sts), sk 4 sc, sc in next 2 sc, FPdc in next 2 dc 2 rows below, sk 2 sc, sc in last 2 sc, turn.

Rep row 3 for all odd rows.

Row 6: Ch 1, sc in 1st 2 sc, FPdc in next 2 dc 2 rows below, sk 2 sc, sc in next 2 sc, FPdc in next 4 dc 2 rows below, sk 4 sc, sc in next 2 sc, FPdc in next 2 dc 2 rows below, sk 2 sc, sc in last 2 sc, turn.

Row 8: Rep row 4.

Row 10: Ch 1, sc in 1st 3 sc, *FPdc in next 4 dc 2 rows below, sk 4 sc, sc in next 2 sc; rep from * to last sc, sc in last sc, turn.

Row 12: Ch 1, sc in 1st 3 sc, *sk 2 dc, FPdc in next 2 dc 2 rows below, FPdc in 2 sk dc 2 rows below (behind prev sts), sk 4 sc, sc in next 2 sc; rep from * across, sc in last sc, turn.

Row 14: Rep row 6.

Row 16: Rep row 6.

Rep rows 3–16 to desired length.

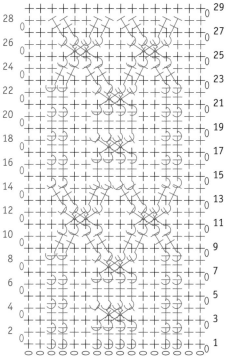

Severin Cable

A single line of post stitches runs through a classic cable pattern to add a touch of argyle to this fabric.

Ch 17 sts.

Row 1 (WS): Hdc in 3rd ch from hk (sk ch counts as hdc) and in ea ch across, turn—16 hdc.

Row 2: Ch 2 (counts as hdc), hdc in next hdc, FPdc around next st (sk st behind prev st), hdc in next 3 sts, sk next 2 hdc, FPdc around next 2 sts, FPdc around sk 2 sts, hdc in next 3 sts, FPdc around next st, hdc in next hdc, hdc in top of t-ch, turn.

Row 3: Ch 2, BPdc around all FPdc and hdc in all hdc, turn.

Row 4: Ch 2 (counts as hdc), hdc in next 3 sts, FPdc2tog around prev dc and next dc (sk 3 hdc), FPdc around next dc, hdc in next 4 dc, FPdc around next dc, FPdc2tog around next 2 dc, sk 2 hdc, hdc in next 3 sts, hdc in top of t-ch, turn.

Rep row 3 for all odd rows.

Row 6: Ch 2 (counts as hdc), hdc in next hdc, FPdc around next 2 dc (sk 2 hdc), hdc in next 2 dc, hdc in next hdc, FPdc around prev and next dc, sk 2 hdc, hdc in next hdc, hdc in next 2 dc, FPdc around prev dc and next dc, hdc in next hdc, hdc in top of t-ch, turn.

Row 8: Ch 2 (counts as hdc), hdc in next hdc, FPdc around next 2 dc, hdc in next 3 hdc, sk 1 dc, FPdc around next dc, FPdc around sk dc, hdc in next 3 hdc, FPdc around next 2 dc, hdc in next hdc, hdc in top of t-ch, turn.

Row 10: Ch 2 (counts as hdc), hdc in next hdc, hdc in next 2 dc, FPdc around 1st of last 2 dc, FPdc2tog around 2nd dc and next dc, sk 2 hdc, hdc in next hdc, hdc in next 2 dc, hdc in next hdc, FPdc2tog around prev and next dc, FPdc around next dc, sk 2 hdc, hdc in next 2 dc, hdc in next hdc, hdc in top of t-ch, turn.

Row 12: Ch 2 (counts as hdc), hdc in next hdc, FPdc around next dc, sk hdc behind dc, hdc in next hdc, hdc in next 2 dc, FPdc around prev and next dc, FPdc around next 2 dc, sk 4 hdc, hdc in next 2 dc, hdc in next hdc, FPdc around prev dc, hdc in next hdc, hdc in top of t-ch, turn.

Rows 14 and 15: Rep rows 2 and 3.

Rep rows 2–15 to desired length.

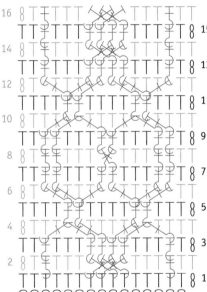

Marcus Cable

The vine network of twisting cables is beautiful on its own; mixed with front and back loop stitches, it becomes a memorable fabric.

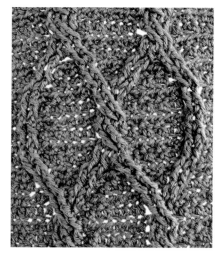

NOTE: After row 2, hdc blp in all hdc blps, hdc flp in all hdc flps when directed to hdc in hdc.

Ch a multiple of 12 sts plus 5.

Row 1 (WS): Hdc in the 3rd ch from the hk (sk ch counts as hdc) and ea ch across, turn.

Row 2: Ch 2 (counts as hdc), [hdc flp in next hdc, hdc blp in next hdc] twice, hdc flp in next hdc, *sk 2 sts, FPdc around next 2 sts, FPdc around prev 2 sts (skipped sts), [hdc blp in next hdc, hdc flp in next hdc] 4 times; rep from * to last 10 sts, sk 2 sts, FPdc around next 2 sts, FPdc around prev 2 sts (skipped sts), [hdc blp in next hdc, hdc flp in next hdc] twice, hdc blp in next hdc, hdc in top of t-ch, turn.

Row 3: Ch 2 (counts as hdc), hdc in all hdc, BPdc around all FPdc, hdc in top of t-ch, turn.

Rows 4 and 5: Rep rows 2 and 3 once.

Row 6: Ch 2 (counts as hdc), hdc in next 3 hdc, *FPdc around next 2 dc (leave 2 hdc unworked), hdc in prev 2 dc and next 2 dc, FPdc around prev 2 dc, sk 2 hdc, hdc in next 4 sts; rep from * to end, turn.

Row 7: Rep row 3.

Row 8: Ch 2 (counts as hdc), hdc in hdc, *FPdc around next 2 dc (leave 2 hdc unworked), hdc in prev 2 dc, [hdc blp in next hdc, hdc flp in next hdc] twice, hdc in next 2 dc, FPdc around prev 2 dc, sk 2 hdc; rep from * to last 2 sts, hdc in next hdc, hdc in top of hdc, turn.

Row 9: Rep row 3.

Row 10: Ch 2 (counts as hdc), hdc in next hdc, FPdc around next 2 dc, change to MC, *hdc in next 8 sts, sk 2 dc, FPdc around next 2 dc, FPdc around 2 prev skipped dc; rep from * to last 12 sts, hdc in next 8 sts, FPdc around next 2 dc, hdc in next hdc, hdc in top of t-ch, turn.

Rows 11–13: Rep row 3; rep row 10; rep row 3.

Row 14: Ch 2 (counts as hdc), hdc in next 3 sts, *FPdc around prev 2 dc, sk 2 hdc, hdc in next 4 sts, FPdc around next 2 dc (leave 2 hdc unworked), hdc in 2 prev sts and next 2 sts; rep from * to end, turn.

Row 15: Rep row 3.

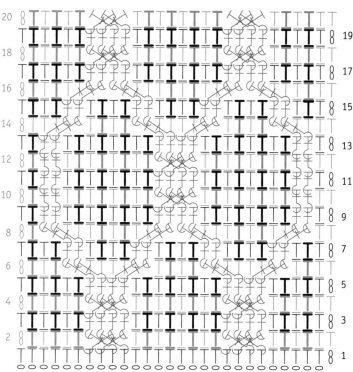

Row 16: Ch 2 (counts as hdc), hdc in next 5 sts, *FPdc around prev 2 dc, sk 4 hdc, FPdc around next 2 dc, hdc in 2 prev dc, hdc in next 6 sts; rep from * to last 10 sts, FPdc around prev 2 dc, sk 4 hdc, FPdc around next 2 dc, hdc in 2 prev dc, hdc in next 3 sts, hdc in top of t-ch, turn.

Row 17: Rep row 3.

Rep rows 2–17 to desired length.

Masterpiece Cable

Aptly named, this cable is a show stopper in projects. Watch your tension when crocheting this pattern, and be prepared to block for the best results.

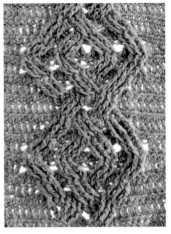

Ch 34 sts.

Row 1 (WS): Dc in 4th ch from hk and ea ch across, turn—32 dc.

Row 2: Ch 3 (counts as dc), dc in next 9 st, [sk 3 sts, FPtr in next 3 sts, FPtr in sk 3 sts] twice, dc in ea st across, turn.

Row 3: Ch 2 (counts as hdc), hdc in next 9 dc, BPdc in ea tr, hdc in ea dc across, hdc in top of t-ch, turn.

Row 4: Ch 3 (counts as dc), dc in next 6 sts, [sk 3 sts, FPtr in next 3 sts, FPtr in skipped 3 sts] 3 times, dc in ea st across, turn.

Row 5: Ch 2 (counts as hdc), hdc in ea dc, BPdc in next 3 tr, hdc in next 3 tr, BPdc in next 6 tr, hdc in next 3 tr, BPdc in next 3 tr, hdc in ea dc, hdc in top of t-ch, turn.

Row 6: Ch 3 (counts as dc), dc in next 3 sts, [sk 3 sts, FPtr in next 3 sts, FPtr in skipped 3 sts] 4 times, dc in ea st across, turn.

Row 7: Ch 2 (counts as hdc), hdc in ea dc, BPdc in next 3 tr, hdc in next 3 tr, BPdc in next 3 tr, hdc in next 6 tr, BPdc in next 3 tr, hdc in next 3 tr, BPdc in next 3 tr, hdc in ea dc, hdc in top of t-ch, turn.

Rows 8–11: Rep row 6; rep row 5; rep row 4; rep row 3.

Rep rows 2–11 to desired length.

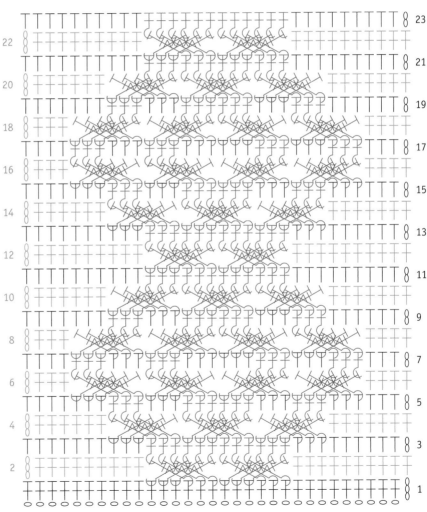

Brennen Cable

Between the clusters and chain spaces, the diamond in the fabric stars in center stage in the pattern. This stitch makes breathtaking shawls.

Back Post Three Double Crochet Cluster (BP3dc-cl): 3 dc-cl around the post of the st indicated from back to front to back.

Back Post Two Treble Crochet Cluster (BP2tr-cl): 2 tr-cl around the post of the st indicated from back to front to back.

Front Post Two Treble Crochet Cluster (FP2tr-cl): 2 tr-cl around the post of the st indicated from front to back to front.

Ch a multiple of 24 sts plus 3.

Row 1 (WS): Dc in 4th ch from hk, dc in next ch, *3 dc-cl in next ch, dc in next 7 ch, sk 2 ch, 2 tr-cl in next ch, ch 1, 2 tr-cl in 1st sk ch, dc in next 7 ch, 3 dc-cl in next ch, dc in next 5 ch; rep from * to end, turn.

Row 2: Ch 3 (counts as dc), *dc in next 8 dc, FP2tr-cl in next tr-cl, ch 1, tr in 1st sk dc (behind tr-cl), ch 1, sk [tr-cl, dc], tr in next dc, ch 1, FP2tr-cl in sk tr-cl (in front of tr), dc in next 9 sts; rep from * across, turn.

Row 3: Ch 3 (counts as dc), *dc in next 6 dc, BP2tr-cl in next tr-cl, ch 1, tr in 1st sk dc (in front of tr-cl), ch 1, sk 1 tr, BP2tr-cl in next tr, ch 1, BP2tr-cl in sk tr, ch 1, sk [tr-cl, dc], tr in next dc, ch 1, BP2tr-cl in sk tr-cl (in behind tr), dc in next 6 sts; BP3dc-cl in next dc; rep from * across to last st, dc in top of t-ch, turn.

Row 4: Ch 3 (counts as dc), *dc in next 4 dc, FP2tr-cl in next tr-cl, ch 1, tr in 1st skipped st, ch 1, FP2tr-cl in next tr-cl, ch 1, tr in sk tr, dc in next ch-1 sp, tr in next tr, ch 1, FP2tr-cl in sk tr-cl, ch 1, sk [tr-cl, dc], tr in next dc, ch 1, FP2tr-cl in sk tr-cl, dc in next 5 sts; rep from * across, turn.

Row 5: Ch 3 (counts as dc), *dc in next 2 dc, BP2tr-cl in next tr-cl, ch 1, tr in 1st skipped st, ch 1, BP2tr-cl in next tr-cl, ch 1, tr in sk tr, dc in next ch-1 sp, dc in next 3 sts, dc in next ch-1 sp, tr in next tr, ch 1, BP2tr-cl in sk tr-cl, ch 1, sk [tr-cl, dc], tr in next dc, ch 1, BP2tr-cl in sk tr-cl, dc in next 3 sts; rep from * across, turn.

Row 6: Ch 3 (counts as dc), *FP2tr-cl in next tr-cl, ch 1, tr in 1st skipped st, ch 1, FP2tr-cl in next tr-cl, ch 1, tr in sk tr, dc in next ch-1 sp, dc in next 7 sts, dc in next ch-1 sp, tr in next tr, ch 1, FP2tr-cl in sk tr-cl, ch 1, sk [tr-cl, dc], tr in next dc, ch 1, FP2tr-cl in sk tr-cl, dc in next st; rep from * across, turn.

Row 7: Ch 3 (counts as dc), *tr in next tr, ch 1, BP2tr-cl in sk tr-cl, ch 1, tr in next tr, ch 1, BP2tr-cl in sk tr-cl, dc in next 9 sts, BP2tr-cl in next tr-cl, ch 1, tr in sk tr, ch 1, BP2tr-cl in next tr-cl, ch 1, tr in sk tr, dc in next st; rep from * across, turn.

Row 8: Ch 3 (counts as dc), *dc in next tr, dc in ch-1 sp, tr in next tr, ch 1, FP2tr-cl in sk tr-cl, ch 1, sk [tr-cl, dc], tr in next dc, ch 1, FP2tr-cl in sk tr-cl, dc in next 5 sts, FP2tr-cl in next tr-cl, ch 1, tr in 1st skipped st, ch 1, FP2tr-cl in next tr-cl, ch 1, tr in sk tr, dc in next ch-1 sp, dc in next 2 sts; rep from * across, turn.

Row 9: Ch 3 (counts as dc), *dc in next 3 sts, dc in ch-1 sp, tr in next tr, ch 1, BP2tr-cl in sk tr-cl, ch 1, sk [tr-cl, dc], tr in next dc, ch 1, BP2tr-cl in sk tr-cl, dc in next st, BP2tr-cl in next tr-cl, ch 1, tr in 1st skipped st, ch 1, BP2tr-cl in next tr-cl, ch 1, tr in sk tr, dc in next ch-1 sp, dc in next 4 sts; rep from * across, turn.

Row 10: Ch 3 (counts as dc), *dc in next 5 sts, dc in ch-1 sp, tr in next tr, ch 1, FP2tr-cl in sk tr-cl, ch 1, sk tr-cl, FP2tr-cl in next tr-cl, ch 1, FP2tr-cl in sk tr-cl, ch 1, FP2tr-cl in next tr-cl, ch 1, tr in sk tr, dc in next ch-1 sp, dc in next 6 sts; rep from * across, turn.

Row 11: Ch 3 (counts as dc), *dc in next 7 sts, dc in ch-1 sp, sk tr-cl, tr in next tr-cl, ch 1, BP2tr-cl in sk tr-cl, ch 1, sk tr-cl, BP2tr-cl in next tr-cl, ch 1, tr in sk tr-cl, dc in next ch-1 sp, dc in next 7 sts, BP3dc-cl in next dc; rep from * across to last st, dc in top of t-ch, turn.

Row 12: Ch 3 (counts as dc), *dc in next 9 sts, dc in ch-1 sp, sk tr-cl, FP2tr-cl in next tr-cl, ch 1, FP2tr-cl in sk tr-cl, dc in next ch-1 sp, dc in next 10 sts; rep from * across to last st, dc in top of t-ch, turn.

Row 13: Ch 3 (counts as dc), *dc in next 2 sts, BP3dc-cl in next dc, dc in next 7 dc, sk tr-cl, BP2tr-cl in next tr-cl, ch 1, BP2tr-cl in sk tr-cl, dc in next 7 sts, BP3dc-cl in next dc, dc in next 3 sts; rep from * across to last st, dc in top of t-ch, turn.

Rep rows 2–13 to desired length.

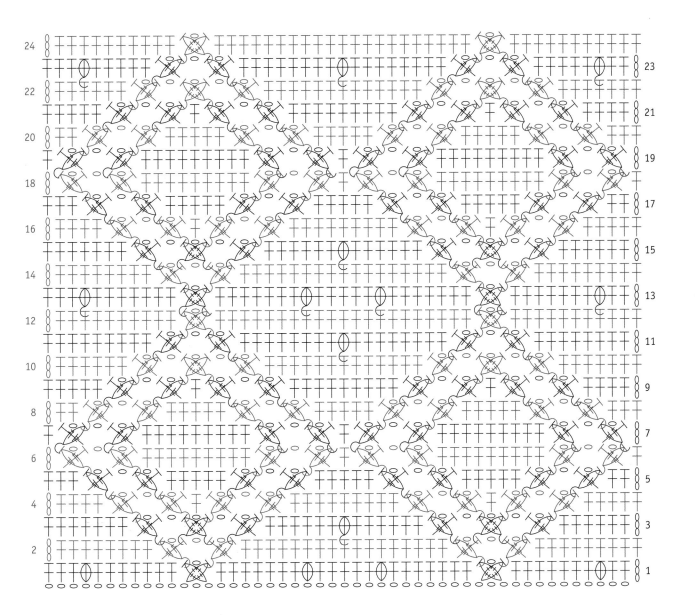

CHAPTER 3

Lace Stitch Patterns

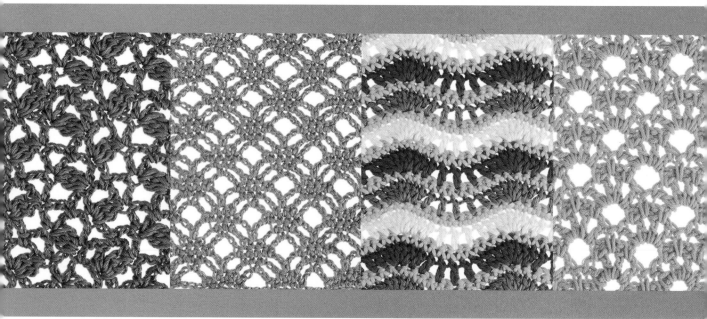

Picot Trellis

The little chain-three picots in the center of the stitches look just like little buds starting to bloom on a trellis.

Ch a multiple of 5 sts plus 2.

Row 1 (RS): Sc in 2nd ch from hk, *ch 5, sk 4 ch, sc in next ch; rep from * across, turn.

Row 2: Ch 6, [sc, ch 3, sc] in 1st ch-5 sp, *ch 5, sk next sc, [sc, ch 3, sc] in next ch-5 sp; rep from * across to last ch-5 sp, ch 2, tr in last sc, turn.

Row 3: Ch 1, sc in tr, *ch 5, sk ch-3 sp, [sc, ch 3, sc] in next ch-5 sp; rep from * across to last ch-5 sp, ch 5, sk ch-3 sp, sc in t-ch sp, turn.

Rep rows 2 and 3 to desired length.

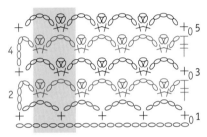

TIP

Chain-space stitch patterns all have one thing in common besides a bunch of chains: blocking. Each of these stitch patterns comes alive when you block it. Their look changes if you stretch them really taut or keep them loose. Either way, you are rewarded in kind when you take the time to block these patterns.

Trefoil Link

This stitch pattern is great on its own or layered on top of a solid fabric.

Trefoil: [Sc, ch 3, sc, ch 5, sc, ch 3, sc] all in ch-sp indicated.

Ch a multiple of 7 sts plus 3.

Row 1 (WS): Sc in 2nd ch from hk, ch 2, sk 2 ch, sc in next ch, ch 3, sk 1 ch, sc in next ch, *ch 4, sk 4 ch, sc in next ch, ch 3, sk 1 ch, sc in next ch; rep from * across to last 3 ch, ch 2, sk 2 ch, sc in last ch, turn.

Row 2: Ch 1, sc in 1st st, ch 2, *trefoil in next ch-3 sp, ch 4, sk ch-4 sp; rep from * to last ch-3 sp, trefoil in last ch-3 sp, ch 2, sk ch-sp, sc in last sc, turn.

Row 3: Ch 6 (counts as tr, ch-2 sp), *sk ch-3 sp, [sc, ch 3, sc] in next ch-5 sp, ch 4, sk next 2 ch-sp; rep from * across to last ch-5 sp, [sc, ch 3, sc] in last ch-5 sp, ch 2, sk last ch-sps, tr in last sc, turn.

Rep rows 2 and 3 to desired length.

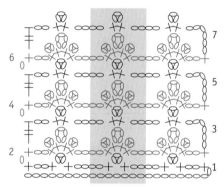

Trefoil Lattice

Alternating v-stitches with trefoils, this fabric mimics a lattice with blooming flowers hanging on it.

V-Stitch (v-st): [Dc, ch 1, dc] in st indicated.

Trefoil: [Ch 3, (sc, ch 4) 3 times, sc, ch 3] in st indicated.

Ch a multiple of 10 sts plus 5.

Row 1 (RS): Dc in 5th ch from hk, *sk 4 ch, trefoil in next ch, sk 4 ch, v-st in next ch; rep from * across, turn.

Row 2: Ch 5 (counts as dc, ch-2 sp), [sc, ch 4, sc, ch 3] in ch-1 sp, sk next ch-4 sp, *v-st in next ch-4 sp, trefoil in next ch-1 sp, sk next ch-4 sp; rep from * across to last trefoil, v-st in next ch-4 sp, ch 3, [sc, ch 4, sc, ch 2, dc] in 4th ch of t-ch, turn.

Row 3: Ch 4 (counts as dc, ch-1 sp), dc in ch-2 sp, *trefoil in next ch-1 sp, sk next ch-4 sp, v-st in next ch-4 sp; rep from * across to last ch-1 sp, trefoil in next ch-1 sp, sk next ch-4 sp, v-st in t-ch, turn.

Rep rows 2 and 3 to desired length.

Last row: Ch 1, sc in dc, *ch 4, sk next ch-4 sp, sc in next ch-4 sp, ch 4, sc in ch-1 sp; rep from * across working last sc in t-ch, fasten off.

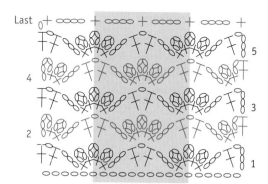

Zen Lattice

The easy rhythm of this stitch pattern can lull you into a peaceful Zen state, hence the name.

Ch a multiple of 8 sts plus 2.

Row 1 (RS): Sc in 2nd ch from hk, sc in next 2 ch, *ch 5, sk 3 ch, sc in next 5 ch; rep from * across to last 6 ch, ch 5, sk 3 ch, sc in last 3 ch, turn.

Row 2: Ch 1, sc in 1st 2 sc, *ch 3, sk next sc, sc in next ch-5 sp, ch 3, sk 1 sc, sc in next 3 sc; rep from * across to last ch-5 sp, ch 3, sc in last ch-5 sp, ch 3, sc in last 2 sc, turn.

Row 3: Ch 1, sc in sc, *ch 3, sk next sc, sc in next ch-3 sp, sc in sc, sc in next ch-3 sp, ch 3, sk 1 sc, sc in next sc; rep from * across, turn.

Row 4: Ch 5 (counts as dc, ch-2 sp), *sc in ch-3 sp, sc in next 3 sc, sc in next ch-3 sp, ch 5, sk sc; rep from * across to last 2 ch-3 sps, sc in ch-3 sp, sc in next 3 sc, sc in next ch-3 sp, ch 2, dc in last sc, turn.

Row 5: Ch 1, sc in dc, *ch 3, sk next sc, sc in next 3 sc, sk next sc, ch 3, sc in ch-5 sp; rep from * across, turn.

Row 6: Ch 1, sc in 1st sc, sc in next ch-3 sp, *ch 3, sk 1 sc, sc in next sc, ch 3, sc in next ch-3 sp, sc in sc, sc in next ch-3 sp; rep from * across to last 2 ch-3 sps, ch 3, sk 1 sc, sc in next sc, ch 3, sk sc, sc in last ch-3 sp, sc in last sc, turn.

Row 7: Ch 1, sc in 1st 2 sc, *ch 5, sk sc, sc in next ch-3 sp, sc in next 3 sc, sc in next ch-3 sp; rep from * across to last 2 ch-3 sps, ch 5, sc in last ch-3 sp, sc in last 2 sc, turn.

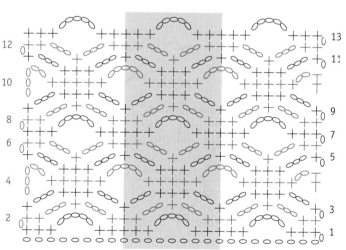

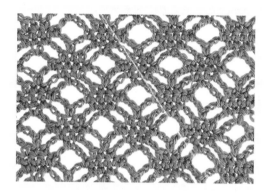

Rep rows 2–7 to desired length.

Zen Shell

This is a fun variation on the Zen stitch pattern with shells completely filling in some of the chain spaces.

Shell (sh): 5 dc in st indicated.

Ch a multiple of 12 sts.

Row 1 (RS): Sc in 8th ch from hk, sc in next 2 ch, *ch 5, sk 3 ch, sc in next 3 ch; rep from * across to last 2 ch, ch 2, dc in last ch, turn.

Row 2: Ch 1, sc in dc, *ch 3, sk sc, sc in next sc, ch 3, sc in ch-5 sp; rep from * across, turn.

Row 3: Ch 1, *sc in sc, sc in ch-3 sp, ch 5, sk sc, sc in next ch-3 sp, sc in sc, sc in next ch-3 sp, sh in sc, sc in next ch-3 sp; rep from * across to last 3 sc, sc in sc, sc in ch-3 sp, ch 5, sk sc, sc in next ch-3 sp, sc in sc, turn.

Row 4: Ch 1, sc in sc, *ch 3, sc in ch-5 sp, ch 3, sk sc, sc in next sc, ch 3, sk sc, sk 2 dc, sc in next dc, ch 3, sk 2 dc, sk sc, sc in next sc; rep from * across to last ch-5 sp, ch 3, sc in ch-5 sp, ch 3, sk sc, sc in next sc, turn.

Row 5: Ch 5, sc in ch-3 sp, sc in sc, sc in ch-3 sp, *ch 5, sk sc, sc in next ch-3 sp, sc in sc, sc in next ch-3 sp; rep from * across to last sc, ch 2, dc in sc, turn.

Row 6: Rep row 2.

Row 7: Ch 1, *sc in sc, sc in ch-3 sp, sh in sc, sc in next ch-3 sp, sc in sc, sc in next ch-3 sp, ch 5, sk sc, sc in next ch-3 sp; rep from * across to last 3 sc, sc in sc, sc in ch-3 sp, sh in sc, sc in next ch-3 sp, sc in sc, turn.

Row 8: Ch 1, sc in sc, *ch 3, sk sc, sk 2 dc, sc in next dc, ch 3, sk 2 dc, sk sc, sc in next sc, ch 3, sk sc, sc in ch-5 sp, ch 3, sk sc, sc in next sc; rep from * across to last sh, ch 3, sk sc, sk 2 dc, sc in next dc, ch 3, sk 2 dc, sk sc, sc in next sc, turn.

Row 9: Rep row 5.

Rep rows 2–9 to desired length, ending with row 8.

Last row: Ch 3 (counts as hdc, ch 1), sc in ch-3 sp, sc in sc, sc in ch-3 sp, *ch 3, sk sc, sc in next ch-3 sp, sc in sc, sc in next ch-3 sp; rep from * across to last sc, ch 1, hdc in last sc. Fasten off.

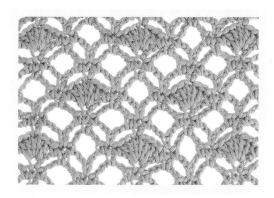

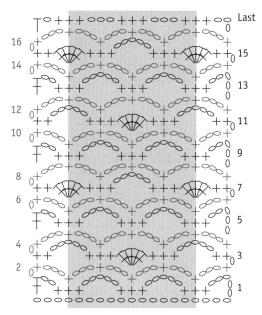

Diamond Lattice

This stitch pattern makes a simple fabric even though the stitch diagram looks complex.

Double Crochet Treble Together (dctrtog): Yo, insert hk into st indicated, pull up lp, yo, pull through 2 lps on hk, yo twice, insert hk into st indicated, pull up lp, yo, pull through 2 lps on hk twice, yo, pull through rem lps on hk.

Ch a multiple of 4 sts plus 2.

Row 1 (RS): Sc in 2nd ch from hk, *ch 2, dc2tog in same ch and ch 4 ch away (sk 3 ch), ch 2, sc in same ch as dc2tog; rep from * across, turn.

Row 2: Ch 4 (counts as tr), dc in next dc2tog, ch 2, sc around prev dc2tog, *ch 2, dc2tog in prev and next dc2tog, ch 2, sc around same dc2tog; rep from * across to last dc2tog, ch 2, dctrtog in prev dc2tog and sc, turn.

Row 3: Ch 1, sc in dctrtog, *ch 2, dc2tog in prev st and next dc2tog, ch 2, sc around dc2tog; rep from * across, ending sc in dctrtog, turn.

Rep rows 2 and 3 to desired length ending with row 2.

Last row: Ch 1, sc in dctrtog, *ch 3, sc in next dc2tog; rep from * across to end, sc in dctrtog. Fasten off.

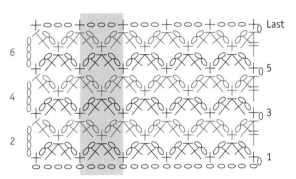

Posy Arcade

A classic net mesh pattern is enlivened with cluster flowers.

Ch a multiple of 8 sts plus 2.

Row 1 (RS): Sc in 2nd ch from hk, *ch 5, sk 3 ch, sc in next ch; rep from * across, turn.

Row 2: Ch 5, *sc in next ch-5 sp, ch 2, 3 dc-cl in next sc, ch 2, sc in next ch-5 sp, ch 5, sk sc; rep from * across to last 2 ch-5 sps, sc in next ch-5 sp, ch 2, 3 dc-cl in next sc, ch 2, sc in next ch-5 sp, ch 2, dc in last sc, turn.

Row 3: Ch 1, sc in dc, ch 5, 3 dc-cl in 1st dc, *sl st in next 3 dc-cl, ch 5, 3 dc-cl in sl st just made, ch 1, sl st in next ch-5 sp, ch 5, 3 dc-cl in sl st just made; rep from * across to last 2 ch-5 sps, sl st in next 3 dc-cl, ch 5, 3 dc-cl in sl st just made, sc in last ch-5 sp, turn.

Row 4: Ch 5, *sc in ch-5 sp, ch 2, 3 dc-cl in sl st, ch 2, sc in next ch-5 sp, ch 5, sk sl st; rep from * across to last 2 ch-5 sps, sc in next ch-5 sp, ch 2, 3 dc-cl in next sl st, ch 2, sc in last ch-5 sp, ch 2, dc in last sc, turn.

Row 5: Ch 1, sc in dc, *ch 5, sk sc, sc in 3 dc-cl, ch 5, sk sc, sc in ch-5 sp; rep from * across, turn.

Row 6: Ch 2, dc in sc, ch 2, sc in next ch-5 sp, ch 5, sk sc, *sc in next ch-5 sp, ch 2, 3 dc-cl in next sc, ch 2, sc in next ch-5 sp, ch 5, sk sc; rep from * across to last ch-5 sp, ch 2, 2 dc-cl in last sc, turn.

Row 7: Ch 1, sc in 2 dc-cl, ch 4, 3 dc-cl in prev st, ch 1, *sl st in next ch-5 sp, ch 5, 3 dc-cl in sl st just made, sl st in next 3 dc-cl, ch 5, 3 dc-cl in sl st just made, ch 1; rep from * across to last ch-5 sp, sl st in last ch-5 sp, ch 5, 3 dc-cl in sl st just made, sc in dc, turn.

Row 8: Ch 2, dc in sc, ch 2, sc in next ch-5 sp, ch 5, sk sl st, *sc in next ch-5 sp, ch 2, 3 dc-cl in sl st, ch 2, sc in next ch-5 sp, ch 5, sk sl st; rep from * across to last ch-5 sp, sc in last ch-5 sp, ch 2, 2 dc-cl in last sc, turn.

Row 9: Ch 1, sc in 2 dc-cl, *ch 5, sk sc, sc in ch-5 sp, ch 5, sk sc, sc in 3 dc-cl; rep from * across to last 3 dc-cl, ch 5, sk sc, sc in ch-5 sp, ch 5, sk sc, sc in last dc, turn.

Rep rows 2–9 to desired length.

Iced Shell

The combination of open chain spaces plus solid shells gives almost a wave stripe look to the fabric.

Ch a multiple of 3 sts plus 2.

Row 1 (RS): Sc in 2nd ch from hk, *ch 3, sk 2 ch, sc in next ch; rep from * across, turn.

Row 2: Ch 3 (counts as dc), dc in 1st sc, *sc in next ch-3 sp, 3 dc in next sc; rep from * across to last ch-3 sp, sc in last ch-3 sp, 2 dc in last sc, turn.

Row 3: Ch 1, sc in 1st dc, *ch 3, skip next 3 sts, sc in next dc; rep from * across, sc in top of t-ch, turn.

Rep rows 2 and 3 to desired length.

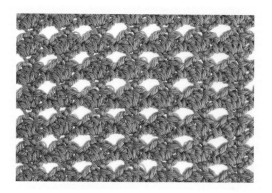

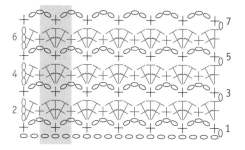

Fairy Shell

Depending on your hook size, this shell pattern can be either very solid or very lacy. Why not try both and see what your favorite is?

Shell (sh): [2 dc, ch 2, 2 dc] in st indicated.

Ch a multiple of 6 sts plus 4.

Row 1 (RS): Sc in 4th ch from hk, *sk 2 ch, sh in next ch, sk 2 ch, [sc, ch 3, sc] in next ch; rep from * across to last 6 ch, sk 2 ch, sh in next ch, sk 2 ch, [sc, ch 1, hdc] in last ch, turn.

Row 2: Ch 3 (counts as dc), 2 dc in hdc, *[sc, ch 3, sc] in ch-2 sp, sh in ch-3 sp; rep from * across to last ch-2 sp, [sc, ch 3, sc] in last ch-2 sp, 3 dc in 3rd ch of t-ch, turn.

Row 3: Ch 3 (counts as hdc, ch 1-sp), sc in 1st dc, *sh in ch-3 sp, [sc, ch 3, sc] in next ch-2 sp; rep from * across to last ch-2 sp, sh in last ch-3 sp, [sc, ch 1, hdc] in top of t-ch, turn.

Rep rows 2 and 3 to desired length.

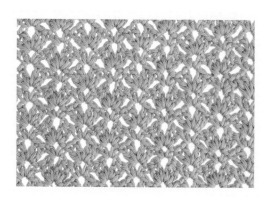

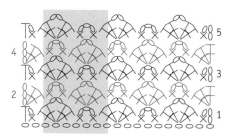

Pistachio Shell

This classic stitch pattern always reminds me of cracked-open pistachio shells when I block it open.

Shell (sh): [(Dc, ch 1) 3 times, dc] in st indicated.

V-Stitch (v-st): [Dc, ch 1, dc] in st indicated.

Ch a multiple of 8 sts plus 2.

Row 1 (RS): Sc in 2nd ch from hk, *ch 1, sk 3 ch, sh in next ch, ch 1, sk 3 ch, sc in next ch; rep from * across to end, turn.

Row 2: Ch 3 (counts as dc), dc in same sc, *ch 2, sk 2 ch-1 sps, [sc, ch 1, sc] in next ch-1 sp, ch 2, sk next 2 ch-1 sps, v-st in next sc; rep from * across to last sc, 2 dc in last sc, turn.

Row 3: Ch 3 (counts as dc), [dc, ch 1, dc] in 1st dc, ch 1, *sk ch-2 sp, sc in next ch-1 sp, ch 1, sk ch-2 sp, sh in next ch-1 sp, ch 1; rep from * across to last ch-1 sp, sc in last ch-1 sp, ch 1, sk ch-2 sp, [dc, ch 1, 2 dc] in top of t-ch, turn.

Row 4: Ch 1, 2 sc in 1st dc, *ch 2, sk 2 ch-1 sps, v-st in next sc, sk 2 ch-1 sps, ch 2, [sc, ch 1, sc] in next ch-1 sp; rep from * across to last sh, ch 2, sk 2 ch-1 sps, v-st in last sc, sk 2 ch-1 sps, ch 2, 2 sc in top of t-ch, turn.

Row 5: Ch 1, sc in 1st sc, *ch 1, sk ch-2 sp, sh in next ch-1 sp, ch 1, sk ch-2 sp, sc in next ch-1 sp; rep from * across to last sc, sc in last sc, turn.

Rep rows 2–5 to desired length.

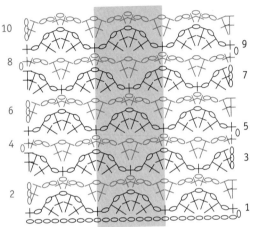

Arcade

When crocheted in a large piece, this stitch pattern looks like little teardrops sprinkled all over a gentle lace.

Shell (sh): [(Dc, ch 1) 3 times, dc] in st indicated.

Single Crochet Spike (sc spike): Insert hk into st indicated 1 row below last, yo and pull up lp around prev row, yo, draw through lps on hk.

Ch a multiple of 6 sts plus 2.

Row 1 (WS): Sc in 2nd ch from hk, ch 1, sk 1 ch, *sc in next ch, ch 3, sk 1 ch, sc in next ch, ch 3, sk 3 ch; rep from * across to last 5 ch, sc in next ch, ch 3, sk 1 ch, sc in next ch, ch 1, sc in last ch, turn.

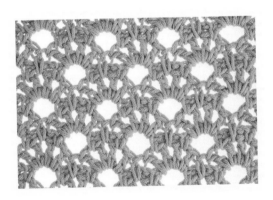

Row 2: Ch 1, sc in sc, *sh in next ch-3 sp, sc spike over next ch-3 sp (sk 1 ch on foundation row) and in next ch on foundation row; rep from * across; sc in last sc, turn.

Row 3: Ch 4 (counts as dc, ch-1 sp), sc in next ch-1 sp, *ch 3, sk ch-1 sp, sc in next ch-1 sp, ch 3, sc in next ch-1 sp; rep from * across to last 2 ch-1 sps, ch 3, sk next ch-1 sp, sc in next ch-1 sp, ch 1, dc in last sc, turn.

Row 4: Ch 3 (counts as dc), [dc, ch 1, dc] in dc, *sc spike over ch-3 sp and in ch-1 sp 1 row below, sh in ch-3 sp; rep from * across to last ch-3 sp, sc spike over ch-3 sp and in ch-1 sp 1 row below, [dc, ch 1, 2 dc] in 3rd ch of t-ch, turn.

Row 5: Ch 1, sc in dc, ch 1, *sc in next ch-1 sp, ch 3, sc in next ch-1 sp, ch 3, sk ch-1 sp; rep from * across to last 2 ch-1 sps, sc in next ch-1 sp, ch 3, sc in last ch-1 sp, ch 1, sc in top of t-ch, turn.

Row 6: Ch 1, sc in sc, *sh in ch-3 sp, sc spike over ch-3 sp and in ch-1 sp 1 row below; rep from * across to last ch-3 sp, sh in last ch-3 sp, sc in last sc, turn.

Rep rows 3–6 to desired length.

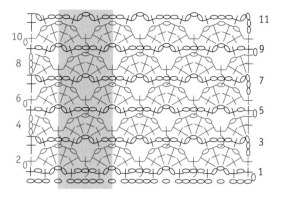

Clunky Lace

Clunky describes not the weight of the fabric, but the short, squat shells that dot the fabric.

Ch a multiple of 6 sts plus 2.

Row 1 (RS): [2 hdc, ch 2, 2 hdc] in 5th ch from hk, *sk 2 ch, 2 dc-cl in next ch, sk 2 ch, [2 hdc, ch 2, 2 hdc] in next ch; rep from * across to last 3 ch, sk 2 ch, hdc in last ch, turn.

Row 2: Ch 2, *[2 sc, ch 2, 2 sc] in next ch-2 sp, sc in 2 dc-cl; rep from * across to last ch-2 sp, [2 sc, ch 2, 2 sc] in last ch-2 sp, hdc in top of t-ch, turn.

Row 3: Ch 2, *[2 hdc, ch 2, 2 hdc] in next ch-2 sp, 2 dc-cl in sc; rep from * across to last ch-2 sp, [2 hdc, ch 2, 2 hdc] in last ch-2 sp, hdc in top of t-ch, turn.

Rep rows 2 and 3 to desired length.

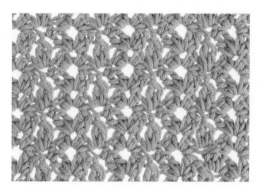

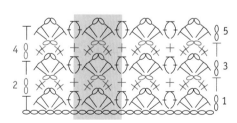

Delmarva

The shell clusters in this stitch pattern transform the fabric from horizontal rows to vertical columns of flowers.

Shell (sh): [(2 tr-cl, ch 1) twice, 2 tr-cl] in st indicated.

Ch a multiple of 10 sts plus 7.

Row 1 (WS): 2 dc in 5th ch from hk, sk ch, 2 dc in next ch (dc group made), *ch 2, sk 2 ch, [sc, ch 2, sc] in next ch, ch 2, sk 2 ch, [2 dc in next ch, sk ch] twice, 2 dc in next ch; rep from * across to last 10 ch, ch 2, sk 2 ch, [sc, ch 2, sc] in next ch, ch 2, sk 2 ch, [2 dc in next ch, sk ch] twice, dc in last ch, turn.

Row 2: Ch 3 (counts as dc), 2 dc btw dc of next 2 dc groups, *sk next ch-2 sp, sh in next ch-2 sp, 2 dc btw dc of next 3 dc groups; rep from * across to last 3 ch-2 sps, sk next ch-2 sp, sh in next ch-2 sp, 2 dc btw dc of next 2 dc groups, dc in top of t-ch, turn.

Row 3: Ch 3 (counts as dc), 2 dc btw dc of next 2 dc groups, *ch 2, sk ch-1 sp, [sc, ch 2, sc] in next 2 tr-cl, ch 2, 2 dc btw dc of next 3 dc groups; rep from * across to last sh, ch 2, sk ch-1 sp, [sc, ch 2, sc] in next 2 tr-cl, ch 2, 2 dc btw dc of next 2 dc groups, dc in top of t-ch, turn.

Rep rows 2 and 3 to desired length.

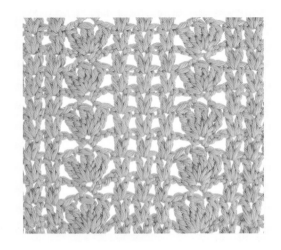

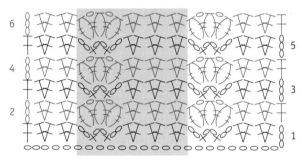

Iris Shell

The cluster stitches perched on top of the shells remind me of little birds sitting delicately on the tops of trees.

Shell (sh): [(Dc, ch 1) 5 times, dc] in st indicated.

Half Shell (half sh): [(Dc, ch 1) twice, 2 dc] in st indicated.

Ch a multiple of 10 sts plus 4.

Row 1 (RS): [(Dc, ch 1) twice, dc] in 4th ch from hk (t-ch counts as dc), *sk 3 ch, sc in next ch, ch 3, sk 1 ch, sc in next ch, sk 3 ch, sh in next ch; rep from * to last 10 ch, sk 3 ch, sc in next ch, ch 3, sk 1 ch, sc in next ch, sk 3 ch, half sh in last ch, turn.

Row 2: Ch 2, dc in 1st dc, ch 3, sc in ch-1 sp, ch 2, sk next ch-1 sp, [sc, ch 3, sc] in ch-3 sp, *ch 2, sk next ch-1 sp, sc in next ch-1 sp, ch 3, 3 dc-cl in next ch-1 sp, ch 3, sc in next ch-1 sp, ch 2, sk next ch-1 sp, [sc, ch 3, sc] in ch-3 sp; rep from * across to last ch-3 sp, ch 2, sk next ch-1 sp, sc in next ch-1 sp, ch 3, 2 dc-cl in top of t-ch, turn.

Row 3: Ch 3, sc in ch-3 sp, sk ch-2 sp, sh in ch-3 sp, *sk ch-2 sp, sc in ch-3 sp, ch 3, sk 3 dc-cl, sc in ch-3 sp, sk ch-2 sp, sh in ch-3 sp; rep from * across to last ch-2 sp, sk ch-2 sp, sc in ch-3 sp, ch 1, hdc in last dc, turn.

Row 4: Ch 3, sc in ch-1 sp, ch 2, sk ch-1 sp, sc in next ch-1 sp, ch 3, 3 dc-cl in next ch-1 sp, ch 3, sc in next ch-1 sp, *ch 2, sk next ch-1 sp, [sc, ch 3, sc] in ch-3 sp, ch 2, sk next ch-1 sp, sc in next ch-1 sp, ch 3, 3 dc-cl in next ch-1 sp, ch 3, sc in next ch-1 sp; rep from * across to last ch-1 sp, ch 2, sk last ch-1 sp, [sc, ch 1, hdc] in last ch-3 sp, turn.

Row 5: Ch 3 (counts as dc), [(dc, ch 1) twice, dc] in ch-1 sp, *sk ch-2 sp, sc in ch-3 sp, ch 3, sk 3 dc-cl, sc in next ch-3 sp, sk ch-2 sp, sh in next ch-3 sp; rep from * to last 3 dc-cl, sk ch-2 sp, sc in ch-3 sp, ch 3, sk 3 dc-cl, sc in next ch-3 sp, sk ch-2 sp, half sh in last ch-3 sp, turn.

Rep rows 2–5 to desired length.

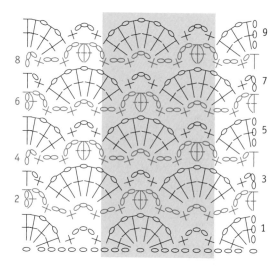

Colonnade

The arches in this stitch pattern make a bold fabric choice, and are best used in scarves or skirts where you want to make a statement.

Single Crochet Spike (sc spike): Insert hk into st indicated 1 row below last row worked, yo and pull up lp around prev row, yo, draw through lps on hk.

Ch a multiple of 7 sts plus 2.

Row 1 (RS): Sc in 2nd ch from hk, ch 1, sk 1 ch, *sc in next ch, ch 4, sk 2 ch, sc in next ch, ch 3, sk 3 ch; rep from * across to last 6 ch, sc in next ch, ch 4, sk 2 ch, sc in next ch, ch 1, sk 1 ch, sc in last ch, turn.

Row 2: Ch 1, sc in 1st sc, *9 dc in ch-4 sp, sc spike over ch-3 sp to center ch of skipped 3-ch on foundation ch; rep from * across to last ch-4 sp, 9 dc in last ch-4 sp, sc in last sc, turn.

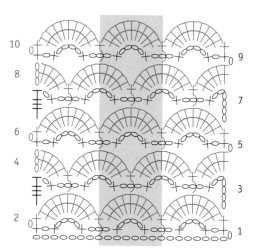

Row 3: Ch 6 (counts as dtr, ch-1 sp), sk 2 dc, sc in next dc, ch 3, sk 3 dc, *sc in next dc, ch 4, sk 4 dc, sc in next dc, ch 3, sk 3 dc; rep from * across to last 3 dc, sc in next dc, ch 1, dtr in last sc, turn.

Row 4: Ch 3 (counts as dc), 4 dc in ch-1 sp, *sc spike over ch-3 sp in center dc, 9 dc in ch-4 sp; rep from * across to last ch-3 sp, sc spike over ch-3 sp in center dc, 5 dc in ch-6 sp, turn.

Row 5: Ch 1, sc in dc, ch 1, sk 1 dc, sc in next dc, *ch 4, sk 4 dc, sc in next dc, ch 3, sk 3 dc, sc in next dc; rep from * across to last 7 dc, ch 4, sk 4 dc, sc in next dc, ch 1, sc in top of t-ch, turn.

Row 6: Ch 1, sc in sc, *9 dc in ch-4 sp, sc spike over ch-3 sp in center dc; rep from * across to last ch-3 sp, 9 dc in last ch-4 sp, sc in last sc, turn.

Rep rows 3–6 to desired length.

Diamond Shell

Alternating diamonds look almost like teardrops on a very versatile fabric.

V-Stitch (v-st): [Dc, ch 3, dc] in st indicated.

Chain a multiple of 10 sts plus 3.

Row 1 (RS): Dc in 4th ch from hk, dc in next ch, sk 2 ch, v-st in next ch, sk 2 ch, *dc in next 5 ch, sk 2 ch, v-st in next ch, sk 2 ch; rep from * across to last 3 ch, dc in last 3 ch, turn.

Row 2: Ch 2, sk 1st 2 dc, dc in next dc, ch 2, 5 dc in ch-3 sp, ch 2, *dc2tog over 1st and 5th dc (sk 2nd, 3rd, and 4th dc) of 5-dc group, ch 2, 5 dc in ch-3 sp, ch 2; rep from * across to last 3 dc, dc2tog over next dc and top of t-ch, turn.

Row 3: Ch 4 (counts as dc and ch 1), dc into top of dc2tog, dc in next 5 dc, *v-st in top of dc2tog, dc in next 5 dc; rep from * across to last dc, [dc, ch 1, dc] in last dc, turn.

Row 4: Ch 3 (counts as dc), 2 dc in 1st dc, ch 2, dc2tog over 1st and 5th dc, ch 2, *5 dc in ch-3 sp, ch 2, dc2tog over 1st and 5th dc, ch 2; rep from * across to t-ch, 3 dc in 3rd ch of t-ch, turn.

Row 5: Ch 3 (counts as dc), dc in next 2 dc, v-st in top of dc2tog, *dc in next 5 dc, v-st in top of dc2tog; rep from * across to last 3 dc, dc in last 3 dc, turn.

Rep rows 2–5 to desired length.

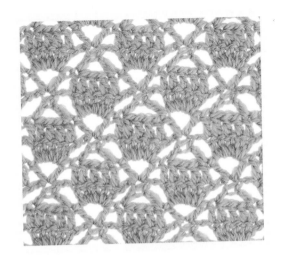

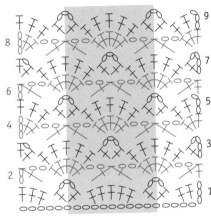

Jumping Shells

This lace separates shells by a row, scattering them all throughout the fabric as if they jumped there.

Ch a multiple of 9 sts plus 6.

Row 1 (RS): Sc in 7th ch from hk (sk ch counts as dc, ch-1 sp), *sk 2 ch, 5 dc in next ch, sk 2 ch, sc in next ch, ch 3, sk 2 ch, sc in next ch; rep from * across to last 8 ch, sk 2 ch, 5 dc in next ch, sk 2 ch, sc in next ch, ch 1, sk 1 ch, dc in last ch, turn.

Row 2: Ch 1, sc in dc, *sk sc, dc in next 2 dc, ch 3, sc in next dc, ch 3, dc in next 2 dc, sk sc, sc in ch-3 sp; rep from * across, ending sc in top of t-ch, turn.

Row 3: Ch 3 (counts as dc), 2 dc in 1st sc, *sk 2 dc, sc in ch-3 sp, ch 3, sc in next ch-3 sp, sk 2 dc, 5 dc in sc; rep from * across to last 2 ch-3 sps, sk 2 dc, sc in ch-3 sp, ch 3, sc in next ch-3 sp, sk 2 dc, 3 dc in last sc, turn.

Row 4: Ch 1, sc in 1st dc, ch 3, dc in next 2 dc, sk sc, sc in ch-3 sp, *sk sc, dc in next 2 dc, ch 3, sc in next dc, ch 3, dc in next 2 dc, sk sc, sc in ch-3 sp; rep from * across to last 3 dc, dc in next 2 dc, ch 3, sc in top of t-ch, turn.

Row 5: Ch 4 (counts as dc, ch-1 sp), *sc in ch-3 sp, sk 2 dc, 5 dc in next sc, sk 2 dc, sc in ch-3 sp, ch 3; rep from * across to last 2 ch-3 sps, sc in ch-3 sp, sk 2 dc, 5 dc in next sc, sk 2 dc, sc in ch-3 sp, ch 1, dc in last sc, turn.

Rep rows 2–5 to desired length.

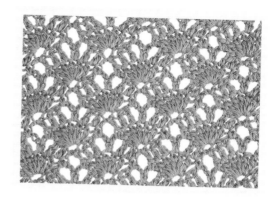

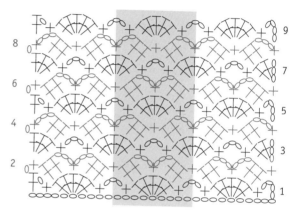

Emma Lace

This delicate lace makes stunning projects, from shawls to blankets.

Picot: Ch 3, sl st in 3rd ch.

Ch a multiple of 8 sts plus 5.

Row 1 (WS): Sc in 6th ch from hk, *ch 5, sk 4 ch, sc in next ch, ch 3, sk 2 ch, sc in next ch; rep from * across to last 7 ch, ch 5, sk 4 ch, sc in next ch, ch 1, hdc in last ch, turn.

Row 2: Ch 1, sc in 1st hdc, sk ch-1 sp, *9 dc in next ch-5 sp, sk next sc, sc in next ch-3 sp; rep from * across, turn.

Row 3: Ch 6 (counts as tr and ch 2), sk 2 dc, *[sl st, ch 3, sl st] in next dc, sc in each of next 3 dc, [sl st, ch 3, sl st] in next dc, ch 5, sk (next 2 dc, sc, next 2 dc); rep from * across to last 7 dc, [sl st, ch 3, sl st] in next dc, sc in each of next 3 dc, [sl st, ch 3, sl st] in next dc, ch 2, sk next 2 dc, tr in last sc, turn.

Row 4: Ch 1, sc in tr, *ch 3, sk next sc, 2 dc in next sc, ch 3, sk next sc, sc in next ch-5 sp, picot; rep from * across to last ch-5 sp, ch 3, sk next sc, 2 dc in next sc, ch 3, sc in 4th ch from t-ch, turn.

Row 5: *Ch 5, sk sc, sc in next ch-3 sp, ch 3, sk next 2 dc, sc in next ch-3 sp; rep from * across to last sc, ch 2, dc in last sc, turn.

Row 6: Ch 3 (counts as dc), 4 dc in ch-2 sp, sk next sc, sc in next ch-3 sp, *9 dc in next ch-5 sp, sk next sc, sc in next ch-3 sp; rep from * across to last ch-5 sp, sk sc, 5 dc in last ch-5 sp, turn.

Row 7: Ch 1, *sc in next 2 dc, [sl st, ch 3, sl st] in next dc, ch 5, sk (next 2 dc, sc, next 2 dc), [sl st, ch 3, sl st] in next dc, sc in next dc; rep from * across to t-ch, sc in top of t-ch, turn.

Row 8: Ch 3 (counts as dc), dc in 1st sc, *ch 3, sk next sc, sc in next ch-5 sp, picot, ch 3, sk next sc, 2 dc in next sc; rep from * across, turn.

Row 9: *Ch 3, sc in next ch-3 sp, ch 5, sc in next ch-3 sp; rep from * across to t-ch, ch 1, hdc in top of t-ch, turn.

Rep rows 2–9 to desired length.

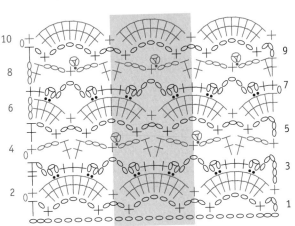

Wallpaper Cluster

The simplicity of the single and double crochet stitches lets the alternating clusters shine in this easygoing fabric.

Ch a multiple of 4 sts.

Row 1 (WS): Sc in 2nd ch from hk, *ch 1, sk 1 ch, sc in next ch; rep from * across to end, turn.

Row 2: Ch 3 (counts as dc), dc in next ch-1 sp, *ch 1, 3 dc-cl in next ch-1 sp, ch 1, dc in next ch-1 sp; rep from * across to end, dc in last sc, turn.

Row 3: Ch 1, sc in 1st dc, *ch 1, sk next st, sc in next ch-1 sp; rep from * across, ch 1, sk next st, sc in top of t-ch, turn.

Row 4: Ch 3 (counts as dc), 3 dc-cl in next ch-1 sp, *ch 1, sk sc, dc in next ch-1 sp, ch 1, sk sc, 3 dc-cl in next ch-1 sp; rep from * across, dc in last sc, turn.

Row 5: Rep row 3.

Rep rows 2–5 to desired length.

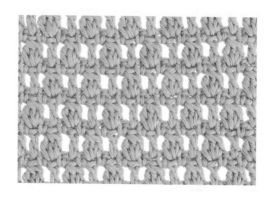

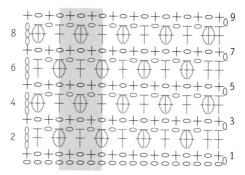

TIP

Blocking can dramatically change the look of lace stitch patterns. There are many ways to block crochet, and each kind of fiber prefers a different method. Of course, you need to test a swatch to see exactly which one will work for your project. I like to try pinning my swatch to my blocking board (a foam board covered in cotton fabric), spraying it with water, and then allowing it to dry. The pin-and-spray method works for many yarns, and for most of the ones I use. For tougher fibers, I sometimes also try dunking in cold water and pinning out, or a quick steam and pinning out. Good luck with your experimenting!

Pebble Lace

Looking for a fabric that is simple, textured, and lacy? You have come to the right place with this pattern. The clusters create little pebbles within a net of lace.

Ch a multiple of 4 sts plus 2.

Row 1 (WS): Sc in 2nd ch from hk, *ch 3, 2 hdc-cl in next ch, ch 1, sk 2 ch, sc in next ch; rep from * across to end, turn.

Row 2: Ch 4, hdc2tog over 3rd and 4th ch, ch 1, *[sc, ch 3, 2 hdc-cl] in next ch-3 sp, ch 1; rep from * to last ch-3 sp, sc in last ch-3 sp, ch 2, hdc3tog over last ch-3 sp twice and last sc, turn.

Row 3: Ch 1, sc in 1st sc, ch 3, 2 hdc-cl in ch-2 sp, ch 1, *[sc, ch 3, 2 hdc-cl] in next ch-3 sp, ch 1; rep from * across to t-ch, sc in top of t-ch, turn.

Rep rows 2 and 3 to desired length.

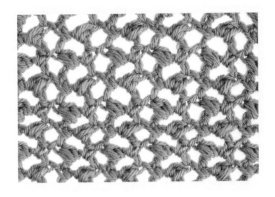

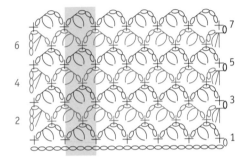

Climbing Vine

This stitch pattern fools you into thinking that it is much more complex than it really is. With only one row repeating, it is easy to memorize and versatile for any project.

Ch a multiple of 8 sts plus 6.

Row 1 (RS): 3 dc-cl in 6th ch from hk (sk ch counts as dc, ch-3 sp), sk 3 ch, dc in next ch, *sk 1 ch, ch 2, sc in next ch, ch 2, sk 1 ch, [dc, ch 3, 3 dc-cl] in next ch, sk 3 ch, dc in next ch; rep from * across to last 4 ch, sk 1 ch, ch 2, sc in next ch, ch 2, sk 1 ch, dc in last ch, turn.

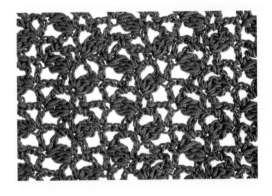

Row 2: Ch 6 (counts as dc, ch-3 sp), 3 dc-cl in 1st dc, *sk sc, dc in next dc, ch 2, sc in next ch-3 sp, ch 2, [dc, ch 3, 3 dc-cl] in next dc; rep from * across to last dc, dc in last dc, ch 2, sc in t-ch sp, ch 2, dc in 3rd ch of t-ch, turn.

Rep row 2 to desired length.

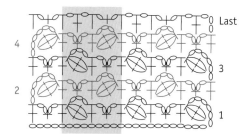

Stone Trellis

The half double cluster is one of the most definitive stitches, with all the yarn overs lining up. The chain spaces in this pattern use that arrangement to their advantage, making the clusters a star.

Ch a multiple of 6 sts plus 2.

Row 1 (RS): Sc in 2nd ch from hk, *ch 3, sk 2 ch, 4 hdc-cl in next ch, ch 4, sk 2 ch, sc in next ch; rep from * across, turn.

Row 2: Ch 1, sc in 1st sc, *ch 3, sc in 4 hdc-cl, ch 3, sc in next sc; rep from * across, turn.

Row 3: Ch 6 (counts as dc, ch 3), sc in next sc, *ch 3, 4 hdc-cl in next sc, ch 4, sc in next sc; rep from * across to last sc, ch 3, dc in last sc, turn.

Row 4: Ch 1, sc in 1st sc, *ch 3, sc in next sc, ch 3, sc in next 4 hdc-cl; rep from * across to last sc, ch 3, sc in last sc, ch 3, sc in 3rd ch of t-ch, turn.

Row 5: Ch 1, sc in 1st sc, *ch 3, 4 hdc-cl in next sc, ch 4, sc in next sc; rep from * across, turn.

Rep rows 2–5 to desired length.

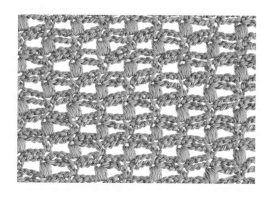

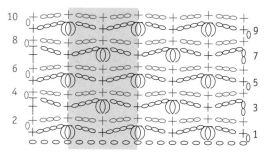

Paragon

The openness of the pattern lulls you into thinking that it will be a delicate fabric, but the shells can hold up to any wear, making this a great pattern for sweaters or blankets.

Shell (sh): [(3 dc-cl, ch 2) twice, 3 dc-cl] in st indicated.

Half Shell (half sh): [3 dc-cl, ch 2, 2 dc-cl] in st indicated.

Ch a multiple of 8 sts plus 2.

Row 1 (RS): Sc in 2nd ch from hk, *sk 3 ch, sh in next ch, sk 3 ch, sc in next ch; rep from * across, turn.

Row 2: Ch 6 (counts as dc, ch-3 sp), *sk next 3 dc-cl, sc in next 3 dc-cl, ch 3, dc in next sc, ch 3; rep from * to last sh, sk next 3 dc-cl, sc in next 3 dc-cl, ch 3, dc in last sc, turn.

Row 3: Ch 2, [dc, ch 2, 3 dc-cl] in 1st dc, *sc in next sc, sh in next dc; rep from * across to last sc, sc in last sc, half sh in 3rd ch of t-ch, turn.

Row 4: Ch 1, sc in 2 dc-cl, *ch 3, dc in next sc, ch 3, sk 3 dc-cl, sc in next 3 dc-cl; rep from * across, sc in last dc, turn.

Row 5: Ch 1, sc in 1st sc, *sh in next dc, sc in next sc; rep from * across, turn.

Rep rows 2–5 to desired length.

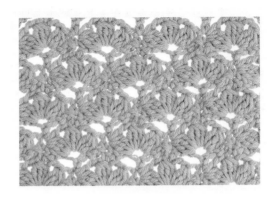

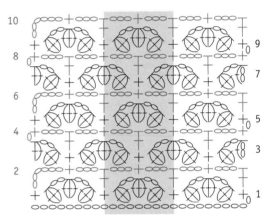

Leaf Bloom

The fairly light blooms of this stitch pattern make exquisite wraps if combined with beads.

Picot: Ch 3, sl st in 3rd ch.

Bloom: [3 dc-cl, picot, ch 5, 3 dc-cl, picot] in st indicated.

Ch a multiple of 12 sts plus 6.

Row 1 (RS): Sc in 8th ch from hk, picot, ch 3, sk 3 ch, sc in next sc, *picot, ch 3, sk 3 ch, sc in next ch, picot, ch 5, sk 3 ch, sc in next ch, picot, ch 3, sk 3 ch, sc in next ch; rep from * across to last 6 ch, picot, ch 3, sk 3 ch, sc in next ch, picot, ch 2, sk 1 ch, dc in last ch, turn.

Row 2: Ch 1, sc in dc, *picot, ch 3, sk 1 picot, bloom in next picot ch-3 sp, ch 3, sc in ch-5 sp; rep from * across to t-ch, sc in t-ch sp, turn.

Row 3: Ch 7 (counts as dtr and ch-2 sp), 3 dc-cl in 1st sc, picot, *ch 3, sc in ch-5 sp, picot, ch 3, sk 1 picot, bloom in next picot ch-3 sp; rep from * across to last bloom, ch 3, sc in ch-5 sp, picot, ch 3, sk 1 picot, 3 dc-cl in last picot ch-3 sp, picot, ch 2, dtr in last sc, turn.

Rep rows 2 and 3 to desired length.

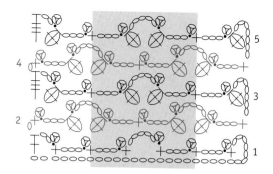

Clover Lattice

By combining clusters and shells, this pattern results in a little clover. This fabric is bold and eye-catching in any shawl project.

Ch a multiple of 8 sts plus 2.

Row 1 (RS): Sc in 2nd ch from hk, *ch 4, sk 3 ch, 4 dc-cl in next ch, ch 4, sk 3 ch, [sc, ch 1, sc] in next ch; rep from * across, sc in last ch, turn.

Row 2: Ch 3 (counts as dc), 2 dc in 1st sc, ch 2, *sc in 4 dc-cl, ch 2, 6 dc in next ch-1 sp, ch 2; rep from * across to last 4 dc-cl, sc in last 4 dc-cl, ch 2, 3 dc in last sc, turn.

Row 3: Ch 7 (counts as dc and ch-4 sp), *[sc, ch 1, sc] in next sc, ch 4, 4 dc-cl between 3rd and 4th dc, ch 4; rep from * across to last sc, [sc, ch 1, sc] in last sc, ch 4, dc in top of t-ch, turn.

Row 4: Ch 1, sc in dc, *ch 2, 6 dc in next ch-1 sp, ch 2, sc in 4 dc-cl; rep from * across, sc in 3rd ch of t-ch, turn.

Row 5: Ch 1, sc in sc, *ch 4, 4 dc-cl between 3rd and 4th dc, ch 4, [sc, ch 1, sc] in next sc; rep from * across, sc in last sc, turn.

Rep rows 2–5 to desired length.

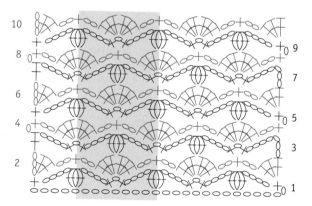

Harriet Lace

You can use this delicate stitch pattern in a wonderful scarf or as an edging to a cardigan, stopping after row 4.

Picot: Ch 3, sl st in 3rd ch.

Shell (sh): [(3 dc-cl, ch 2) twice, 3 dc-cl] in st indicated.

V-Stitch (v-st): [Dc, ch 2, dc] in st indicated.

Ch a multiple of 6 sts plus 3.

Row 1 (WS): Hdc in 6th ch from hk (sk ch counts as hdc and ch-1 sp), *ch 1, sk 1 ch, hdc in next ch; rep from * across, turn.

Row 2: Ch 1, sc in ea hdc and ch-1 sp across to t-ch, sc in 1st and 2nd ch of t-ch, turn.

Row 3: Ch 1, sc in 1st sc, ch 2, sk 2 sc, v-st in next sc, ch 2, sk 2 sc, sc in next sc, *picot, ch 2, sk 2 sc, v-st in next sc, ch 2, sk 2 sc, sc in next sc; rep from * across to end, turn.

Row 4: Ch 3 (counts as dc), *sh in next v-st ch-2 sp, ch 1; rep from * across to last v-st, sh in next v-st ch-2 sp, dc in last sc, turn.

Row 5: Ch 3 (counts as hdc, ch-1 sp), hdc in next ch-2 sp, ch 1, hdc in next ch-2 sp, *ch 1, hdc in next ch-1 sp, [ch 1, hdc in next ch-2 sp] twice; rep from * across to last sh, ch 1, hdc in top of t-ch, turn.

Rep rows 2–5 to desired length.

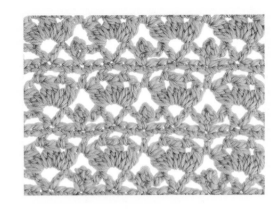

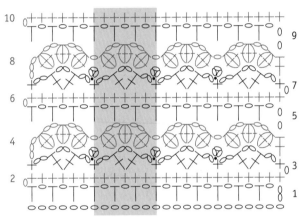

Flower Diamond

This stitch pattern takes a plain cluster and combines it with others to create flowers highlighted on each side with double crochet lines.

Ch a multiple of 16 sts plus 2.

Row 1 (RS): Sc in 2nd ch from hk, *ch 2, dc in next 5 ch, sk 2 ch, sc in next ch, sk 2 ch, dc in next 5 ch, ch 2, sc in next ch; rep from * across, turn.

Row 2: Ch 6 (counts as tr, ch-2 sp), sc in ch-2 sp, *ch 4, 2 tr-cl in sc just made, 3 tr-cl in next sc, ch 4, 2 tr-cl in 3 tr-cl just made, sc in next ch-2 sp, ch 5, sc in next ch-2 sp; rep from * across to last sc, ch 4, 2 tr-cl in sc just made, 3 tr-cl in next sc, ch 4, 2 tr-cl in 3 tr-cl just made, sc in next ch-2 sp, ch 2, tr in last sc, turn.

Row 3: Ch 1, sc in tr, *ch 2, sc in next sc, ch 5, sk 2 tr-cl, 3 tr-cl in next 3 tr-cl, ch 5, sc in next sc, ch 2, sc in next ch-5 sp; rep from * across, turn.

Row 4: Ch 1, sc in 1st sc, *5 dc in next ch-5 sp, ch 2, sc in 3 tr-cl, ch 2, 5 dc in next ch-5 sp, sk next sc, sc in next sc; rep from * across, turn.

Row 5: Ch 3, tr in 1st sc, ch 4, 2 tr-cl in tr just made, *sc in ch-2 sp, ch 5, sc in next ch-2 sp, ch 4, 2 tr-cl in sc just made, 3 tr-cl in next sc, ch 4, 2 tr-cl in 3 tr-cl just made; rep from * across to last 2 ch-2 sps, sc in next ch-2 sp, ch 5, sc in next ch-2 sp, ch 4, 2 tr-cl in sc just made, 2 tr-cl in last sc, turn.

Row 6: Ch 3, tr in 2 tr-cl, ch 5, *sc in next sc, ch 2, sc in ch-5 sp, ch 2, sc in next sc, ch 5, 3 tr-cl in next 3 tr-cl, ch 5; rep from * across to last ch-5 sp, sc in next sc, ch 2, sc in next ch-5 sp, ch 2, sc in next sc, ch 5, 2 tr-cl in last tr, turn.

Row 7: Ch 1, sc in 2 tr-cl, *ch 2, 5 dc in ch-5 sp, sk next sc, sc in next sc, 5 dc in next ch-5 sp, ch 2, sc in 3 tr-cl; rep from * across to last tr, sc in last tr, turn.

Rep rows 2–7 to desired length.

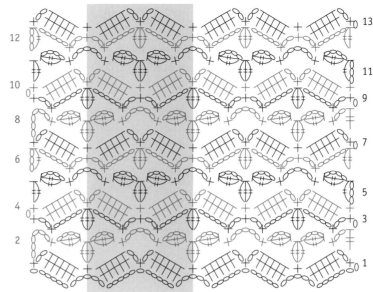

Cluster Stitches vs. Decreases

Have you ever gotten confused between clusters and decreases? It's easy to do since their definitions are nearly identical. There is one quick trick you can use to figure out whether you will be going through one or multiple stitches to make either a cluster or a decrease: look at the shape. If the stitch looks like an oval or a circle, then it is a cluster. If it looks like a triangle or an inverted V, then it is a decrease. Decreases go in multiple stitches and end as one, thus forming those triangles. And clusters start and end as one stitch, so all those extra yarn overs naturally pop out to become a circle. Check out the stitch patterns here and you will see this immediately.

Simple Chevron

The most basic of wave patterns creates V-shaped vertical columns. Vary the look by changing colors after each row.

Ch a multiple of 13 plus 2.

Row 1 (RS): Sc in 2nd ch from hk, sc in same ch, *sc in next 5 ch, sk 2 ch, sc in next 5 ch, 3 sc in next ch; rep from * to last ch, 2 sc in last ch, turn.

Row 2: Ch 1, 2 sc in 1st sc, *sc in next 5 sc, sk 2 sc, sc in next 5 sc, 3 sc in next sc; rep from * across to last sc, 2 sc in last sc, turn.

Rep row 2 to desired length.

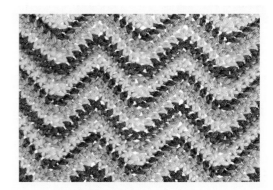

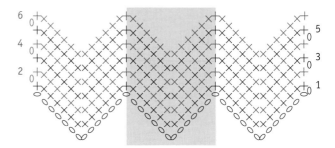

TIP

Liven Up Your Waves

You can easily enliven all these waves by changing where you insert the hook. Try changing the patterns by doing one row in the front loop of all the stitches and in the back loop on the next row. You will get very defined lines on each row, highlighting the wave. Try going between the stitches instead of the top loops, or spike every few stitches; each will change the wave slightly. You can get many more patterns than the ones shown just by making these simple changes.

Peephole Chevron

This is a twist on the double crochet chevron, with chain spaces instead of the shell at the ridges of the wave. The chain spaces and skipped stitches create teardrops in the fabric.

Ch a multiple of 10 sts plus 5.

Row 1 (RS): Dc in 4th ch from hk, *dc in next 4 ch, sk 2 ch, dc in next 4 ch, ch 2; rep from * across to last 11 ch, dc in next 4 ch, sk 2 ch, dc in next 4 ch, 2 dc in last ch, turn.

Row 2: Ch 3 (counts as dc), dc in 1st dc, *dc in next 4 dc, sk 2 dc, dc in next 3 dc, [dc, ch 2, dc] in next ch-2 sp; rep from * across to last ch-2 sp, dc in next 3 dc, sk 2 dc, dc in next 4 dc, 2 dc in top of t-ch, turn.

Rep row 2 to desired length.

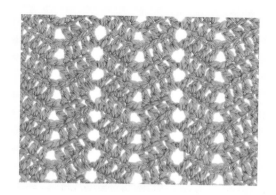

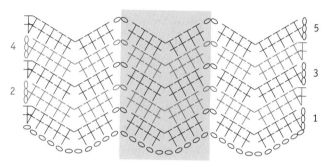

Simple Wave

When you add a row of single crochet between undulating double crochet rows, the chevron softens to a gentle wave. Try changing colors every other row to highlight the wave.

Ch a multiple of 12 sts plus 5.

Row 1 (RS): Dc in 4th ch from hk (sk 3 ch counts as dc), *[sk next ch, dc in next ch] twice, dc in next ch, 5 dc in next ch, dc in ea of next 2 ch, [sk 1 ch, dc in next ch] twice; rep from * across, dc in last ch, turn.

Row 2: Ch 1, sc in ea dc across, turn.

Row 3: Ch 3 (counts as 1 dc), dc in next sc, *[sk 1 sc, dc in next sc] twice, dc in next sc, 5 dc in next sc, dc in ea of next 2 sc, [sk 1 sc, dc in next sc] twice; rep from * across, dc in last sc, turn.

Rep rows 2 and 3 to desired length.

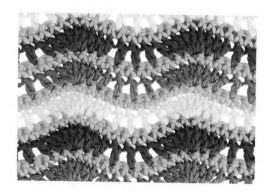

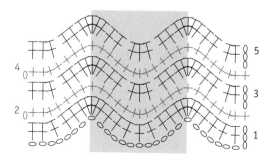

Corolla Wave

When you sprinkle chain spaces in the taller rows, this wave becomes more elegant and dressier—great for shawls and scarves.

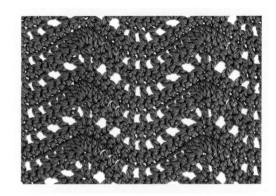

Ch a multiple of 16 sts plus 5.

Row 1 (RS): Dc in 4th ch from hk (sk 3 ch counts as 1 dc), *[sk next ch, dc in next ch] twice, dc in ea of next 3 ch, 5 dc in next ch, dc in ea of next 4 ch, [sk 1 ch, dc in next ch] twice; rep from * across, dc in last ch, turn.

Row 2: Ch 1, sc in ea dc across, turn.

Row 3: Ch 3 (counts as 1 dc), dc in next sc, *[sk 1 sc, dc in next sc] twice, [ch 1, sk 1 sc, dc in next sc] twice, [ch 1, dc] twice in prev sc, [ch 1, sk 1 sc, dc in next sc] twice, [sk 1 sc, dc in next sc] twice; rep from * across, dc in last sc, turn.

Row 4: Ch 1, sc in ea dc and ch-1 sp across, turn.

Row 5: Ch 3 (counts as 1 dc), dc in next sc, *[sk 1 sc, dc in next sc] twice, dc in ea of next 3 sc, 5 dc in next sc, dc in ea of next 4 sc, [sk 1 sc, dc in next sc] twice; rep from * across, dc in last sc, turn.

Rep rows 2–5 to desired length.

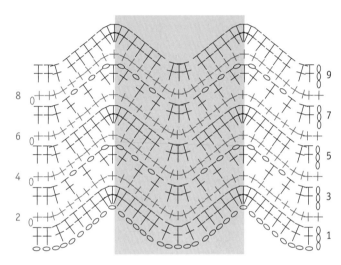

Atlantic Wave

The front post stitches in this pattern make the wave stand out and say "hi." Use it wherever you need a dramatic statement.

Ch a multiple of 14 sts plus 5.

Row 1 (RS): Dc in 4th ch from hk (sk 3 ch counts as 1 dc), *[sk next ch, dc in next ch] twice, dc in next ch, 2 dc in next ch, 3 dc in next ch, 2 dc in next ch, dc in next 2 ch, [sk 1 ch, dc in next ch] twice; rep from * across, dc in last ch, turn.

Row 2: Ch 1, sc in ea dc across, turn.

Row 3: Ch 3 (counts as 1 dc), dc in next dc, *[sk 1 sc, dc in next sc] twice, dc in next sc, 2 dc in next sc, 3 dc in next sc, 2 dc in next sc, dc in next 2 sc, [sk 1 sc, dc in next sc] twice; rep from * across, dc in last sc, turn.

Row 4: Ch 1, sc in 1st dc, FPsc around ea dc across to t-ch, sc in top of t-ch, turn.

Rows 5–10: Rep rows 3 and 4 three times.

Row 11: Ch 4 (counts as 1 tr), tr in ea sc across, turn.

Rep rows 2–11 to desired length.

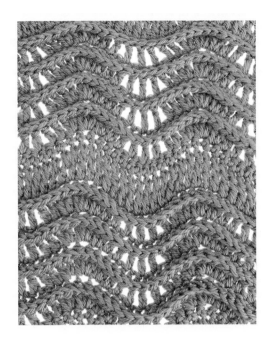

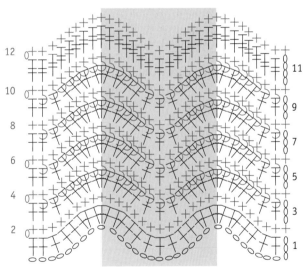

Pacific Wave

The puff stitch of the clusters combined with the triangle shapes of the decrease stitches transform this wave pattern into an interesting, textured lace fabric.

Ch a multiple of 17 sts plus 4.

Row 1 (RS): Dc2tog over 4th and 5th ch, *dc2tog over next 2 ch twice, (ch 1, 3 dc-cl in next ch) 5 times, ch 1, (dc2tog over next 2 ch) 4 times; rep from * across to last ch, dc in last ch, turn.

Row 2: Ch 1, sc in ea st across, turn.

Row 3: Ch 3 (counts as dc), *dc2tog over next 2 sc 3 times, (ch 1, 3 dc-cl in next sc) 5 times, ch 1, (dc2tog over next 2 sc) 3 times; rep from * across to last ch, dc in last ch, turn.

Rep rows 2 and 3 to desired length.

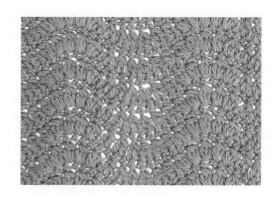

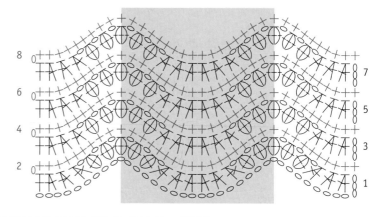

PINEAPPLE STITCH PATTERNS

Spider

The chain spaces all converging onto the diamond between the groups of double crochet look like a spider web when crocheted. This intricate pattern is great for small garments, like shrugs or wraps.

Ch a multiple of 14 sts plus 5.

Row 1 (RS): Dc in 4th ch from hk (sk ch counts as dc), dc in next ch, *ch 3, sk next 3 ch, sc in next 5 ch, ch 3, sk next 3 ch, dc in next 3 ch; rep from * across, turn.

Row 2: Ch 4 (counts as dc, ch-1 sp), *sk 3 dc, 3 dc in ch-3 sp, ch 3, sk next sc, sc in next 3 sc, ch 3, sk next sc, 3 dc in ch-3 sp, ch 1; rep from * across, dc in top of t-ch, turn.

Row 3: Ch 3 (counts as dc), dc in ch-1 sp, *ch 3, sk next 3 dc, 3 dc in ch-3 sp, ch 3, sk next sc, dc in next sc, ch 3, sk next sc, 3 dc in ch-3 sp, ch 3, sk next 3 dc, dc in ch-1 sp; rep from * across, dc in 3rd ch of t-ch, turn.

Row 4: Ch 1, sc in 1st 2 dc, *sc in next ch-3 sp, ch 3, sk 3 dc, 3 dc in next ch-3 sp, ch 1, 3 dc in next ch-3 sp, ch 3, sk 3 dc, sc in next ch-3 sp, sc in dc; rep from * across, sc in top of t-ch, turn.

Row 5: Ch 1, sc in 1st 3 sc, *sc in next ch-3 sp, ch 3, sk next 3 dc, 3 dc in ch-1 sp, ch 3, sk 3 dc, sc in next ch-3 sp, sc in next 3 sc; rep from * across, turn.

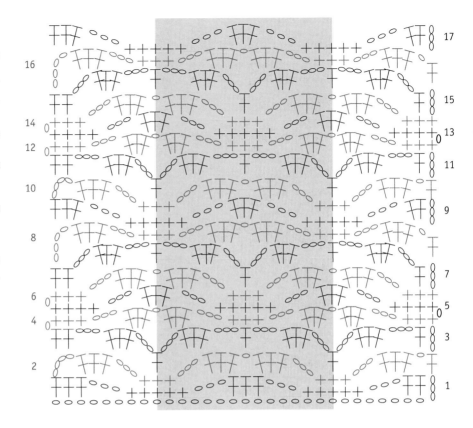

Row 6: Ch 1, sc in 1st 3 sc, *ch 3, sk 1 sc, 3 dc in next ch-3 sp, ch 1, sk 3 dc, 3 dc in next ch-3 sp, ch 3, sk 1 sc, sc in next 3 sc; rep from * across, turn.

Row 7: Ch 3 (counts as dc), dc in next sc, *ch 3, sk 1 sc, 3 dc in next ch-3 sp, ch 3, sk 3 dc, dc in ch-1 sp, ch 3, sk 3 dc, 3 dc in next ch-3 sp, ch 3, sk 1 sc, dc in next sc; rep from * across, dc in last sc, turn.

Row 8: Ch 4 (counts as dc, ch-1 sp), *3 dc in next ch-3 sp, ch 3, sk 3 dc, sc in next ch-3 sp, sc in dc, sc in next ch-3 sp, ch 3, sk 3 dc, 3 dc in next ch-3 sp, ch 1; rep from * across, dc in top of t-ch, turn.

Row 9: Ch 3 (counts as dc), 2 dc in ch-1 sp, *ch 3, sk 3 dc, sc in next ch-3 sp, sc in next 3 sc, sc in next ch-3 sp, ch 3, sk 3 dc, 3 dc in ch-1 sp; rep from * across, turn.

Rep rows 2–9 to desired length.

Berry Lace

This shortened pineapple stitch pattern makes a lovely fabric for all types of garments.

Shell (sh): [(Ch 1, dc) 6 times, ch 1] in st indicated.

V-Stitch (v-st): [Dc, ch 3, dc] in ch-sp indicated.

Ch a multiple of 17 sts plus 4.

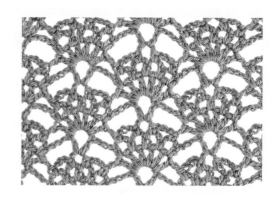

Row 1 (RS): Sc in 5th ch from hk, ch 3, sk 2 ch, sc in next ch, *sk 3 ch, sh in next ch, sk 3 ch, [sc in next ch, ch 3, sk 2 ch] 3 times, sc in next ch; rep from * across to last 13 ch, sk 3 ch, sh in next ch, sc in next ch, ch 3, sk 2 ch, sc in next ch, ch 1, sk 1 ch, hdc in last ch, turn.

Row 2: Ch 4 (counts as dc, ch 1), dc in hdc, ch 3, *sk 1st dc on sh, [sc in next ch-1 sp, ch 3] 4 times, sc in next ch-1 sp, ch 3, sk 1st ch-3 sp, v-st in next ch-3 sp, ch 3, sk last ch-3 sp; rep from * across to last sh, sk 1 ch-1 sp on sh, [sc in next ch-1 sp, ch 3] 4 times, sc in next ch-1 sp, ch 3, sk next ch-3 sp, [dc, ch 1, dc] in 2nd ch of t-ch, turn.

Row 3: Ch 3 (counts as dc), [dc, ch 1] 3 times in ch-1 sp, sk next ch-3 sp *[sc in next ch-3 sp, ch 3] 3 times, sc in next ch-3 sp, sk next ch-3 sp, sh in next v-st, sk next ch-3 sp; rep from * across to last 5 ch-3 sps, [sc in next ch-3 sp, ch 3] 3 times, sc in next ch-3 sp, sk next ch-3 sp, [(ch 1, dc) 3 times, dc] in t-ch sp, turn.

Row 4: Ch 1, sc in 1st dc, [ch 3, sc in next ch-1 sp] twice, *ch 3, sk 1st ch-3 sp, [dc, ch 3, dc] in next ch-3 sp, sk last ch-3 sp, sk 1st dc on sh, [sc in next ch-1 sp, ch 3] 4 times, sc in next ch-1 sp; rep from * across to last sh, ch 3, sk 1st ch-3 sp, [dc, ch 3, dc] in next ch-3 sp, sk last ch-3 sp, sk 1st dc on sh, [sc in next ch-1 sp, ch 3] twice, sc in top of t-ch, turn.

Row 5: Ch 3 (counts as hdc, ch-1 sp), sc in next ch-3 sp, ch 3, sc in next ch-3 sp, *sk next ch-3 sp, sh in next ch-3 sp, sk next ch-3 sp, [sc in next ch-3 sp, ch 3] 3 times, sc in next ch-3 sp; rep from * across to last 5 ch-3 sps, sk next ch-3 sp, sh in next ch-3 sp, sk next ch-3 sp, sc in next ch-3 sp, ch 3, sc in next ch-3 sp, ch 1, hdc in last sc, turn.

Rep rows 2–5 to desired length.

Blackberry Jam

The stacking of the pineapples in this stitch pattern highlights them in vertical columns.

Shell (sh): [(Dc, ch 1) 4 times, dc] in st indicated.

Ch a multiple of 12 sts plus 2.

Row 1 (RS): Sc in 2nd ch from hk, *ch 3, sk 5 ch, sh in next ch, sk 5 ch, sc in next ch; rep from * across, turn.

Row 2: Ch 3 (counts as dc), 2 dc in same sc, *ch 1, [sc in next ch-1 sp, ch 3] 3 times, sc in next ch-1 sp, ch 1, [2 dc, ch 1, 2 dc] in next sc; rep from * to last sc, 3 dc in last sc, turn.

Row 3: Ch 3 (counts as dc), 2 dc in same dc, *ch 2, [sc in next ch-3 sp, ch 3] twice, sc in next ch-3 sp, ch 2, sk 1 ch-1 sp, [2 dc, ch 1, 2 dc] in next ch-1 sp; rep from * across to t-ch, 3 dc in top of t-ch, turn.

Row 4: Ch 3 (counts as dc), 2 dc in same dc, *ch 3, [sc in next ch-3 sp, ch 3] twice, [2 dc, ch 1, 2 dc] in next ch-1 sp; rep from * across to t-ch, 3 dc in top of t-ch, turn.

Row 5: Ch 1, sc in 1st dc, *ch 3, sk next ch-3 sp, sh in next ch-3 sp, ch 3, sc in next ch-1 sp; rep from * across to t-ch, sc in top of t-ch, turn.

Rep rows 2–5 to desired length.

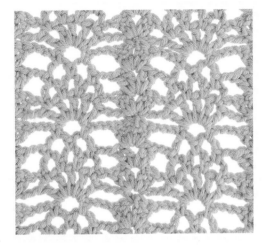

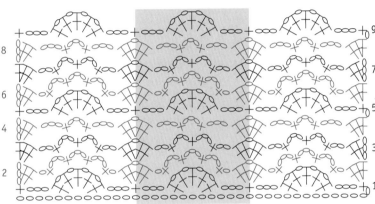

Strawberry Lace

Chain spaces let the pineapples in this pattern stand out. This delicate fabric works well for fancy scarves.

Shell (sh): [(Dc, ch 1) 4 times, dc] in st indicated.

V-Stitch (v-st): [Dc, ch 1, dc] in st indicated.

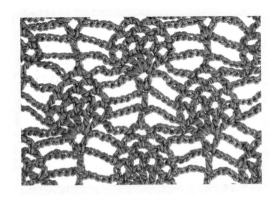

Ch a multiple of 16 sts plus 8.

Row 1 (RS): Sc in 12th ch from hk, [ch 3, sk 1 ch, sc in next ch] 4 times, ch 5, sk 3 ch, dc in next ch, *ch 5, sk 3 ch, [sc in next ch, sk next ch, ch 3] 4 times, sc in next ch, ch 5, sk 3 ch, dc in next ch; rep from * across, turn.

Row 2: Ch 8, [sc in next ch-3 sp, ch 3] 3 times, sc in next ch-3 sp, ch 5, *dc in next dc, ch 5, [sc in next ch-3 sp, ch 3] 3 times, sc in next ch-3 sp, ch 5; rep from * across to t-ch, dc in 6th ch of t-ch, turn.

Row 3: Ch 3 (counts as dc), dc in 1st dc, *ch 5, [sc in next ch-3 sp, ch 3] twice, sc in next ch-3 sp, ch 5, v-st in next dc; rep from * across to t-ch, 2 dc in 3rd ch of t-ch, turn.

Row 4: Ch 4, v-st in 1st dc, *ch 5, sc in next ch-3 sp, ch 3, sc in next ch-3 sp, ch 5, sh in ch-1 sp; rep from * across to t-ch, [(dc, ch 1) twice, dc] in 3rd ch of t-ch, turn.

Row 5: Ch 1, *[sc in dc, ch 3] twice, sc in next dc, ch 5, dc in ch-3 sp, ch 5, [sc in next dc, ch 3] twice; rep from * across to t-ch, sc in 3rd ch of t-ch, turn.

Row 6: Ch 4, sc in next ch-3 sp, ch 3, sc in next ch-3 sp, ch 5, dc in next dc, ch 5, *[sc in next ch-3 sp, ch 3] 3 times, sc in next ch-3 sp, ch 5, dc in next ch-3 sp, ch 5; rep from * across to last 2 ch-3 sps, sc in next ch-3 sp, ch 3, sc in next ch-3 sp, ch 1, dc in last sc, turn.

Row 7: Ch 1, sc in dc, *ch 3, sc in next ch-3 sp, ch 5, v-st in next dc, ch 5, sc in next ch-3 sp, ch 3, sc in next ch-3 sp; rep from * across to t-ch, sc in t-ch, turn.

Row 8: Ch 4, sc in ch-3 sp, *ch 5, sh in ch-1 sp, ch 5, sc in ch-3 sp, ch 3, sc in next ch-3 sp; rep from * across to last v-st, ch 5, sh in ch-1 sp, ch 5, sc in ch-3 sp, ch 1, dc in last sc, turn.

Row 9: Ch 8, *[sc in dc, ch 3] 4 times, sc in next dc, ch 5, dc in next ch-3 sp, ch 5; rep from * across to t-ch, dc in 3rd ch of t-ch, turn.

Rep rows 2–9 to desired length.

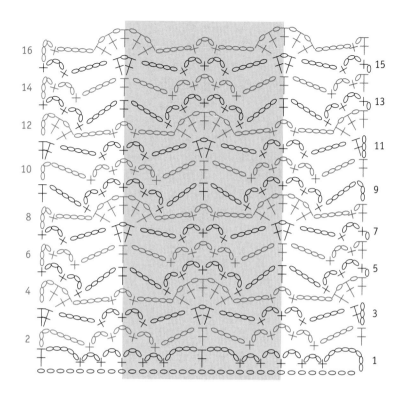

Columbia Lace

This pineapple lace has small berries centered in a network of double crochet. The fabric is wearable enough for shawls and works for tablecloths as well.

Shell (sh): [Ch 1, (tr, ch 1) 6 times] in st indicated.

Half Shell (half sh): [(Tr, ch 1) twice, tr] in st indicated.

Double Crochet Triple Treble Together (dcttrtog): Yo, insert hk into st indicated, yo, draw up lp, yo, draw through 2 lps on hk, yo 4 times, insert hk into st indicated, yo, draw up lp, *yo, draw through 2 lps on hk; rep from * 4 times total, yo, draw through last lps on hk.

Ch a multiple of 20 sts plus 8.

Row 1 (RS): Sc in 10th ch from hk, *ch 5, sk 4 ch, dc in next 3 ch, ch 3, sk 1 ch, dc in next 3 ch, ch 5, sk 4 ch, sc in next ch, ch 6, sk 3 ch, sc in next ch; rep from * across to last 18 ch, ch 5, sk 4 ch, dc in next 3 ch, ch 3, sk 1 ch, dc in next 3 ch, ch 5, sk 4 ch, sc in next ch, ch 2, sk 1 ch, dtr in last ch, turn.

Row 2: Ch 4 (counts as tr), half sh in ch-2 sp, ch 1, *sc in ch-5 sp, ch 3, [3 dc, ch 3, 3 dc] in next ch-3 sp, ch 3, sc in next ch-5 sp, sh in ch-6 sp, sc in next ch-5 sp, ch 3, [3 dc, ch 3, 3 dc] in next ch-3 sp, ch 3; rep from * across to last ch-5 sp, sc in next ch-5 sp, ch 1, [half sh, tr] in last ch-7 sp, turn.

Row 3: Ch 1, sc in 1st tr, [ch 3, sc in next ch-1 sp] twice, ch 3, *sk next ch-1 sp, sk next ch-3 sp, [3 dc, ch 3, 3 dc] in next ch-3 sp, ch 3, sk next ch-3 sp, sk next ch-1 sp, [sc in next ch-1 sp, ch 3] 5 times; rep from * across to last 3 ch-3 sps, sk next ch-1 sp, sk next ch-3 sp, [3 dc, ch 3, 3 dc] in next ch-3 sp, ch 3, sk next ch-3 sp, sk next ch-1 sp, [sc in next ch-1 sp, ch 3] twice, sc in top of t-ch, turn.

Row 4: Ch 3 (counts as hdc, ch-1 sp), sc in next ch-3 sp, ch 3, sc in next ch-3 sp, ch 3, *sk next ch-3 sp, [3 dc, ch 3, 3 dc] in next ch-3 sp, ch 3, sk next ch-3 sp, [sc in next ch-3 sp, ch 3] 4 times; rep from * across to last 3 ch-3 sps, sk next ch-3 sp, [3 dc, ch 3, 3 dc] in next ch-3 sp, ch 3, sk next ch-3 sp, sc in next ch-3 sp, ch 3, sc in next ch-3 sp, ch 1, hdc in last sc, turn.

Row 5: Ch 1, sc in hdc, ch 3, sc in next ch-3 sp, ch 3, *sk next ch-3 sp, [3 dc, ch 3, dc, ch 3, 3 dc] in next ch-3 sp, ch 3, sk next ch-3 sp, [sc in next ch-3 sp, ch 3] 3 times; rep from * across to last 3 ch-3 sps, sk next ch-3 sp, [3 dc, ch 3, dc, ch 3, 3 dc] in next ch-3 sp, ch 3, sk next ch-3 sp, sc in next ch-3 sp, ch 3, sc in last ch-3 sp, turn.

Row 6: Ch 3 (counts as hdc, ch-1 sp), sc in next ch-3 sp, ch 3, sk next ch-3 sp, *[(3 dc, ch 3, 3 dc) in next ch-3 sp] twice, ch 3, sk next ch-3 sp, sc in next ch-3 sp, ch 3, sc in next ch-3 sp, ch 3, sk next ch-3 sp; rep from * across to last 4 ch-3 sps, [(3 dc, ch 3, 3 dc) in next ch-3 sp] twice, ch 3, sk next ch-3 sp, sc in next ch-3 sp, ch 1, hdc in last sc, turn.

Row 7: Ch 1, sc in hdc, *ch 3, sk next ch-3 sp, [3 dc, ch 3, 3 dc] in next ch-3 sp, ch 5, [3 dc, ch 3, 3 dc] in next ch-3 sp, ch 3, sk next ch-3 sp, sc in next ch-3 sp; rep from * across to t-ch, sc in t-ch, turn.

Row 8: Ch 6 (counts as ttr), sk next ch-3 sp, [dc, ch 3, 3 dc] in next ch-3 sp, *ch 6, sc in ch-5 sp, ch 6, 3 dc in next ch-3 sp, ch 3, dc2tog in [prev ch-3 sp, sk 2 ch-3 sps, and next ch-3 sp], ch 3, 3 dc in prev ch-3 sp; rep from * across to last ch-5 sp, ch 6, sc in ch-5 sp, ch 6, 3 dc in next ch-3 sp, ch 3, dcttrtog in prev ch-3 sp and last sc, turn.

Row 9: Ch 5 (counts as tr, ch-1 sp), *3 dc in ch-3 sp, ch 5, sc in next ch-6 sp, ch 6, sc in next ch-6 sp, ch 5, 3 dc in next ch-3 sp, ch 3; rep from * across to last dc, ch 1, tr in last dc, turn.

Row 10: Ch 4 (counts as dc, ch-1 sp), 3 dc in ch-1 sp, *ch 3, sc in next ch-5 sp, sh in next ch-6 sp, sc in next ch-5 sp, ch 3, [3 dc, ch 3, 3 dc] in next ch-3 sp; rep from * across to last ch-3 sp, ch 3, sc in next ch-5 sp, sh in next ch-6 sp, sc in next ch-5 sp, ch 3, [3 dc, ch 1, dc] in last ch-5 sp, turn.

Row 11: Ch 4 (counts as dc, ch-1 sp), 3 dc in ch-1 sp, *ch 3, sk ch-3 sp, sk ch-1 sp, [sc in next ch-1 sp, ch 3] 5 times, sk next ch-1 sp, sk next ch-3 sp, [3 dc, ch 3, 3 dc] in next ch-3 sp; rep from * across to last 2 ch-3 sps, ch 3, sk next ch-3 sp, sk next ch-1 sp, [sc in next ch-1 sp, ch 3] 5 times, sk next ch-1 sp, sk next ch-3 sp, [3 dc, ch 1, dc] in last ch-4 sp, turn.

Row 12: Ch 4 (counts as dc, ch-1 sp), 3 dc in ch-1 sp, *ch 3, sk next ch-3 sp, [sc in next ch-3 sp, ch 3] 4 times, sk next ch-3 sp, [3 dc, ch 3, 3 dc] in next ch-3 sp; rep from * across to last 6 ch-3 sps, ch 3, sk next ch-3 sp, [sc in next ch-3 sp, ch 3] 4 times, sk next ch-3 sp, [3 dc, ch 1, dc] in last ch-4 sp, turn.

Row 13: Ch 6 (counts as dc, ch-3 sp), 3 dc in ch-1 sp, *ch 3, sk ch-3 sp, [sc in next ch-3 sp, ch 3] 3 times, sk next ch-3 sp, [3 dc, ch 3, dc, ch 3, 3 dc] in next ch-3 sp; rep from * across to last 5 ch-3 sps, ch 3, sk next ch-3 sp, [sc in next ch-3 sp, ch 3] 3 times, sk next ch-3 sp, [3 dc, ch 3, dc] in last ch-4 sp, turn.

Row 14: Ch 3 (counts as dc), *[3 dc, ch 3, 3 dc] in next ch-3 sp, ch 3, sk next ch-3 sp, [sc in next ch-3 sp, ch 3] twice, sk next ch-3 sp, [3 dc, ch 3, 3 dc] in next ch-3 sp; rep from * across to t-ch, [3 dc, ch 3, 3 dc] in t-ch sp, dc in 3rd ch of t-ch, turn.

Row 15: Ch 7 (counts as dtr, ch-2 sp), *[3 dc, ch 3, 3 dc] in next ch-3 sp, ch 3, sk next ch-3 sp, sc in next ch-3 sp, ch 3, sk next ch-3 sp, [3 dc, ch 3, 3 dc] in next ch-3 sp, ch 5; rep from * across to t-ch, ch 2, dtr in top of t-ch, turn.

Row 16: Ch 1, sc in dtr, *ch 6, 3 dc in next ch-3 sp, ch 3, dc2tog in [prev ch-3 sp, sk 2 ch-3 sps, and next ch-3 sp], ch 3, 3 dc in prev ch-3 sp, ch 6, sc in next ch-5 sp; rep from * across, sc in 4th ch of t-ch, turn.

Row 17: Ch 7 (counts as dtr, ch-2 sp), *sc in next ch-6 sp, ch 5, 3 dc in next ch-3 sp, ch 3, 3 dc in next ch-3 sp, ch 5, sc in next ch-6 sp, ch 6; rep from * across to last 2 ch-6 sps, sc in next ch-6 sp, ch 5, 3 dc in next ch-3 sp, ch 3, 3 dc in next ch-3 sp, ch 5, sc in next ch-6 sp, ch 2, dtr in last sc, turn.

Rep rows 2–17 to desired length.

Pineapple

This classic pineapple stitch pattern makes beautiful lace when crocheted in thread, from bedspreads to wedding shawls.

Shell (sh): [2 dc, ch 2, 2 dc] in st indicated.

Ch a multiple of 31 sts plus 2.

Row 1 (RS): Sc in 2nd ch from hk, *[ch 3, sk 1 ch, sc in next ch] 3 times, ch 3, sk 5 ch, sh in next ch, ch 1, sk 5 ch, sh in next ch, ch 3, sk 5 ch, [sc in next ch, ch 3, sk 1 ch] 3 times; rep from * across, sc in last ch, turn.

Row 2: Ch 4 (counts as dc, ch 1), sc in next ch-3 sp, *[ch 3, sc in next ch-3 sp] twice, ch 3, sh in next ch-2 sp, sh in next ch-1 sp, sh in next ch-2 sp, sk 1 ch-3 sp, [ch 3, sc in next ch-3 sp] 3 times; rep from * across to last ch-3 sp, ch 1, dc in last sc, turn.

Row 3: Ch 1, sc in dc, *[ch 3, sc in next ch-3 sp] twice, ch 3, [sh in next ch-2 sp, ch 1] twice, sh in next ch-2 sp, sk 1 ch-3 sp, [ch 3, sc in next ch-3 sp] twice; rep from * across to last ch-4 sp, ch 3, sc in 3rd ch of t-ch, turn.

Row 4: Ch 4, sc in next ch-3 sp, *ch 3, sc in next ch-3 sp, ch 3, [sh in next ch-2 sp, ch 2] twice, sh in next ch-2 sp, sk 1 ch-3 sp, [ch 3, sc in next ch-3 sp] twice; rep from * across to last sc, ch 1, dc in last sc, turn.

Row 5: Ch 1, sc in dc, *ch 3, sc in ch-3 sp, ch 3, sh in next ch-2 sp, ch 1, sk 1 ch-2 sp, 9 tr in next ch-2 sp, sk 1 ch-2 sp, ch 1, sh in next ch-2 sp, sk 1 ch-3 sp [ch 3, sc in next ch-3 sp] twice; rep from * across to t-ch, sc in t-ch, turn.

Row 6: Ch 4, *sc in next ch-3 sp, ch 3, sh in next ch-2 sp, ch 2, [sc, ch 3] in next 8 tr, sc in next tr, ch 2, sh in next ch-2 sp, sk 1 ch-3 sp, ch 3, sc in next ch-3 sp, ch 3; rep from * across to last sc, ch 1, dc in last sc, turn.

Row 7: Ch 1, sc in dc, *ch 3, sh in next ch-2 sp, ch 3, [sc in next ch-3 sp, ch 3] 8 times, sk 1 ch-2 sp, sh in next ch-2 sp, ch 3, sk next ch-3 sp, sc in next ch-sp; rep from * across, turn.

Row 8: Ch 5, *sh in next ch-2 sp, ch 3, sk next ch-3 sp, [sc in next ch-3 sp, ch 3] 7 times, sk next ch-3 sp, sh in next ch-2 sp, ch 1; rep from * across (do not ch 1), dtr in last sc, turn.

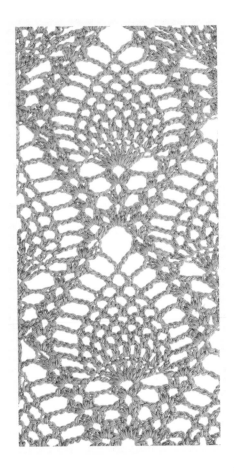

Row 9: Ch 3 (counts as dc), 2 dc in dtr, *sh in next ch-2 sp, ch 3, sk 1 ch-3 sp, [sc in next ch-3 sp, ch 3] 6 times, sh in next ch-2 sp, sh in next ch-1 sp; rep from * across to t-ch, 3 dc in top of t-ch, turn.

Row 10: Ch 3 (counts as dc), 2 dc in 1st dc, ch 1, *sh in next ch-2 sp, ch 3, sk 1 ch-3 sp, [sc in next ch-3 sp, ch 3] 5 times, [sh in next ch-2 sp, ch 1] twice; rep from * across to t-ch (do not sh or ch 1), 3 dc in top of t-ch, turn.

Row 11: Ch 3 (counts as dc), 2 dc in 1st dc, ch 2, *sh in next ch-2 sp, ch 3, sk 1 ch-3 sp, [sc in next ch-3 sp, ch 3] 4 times, [sh in next ch-2 sp, ch 2] twice; rep from * across to t-ch (do not sh or ch 2), 3 dc in top of t-ch, turn.

Row 12: Ch 4 (counts as tr), 4 tr in 1st dc, *ch 1, sk 1 ch-2 sp, sh in next ch-2 sp, ch 3, sk next ch-3 sp, [sc in next ch-3 sp, ch 3] 3 times, sh in next ch-2 sp, ch 1, sk 1 ch-2 sp, 9 tr in next ch-2 sp; rep from * across to t-ch, 5 tr in top of t-ch, turn.

Row 13: Ch 1, sc in 1st tr, *[ch 3, sc] in next 4 tr, ch 2, sh in next ch-2 sp, ch 3, sk 1 ch-3 sp, [sc in next ch-3 sp, ch 3] twice, sh in next ch-2 sp, ch 2, [sc, ch 3] in next 4 tr, sc in next st; rep from * across, turn.

Row 14: Ch 4, *[sc in next ch-3 sp, ch 3] 4 times, sh in next ch-2 sp, ch 3, sk 1 ch-3 sp, sc in next ch-3 sp, ch 3, sh in next ch-2 sp, ch 3, [sc in next ch-3 sp, ch 3] 4 times; rep from * across to last sc (do not ch 3), ch 1, dc in last sc, turn.

Row 15: Ch 1, sc in dc, *[ch 3, sc in next ch-3 sp] 3 times, ch 3, sh in next ch-2 sp, ch 1, sh in next ch-2 sp, sk 1 ch-3 sp, [ch 3, sc in next ch-3 sp] 4 times; rep from * across to t-ch, sc in t-ch, turn.

Rep rows 2–15 to desired length.

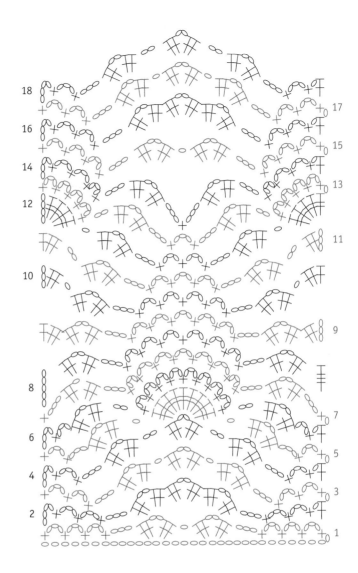

Kiwi Lace

The modern drop shape mixed with the classic pineapple pattern makes for a stunning fabric that will turn heads in any project.

Shell (sh): [(Tr, ch 1) 6 times, tr] in st indicated.

Half Shell (half sh): [(Tr, ch 1) twice, tr] in st indicated.

Ch a multiple of 20 sts plus 6.

Row 1 (RS): Sc in 8th ch from hk, *ch 8, sk 5 ch, tr in next 5 ch, ch 8, sk 5 ch, sc in next ch, ch 5, sk 3 ch, sc in next ch; rep from * across to last 18 ch, ch 8, sk 5 ch, tr in next 5 ch, ch 8, sk 5 ch, sc in next ch, ch 2, sk 1 ch, tr in last ch, turn.

Row 2: Ch 1, sc in tr, *ch 9, tr in next 2 tr, [tr, ch 5, tr] in next tr, tr in next 2 tr, ch 9, sc in next ch-5 sp; rep from * across, turn.

Row 3: Ch 8 (counts as tr, ch-4 sp), *tr in next 3 tr, ch 3, [tr, ch 3, tr] in next ch-5 sp, ch 3, tr in next 3 tr, ch 9; rep from * across to last 6 tr, tr in next 3 tr, ch 3, [tr, ch 3, tr] in next ch-5 sp, ch 3, tr in next 3 tr, ch 4, tr in last sc, turn.

Row 4: Ch 7 (counts as tr, ch-2 sp), *tr in next 3 tr, ch 2, sk 1 ch-3 sp, sh in next ch-3 sp, ch 2, tr in next 3 tr, ch 5; rep from * across to last 8 tr, tr in next 3 tr, ch 2, sk 1 ch-3 sp, sh in next ch-3 sp, ch 2, tr in next 3 tr, ch 2, tr in 4th ch of t-ch, turn.

Row 5: Ch 5 (counts as tr, ch-1 sp), *tr in next 3 tr, ch 5, sk ch-2 sp, [sc, ch 5] in next 6 ch-1 sps, tr in next 3 tr, ch 3; rep from * across to last sh, tr in next 3 tr, ch 5, sk ch-2 sp, [sc, ch 5] in next 6 ch-1 sps, tr in next 3 tr, ch 1, tr in 4th ch of t-ch, turn.

Row 6: Ch 4 (counts as tr), *tr in next 3 tr, ch 5, sk 1 ch-5 sp, [sc, ch 5] in next 5 ch-5 sps, tr in next 3 tr, ch 1; rep from * across to t-ch, do not ch 1, tr in 4th ch of t-ch, turn.

Row 7: Ch 3, tr in 1st 3 tr, *ch 6, sk 1 ch-5 sp, [sc, ch 5] in next 3 ch-5 sps, sc in next ch-5 sp, ch 6, tr in next 2 tr, tr2tog over next 2 tr, tr in next 2 tr; rep from * across to last 6 ch-5 sps, ch 6, sk 1 ch-5 sp, [sc, ch 5] in next 3 ch-5 sps, sc in next ch-5 sp, ch 6, tr in next 2 tr, tr2tog over last tr and t-ch, turn.

Row 8: Ch 4 (counts as tr), tr in next 2 tr, *ch 7, sk ch-6 sp, [sc, ch 5] twice in next ch-5 sp, sc in next ch-5 sp, ch 7, tr in next 5 tr; rep from * across to last 3 tr, tr in last 3 tr, turn.

Row 9: Ch 4 (counts as tr), tr in next 2 tr, *ch 8, sk ch-7 sp, sc in next ch-5 sp, ch 5, sc in next ch-5 sp, ch 8, tr in next 5 tr; rep from * across to last 2 ch-5 sps, ch 8, sk ch-7 sp, sc in next ch-5 sp, ch 5, sc in next ch-5 sp, ch 8, tr in next 2 tr, tr in top of t-ch, turn.

Row 10: Ch 7 (counts as dtr, ch 2), tr in 1st 3 tr, *ch 9, sc in next ch-5 sp, ch 9, tr in next 2 tr, [tr, ch 5, tr] in next tr, tr in next 2 tr; rep from * across to last ch-5 sp, ch 9, sc in next ch-5 sp, ch 9, tr in next 2 tr, [tr, ch 2, dtr] in top of t-ch, turn.

Row 11: Ch 6 (counts as dtr, ch 1), tr in dtr, ch 3, tr in next 3 tr, *ch 9, tr in next 3 tr, ch 3, [tr, ch 3, tr] in next ch-5 sp, ch 3, tr in next 3 tr; rep from * across to last 2 ch-9 sps, ch 9, tr in next 3 tr, ch 3, [tr, ch 1, dtr] in 5th ch of t-ch, turn.

Row 12: Ch 5 (counts as tr, ch 1), half sh in ch-1 sp, *ch 2, tr in next 3 tr, ch 5, tr in next 3 tr, ch 2, sk 1 ch-3 sp, sh in next ch-3 sp; rep from * across to last 7 tr, ch 2, tr in next 3 tr, ch 5, tr in next 3 tr, ch 2, sk 1 ch-3 sp, [half sh, ch 1, tr] in t-ch sp, turn.

Row 13: Ch 6, [sc, ch 5] in next 3 ch-1 sps, tr in next 3 tr, *ch 3, tr in next 3 tr, ch 5, sk ch-2 sp, [sc, ch 5] in next 6 ch-1 sps, tr in next 3 tr; rep from * across to last 6 tr, tr in next 3 tr, [ch 5, sc] twice, ch 5, [sc, ch 2, tr] in t-ch, turn.

Row 14: Ch 1, sc in tr, ch 5, [sc, ch 5] in next 2 ch-5 sps, tr in next 3 tr, *ch 1, tr in next 3 tr, ch 5, sk 1 ch-5 sp, [sc, ch 5] in next 5 ch-5 sps, tr in next 3 tr; rep from * across to last 3 tr, ch 1, tr in next 3 tr, sk 1 ch-5 sp, [ch 5, sc] in last 3 ch-sps, turn.

Row 15: Ch 6, sc in next ch-5 sp, ch 5, sc in next ch-5 sp, ch 6, *tr in next 2 tr, tr2tog over next 2 tr, tr in next 2 tr, ch 6, sk 1 ch-5 sp, [sc, ch 5] in next 3 ch-5 sps, sc in next ch-5 sp, ch 6; rep from * across to last 6 tr, tr in next 2 tr, tr2tog over next 2 tr, tr in next 2 tr, ch 6, sk 1 ch-5 sp, sc in next ch-5 sp, ch 5, sc in next ch-5 sp, ch 2, tr in last sc, turn.

Row 16: Ch 1, sc in tr, ch 5, sc in next ch-5 sp, ch 7, *tr in next 5 tr, ch 7, [sc, ch 5] in next 2 ch-5 sps, sc in next ch-5 sp, ch 7; rep from * across to last 5 tr, tr in next 5 tr, ch 7, sc in next ch-5 sp, ch 5, sc in t-ch, turn.

Row 17: Ch 6, sc in next ch-5 sp, ch 8, *tr in next 5 tr, ch 8, sc in next ch-5 sp, ch 5, sc in next ch-5 sp, ch 8; rep from * across to last 5 tr, tr in next 5 tr, ch 8, sc in next ch-5 sp, ch 2, tr in last sc, turn.

Rep rows 2–17 to desired length.

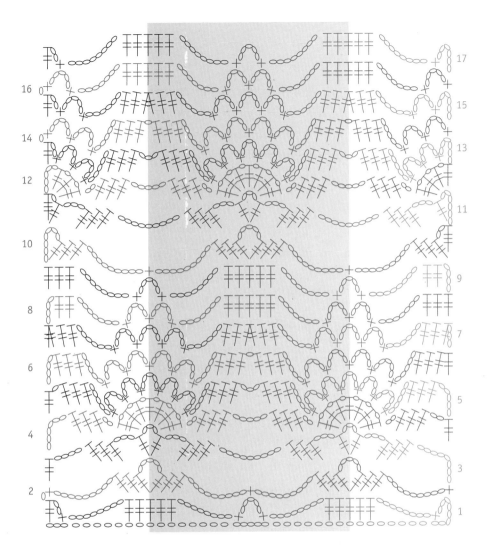

TIP

Pineapple stitch patterns are not difficult because of fancy stitches, but are challenging because they have long row repeats. Staying on track with what row you are on is the hardest part. Using stick-on notes or a highlighter to mark off finished rows helps quite a lot.

CHAPTER 4

Unique
Lace Stitch
Patterns

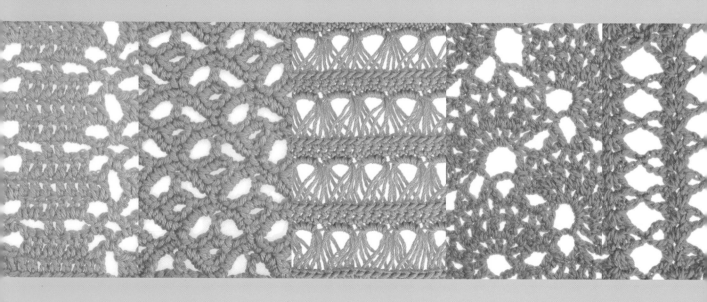

Dermot Filet Stitch

Filet in its natural simplicity is symmetrical and mathematical and appeals to the engineer side of all of us.

Ch a multiple of 16 sts plus 3.

Row 1 (RS): Dc in 4th ch from hk, dc in next 7 ch, [ch 1, sk next ch, dc in next ch] 4 times, *dc in next 8 ch, [ch 1, sk next ch, dc in next ch] 4 times; rep from * across to end, turn.

Row 2: Ch 4 (counts as dc, ch 1), [dc in next dc, ch 1] 3 times, *dc in next 8 dc, [dc in next dc, ch 1] 4 times; rep from * to last 9 sts, dc in ea st across, turn.

Row 3: Ch 3 (counts as dc), *dc in next 8 dc, [ch 1, dc in next dc] 4 times; rep from * across to end, turn.

Row 4: Rep row 3.

Rows 5 and 6: Rep rows 2 and 3.

Row 7: Rep row 3.

Rep rows 2–7 to desired length.

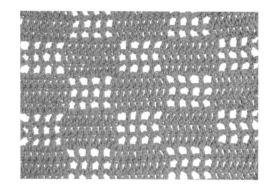

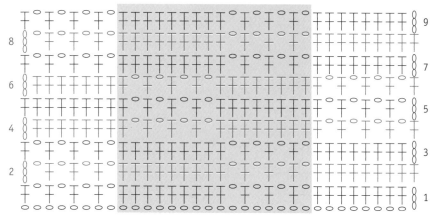

TIP

Filet patterns are made from double crochet stitches and chain spaces. The smaller the number of chains, the taller the rectangular voids will appear, and the more chains, the wider the void will be. You can make up any pattern with graph paper: color in the spaces you want to fill in completely with double crochets, and leave the spaces open where you will just chain.

Keelan Filet Stitch

This Greek-inspired design makes quite a statement in projects from tablecloths to edgings.

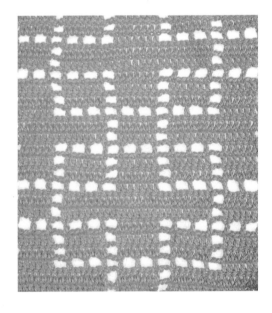

Ch a multiple of 36 sts plus 9.

Row 1 (RS): Dc in 4th ch from hk, dc in next ch, *dc in next 13 ch, ch 2, sk 2 ch, dc in next 7 ch, ch 2, sk 2 ch, dc in next 12 ch; rep from * across to last 4 ch, dc in last 4 ch, turn.

Row 2: Ch 3 (counts as dc), dc in next 2 dc, *dc in next 13 dc, ch 2, sk ch-sp, dc in next 7 dc, ch 2, sk ch-sp, dc in next 12 dc; rep from * across to last 4 dc, dc in last 4 dc, turn.

Row 3: Ch 3 (counts as dc), dc in next 2 dc, *dc in next 4 dc, [ch 2, sk 2 sts, dc in next dc] 10 times, dc in next 2 dc; rep from * across to last 4 dc, dc in ea st, turn.

Row 4: Ch 3 (counts as dc), dc in next 2 dc, *dc in next 4 dc, [ch 2, sk ch-sp, dc in next 7 sts] 3 times, ch 2, sk ch-sp, dc in next 3 dc; rep from * across to last 4 dc, dc in ea st, turn.

Row 5: Rep row 4.

Row 6: Ch 4 (counts as dc, ch 1), sk 3 dc, *[dc in next dc, ch 2, sk 2 sts] 5 times, dc in next 7 dc, [ch 2, sk 2 sts, dc in next dc] 4 times, ch 2, sk 2 sts; rep from * across to last 4 dc, dc in next dc, ch 2, dc in top of t-ch, turn.

Row 7: Ch 3 (counts as dc), dc in next 2 dc, *dc in next 4 dc, ch 2, sk ch-sp, dc in next 25 sts, ch 2, sk ch-sp, dc in next 3 dc; rep from * across to last 4 dc, dc in ea st, turn.

Row 8: Rep row 7.

Row 9: Rep row 6.

Rows 10 and 11: Rep row 4.

Row 12: Rep row 3.

Row 13: Rep row 2.

Rep rows 2–13 to desired length.

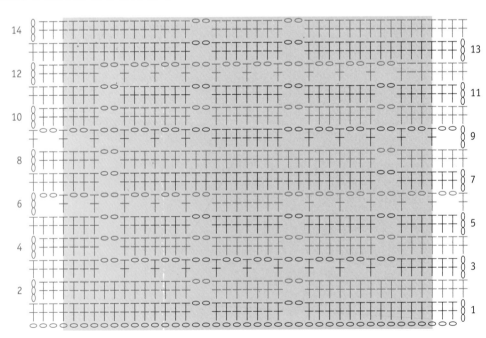

Rebecca Filet Stitch

The voids in this filet are tear shaped, which creates a great fabric for classic tennis vests.

Ch a multiple of 16 sts plus 15.

Row 1 (WS): Dc in 4th ch from hk and ea ch across, turn.

Row 2: Ch 3 (counts as dc), dc in ea st across, turn.

Row 3: Ch 3 (counts as dc), dc in next 5 dc, *ch 3, sk 1 dc, dc in next 15 dc; rep from * across to last 7 sts, ch 3, sk 1 dc, dc in ea st across, turn.

Row 4: Ch 3 (counts as dc), dc in next 3 dc, *ch 2, sc in ch-3 sp, ch 2, sk 2 dc, dc in next 11 dc; rep from * across to last ch-3 sp, ch 2, sc in last ch-3 sp, ch 2, sk 2 dc, dc in last 4 sts, turn.

Rows 5 and 6: Rep row 2.

Row 7: Ch 3 (counts as dc), dc in next 5 dc, *dc in next 8 dc, ch 3, sk 1 dc, dc in next 7 dc; rep from * across to last 7 sts, dc in ea st across, turn.

Row 8: Ch 3 (counts as dc), dc in next 5 dc, *dc in next 6 dc, ch 2, sc in ch-3 sp, ch 2, sk 2 dc, dc in next 5 dc; rep from * across to last 7 sts, dc in last 7 sts, turn.

Row 9: Rep row 2.

Rep rows 2–9 to desired length.

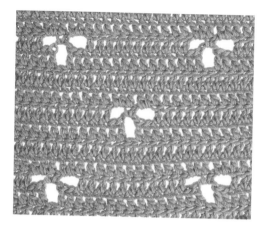

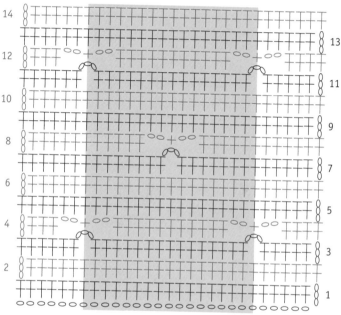

Granya Filet Stitch

Flower-like voids fill this classic filet pattern, making it great for shawls and skirts.

Ch a multiple of 10 sts plus 3.

Row 1 (RS): Dc in 4th ch from hk and ea ch across, turn.

Row 2: Ch 5 (counts as dc, ch-2 sp), dc in 1st dc, *sk 2 dc, dc in next 5 dc, sk 2 dc, [(dc, ch 2) twice, dc] in next dc: rep from * across to last 11 sts, sk 2 dc, dc in next 5 dc, sk 2, [dc, ch 2, dc] in top of t-ch, turn.

Row 3: Ch 2, dc in ch-2 sp, ch 2, *dc in next 5 dc, ch 2, dc3tog over [next ch-2 sp, next dc, next ch-2 sp], ch 2; rep from * to last ch-2 sp, ch 2, dc2tog over last ch-2 sp and 3rd ch of t-ch, turn.

Row 4: Ch 3 (counts as dc), dc in ea st across, turn.

Row 5: Ch 3 (counts as dc), dc in next 2 dc, *sk 2 dc, [(dc, ch 2) twice, dc] in next dc, sk 2 dc, dc in next 5 dc; rep from * across to last 8 sts, sk 2 dc, [(dc, ch 2) twice, dc] in next dc, sk 2 dc, dc in last 3 sts, turn.

Row 6: Ch 3 (counts as dc), dc in next 2 dc, *ch 2, dc3tog over [next ch-2 sp, next dc, next ch-2 sp], ch 2, dc in next 5 dc; rep from * to last 2 ch-2 sps, ch 2, dc3tog over [next ch-2 sp, next dc, last ch-2 sp], ch 2, dc in last 3 sts, turn.

Row 7: Rep row 4.

Rep rows 2–7 to desired length.

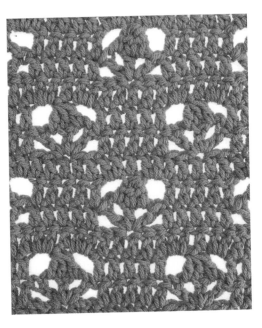

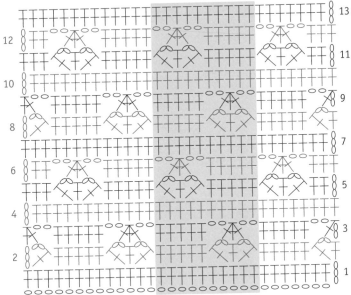

Mairenn Filet Stitch

The classic filet pattern is broken with chain spaces to give a blooming vine look in vertical columns across the fabric.

Ch a multiple of 12 sts plus 4.

Row 1 (RS): Dc in 4th ch from hk, dc in next 4 dc, ch 3, sk 2 ch, dc in next 5 dc, *dc in next 5 ch, ch 3, sk 2 ch, dc in next 5 ch; rep from * across to last ch, dc in last ch, turn.

Row 2: Ch 3 (counts as dc), *dc in next 3 dc, ch 3, sc in next ch-3 sp, ch 3, sk 2 dc, dc in next 3 dc; rep from * across to t-ch, dc in top of t-ch, turn.

Row 3: Ch 3 (counts as dc), *dc in next dc, [ch 3, sc in next ch-3 sp] twice, ch 3, sk 2 dc, dc in next dc; rep from * across to t-ch, dc in top of t-ch, turn.

Row 4: Ch 3 (counts as dc), *dc in next dc, 2 dc in next ch-3 sp, ch 3, sc in next ch-3 sp, ch 3, 2 dc in next ch-3 sp, dc in next dc; rep from * across to t-ch, dc in top of t-ch, turn.

Row 5: Ch 3 (counts as dc), *dc in next 3 dc, 2 dc in next ch-3 sp, ch 3, 2 dc in next ch-3 sp, dc in next 3 dc; rep from * across to t-ch, dc in top of t-ch, turn.

Rep rows 2–5 to desired length.

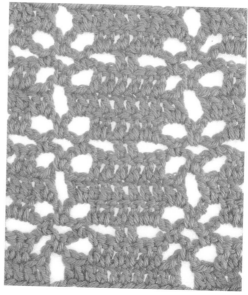

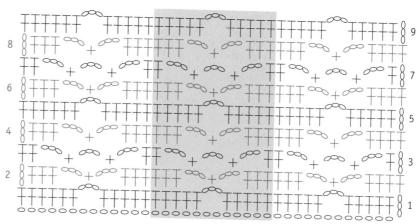

Ella

This lace is dotted with diamonds throughout the even rows. The resulting fabric is strong enough for bag handles or headbands.

Ch a multiple of 6 sts.

Row 1 (WS): Sc in 9th ch from hk (sk ch counts as ch-3 sp and dc), *ch 3, sk 2 ch, dc in next ch, ch 3, sk 2 ch, sc in next ch; rep from * across to last 3 ch, ch 3, sk 2 ch, dc in last ch, turn.

Row 2a: Ch 1, 2 sc in 1st dc, 3 sc in ch-3 sp, sc in next sc, 2 sc in next ch-3 sp, turn, ch 2, sk back 5 sc, sl st in 5th sc, turn.

Row 2b: 3 sc in ch-2 sp, sc in prev ch-3 sp, 3 sc in next dc, 3 sc in next ch-3 sp, sc in next sc, 2 sc in next ch-3 sp, turn, ch 2, sk back 5 sc, sl st in 5th sc, turn.

Rep Row 2b across to last ch-sp.

Row 2 last: 3 sc in last ch-2 sp, sc in prev ch-sp, 2 sc in top of 5th ch of t-ch, turn.

Row 3: Ch 1, sc in sc, *ch 3, sk 3 sc, dc in next sc (middle sc of 3 sc in ch-2 sp), ch 3, sk 3 sc, sc in next sc (middle sc of 3 sc in dc); rep from * across, turn.

Row 4a: Ch 1, sc in sc, 2 sc in ch-3 sp, turn, ch 1, hdc in 1st sc, turn.

Row 4b: Ch 1, sc in hdc, sc in ch-1 sp, sc in prev ch-3 sp, 3 sc in dc, 3 sc in next ch-3 sp, sc in next sc, 2 sc in next ch-3 sp, turn, ch 2, sk back 5 sc, sl st in 5th turn, turn.

Row 4c: 3 sc in ch-2 sp, sc in prev ch-3 sp, 3 sc in next dc, 3 sc in next ch-3 sp, sc in next sc, 2 sc in next ch-3 sp, turn, ch 2, sk back 5 sc, sl st in 5th sc, turn.

Rep Row 4c across to last 2 ch-3 sps.

Row 4 (last 1): 3 sc in ch-2 sp, sc in prev ch-3 sp, 3 sc in next dc, 3 sc in next ch-3 sp, sc in last sc, ch 3, turn, sk back 3 sc, sl in 3rd sc, turn.

Row 4 (last 2): 2 sc in last ch-3 sp, turn.

Row 5: Ch 6 (counts as dc, ch-3 sp), *sk 3 sc, sc in next sc, ch 3, sk 3 sc, dc in next sc, ch 3; rep from * across to last 8 sc, sk 3 sc, sc in next sc, ch 3, sk 3 sc, dc in last sc, turn.

Rep rows 2–5 to desired length, ending with a row 4.

Last row: Ch 1, sc in 1st sc, *ch 2, sk 3 sc, hdc in next sc, ch 2, sk 3 sc, sc in next sc; rep from * across, turn.

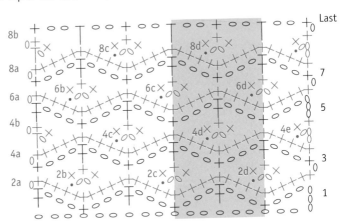

Akalena

This highly geometrical lace is actually pretty delicate, so use it in projects that will be well cared for.

Picot: Ch 3, sl st in 1st ch.

Stitch pattern is a multiple of 17 sts plus 6.

Row 1 (RS): Ch 12, sl st in 12th ch from hk, *ch 17, sl st in 12th ch from hk; rep from * across, ch 11, turn.

Row 2: Ch 1, 3 sc in 2nd ch from hk, [picot, sc in next 2 ch] twice, sk 1 ch, sc in next 5 ch, *[(2 sc, picot) twice, 5 sc, (picot, 2 sc) twice] in next ch-12 sp, sc in next 5 ch; rep from * across to last ch-12 sp, [(2 sc, picot) twice, 3 sc] in last ch-12 sp, turn.

Row 3: Sl st in 1st sc, ch 12, sl st in same sc, *ch 5, sk 17 sc, sl st in next sc, ch 12, sl st in same ch; rep from * across to last 18 sts, ch 5, sk 17 sc, sl st in last sc, ch 6, turn.

Rep rows 2 and 3 to desired length, ending with a row 2.

Last row: Sl st in 1st ch, *ch 5, sk 17 sc, sl st in next sc; rep from * across, fasten off.

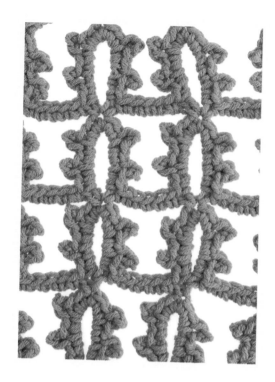

TIP

Short rows in crochet are one of those great mysteries in crafting. In knitting you can add them to get more height in your rows; in crochet you can go in any direction and get more height, new shapes, and new patterns, all in the same row. Since you will be turning back and forth quite a bit and the right and wrong sides will start to get muddled, be sure to keep track of where you are on the diagram by crossing off what you have already crocheted.

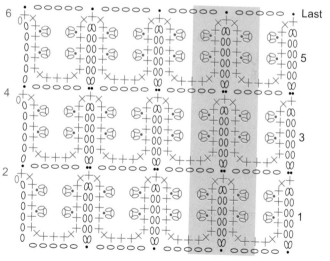

Tatianna

This Baroque-inspired stitch pattern looks amazing as a cuff, or join multiple strips together for unstoppable skirts.

Ch 10 sts.

Row 1 (RS): Sc in 2nd ch from hk, sc in next 2 ch, 2 sc in next ch, 3 sc in next ch, 2 sc in next ch, sc in last 3 ch, do not turn.

Row 2a: Ch 4, tr in 1st ch, do not turn.

Row 2b: 5 sc around post of tr, 5 sc in ch-4 sp (creates a little circle), ch 5, tr in 2nd ch, do not turn.

Row 2c: 5 sc around post of tr, 5 sc in ch-4 sp, ch 4, sk 5 sc on prev row, sc in next 3 sc, ch 8, tr in 5th ch, do not turn.

Row 2d: 5 sc around post of tr, 5 sc in ch-4 sp, ch 5, tr in 2nd ch, do not turn.

Row 2e: 5 sc around post of tr, 5 sc in ch-4 sp, sl st to 1st sc on prev row, do not turn.

Row 3: Sc in next 5 sc, [sc, ch 3, sc] in next ch-1 sp, sc in next 5 sc, 5 sc in next ch-4 sp, sc in next 3 sc, 5 sc in next ch-4 sp, sc in next 5 sc, [sc, ch 3, sc] in next ch-1 sp, sc in next 5 sc, sl st to last sc on row 1, turn.

Row 4: Sl st in next 12 sc, sc in next 3 sc, ch 5, sk 7 sc, sc in next 3 sc, turn.

Row 5: Ch 1, sc in next 3 sc, 7 sc in ch-5 sp, sc in next 3 sc, do not turn.

Rep rows 2–5 to desired length.

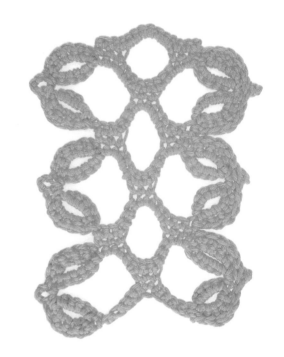

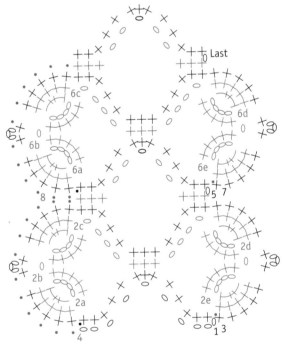

Raya Clover

This classic clover lattice pattern makes a unique and eye-catching fabric, so use it when you need a bit of fabulous in your project.

Lower Petal: [Ch 3, 2 dc] in ring indicated, sl st to next ch-7 sp on prev row, [ch 3, sl st, ch 3, 2 dc] in same ring.

Upper Petal: [Ch 3, sl st, ch 3, 2 dc, ch 3, sl st, ch 3, 2 dc] in ch-sp indicated.

Stitch pattern is a multiple of the entire clover.

Row 1 (RS): Ch 7, sl st in 4th ch from hk (forming ring), [ch 3, 2 dc, ch 3, sl st] in ring, [ch 3, 2 dc] in same ring, *ch 11, sl st to 4th ch from hk, [ch 3, 2 dc, ch 3, sl st, ch 3, 2 dc] in ring; rep from * to 1 less clover than desired width, ch 11, sl st to 4th ch from hk, [(ch 3, 2 dc, ch 3, sl st) 3 times] ch 3, 2 dc] in last ring, do not turn.

Row 2: *Sk 2 ch, sl st in next ch, ch 7, sl st in next dc, upper petal in next ring; rep from * across to last ring, [ch 3, sl st, ch 3, 2 dc] in last ring, sk 2 ch, sl st to next ch.

Row 3: *Ch 10, sl st to 4th ch from hk, lower petal in ring, ch 3, sk next ch-3 sp (petal), sl st to next ch-3 sp; rep from * across, do not turn.

Row 4: Ch 10, turn, *sl st to next dc, upper petal in next ring, sk 2 ch, sl st to next ch, ch 7; rep from * across to last ring, sl st to next dc, upper petal in last ring, sk 2 ch, sl st to next ch, do not turn.

Row 5: Ch 10, sl st to 4th ch from hk, ch 3, 2 dc in ring, ch 3, sk next ch-3 sp, sl st in next ch-3 sp, *ch 10, sl st to 4th ch from hk, lower petal in ring, ch 3, sk next ch-3 sp, sl st to next ch-3 sp; rep from * across to last ring, ch 10, sl st to 4th ch from hk, [lower petal, upper petal] in last ring, do not turn.

Rep rows 2–5 to desired length.

Stivlana

The net of stars in this stitch pattern is stellar in shawls and wraps.

Stitch pattern is a multiple of the star.

Row 1 (RS): Ch 11, tr in 8th ch from hk, *ch 14, tr in 8th ch from hk; rep from * to desired width, do not turn.

Row 2: Ch 7, tr in next tr, ch 7, tr2tog in top of prev tr and next ch (at base of tr on prev row), sk 2 ch, sc in next ch, *ch 3, tr in next tr, ch 7, tr2tog in top of prev tr and next ch on prev row, ch 3, sk 2 ch, sc in next ch; rep from * across, turn.

Row 3: Ch 1, sc in sc, ch 7, *sc in next ch-7 sp, ch 7, sc in next sc, turn, sc in prev ch, hdc in next ch, dc in next ch, tr in next ch, ch 3, turn; rep from * across to last 2 ch-7 sps, ch 7, sc in last ch-7 sp, turn, sc in prev ch, hdc in next ch, dc in next ch, tr in next ch, do not turn.

Row 4: Ch 8, sc in 2nd ch from hk, hdc in next ch, dc in next ch, tr2tog in next ch and next ch on prev row (at base of tr), dc in next ch, hdc in next ch, sc in next ch, sl st to next sc, *sc in next ch, hdc in next ch, dc in next ch, tr in next tr, ch 4, sc in 2nd ch from hk, hdc in next ch, dc in next ch, tr2tog in top of last tr and next ch on prev row (same ch as prev tr), dc in next ch, hdc in next ch, sc in next ch, sl st to next sc; rep from * to last ch-7 sp, sc in next ch, hdc in next ch, dc in next ch, tr in next ch, do not turn.

Row 5: Ch 10, turn, sc in next sl st, ch 3, turn, sk 3 ch of ch-10 sp, tr in next ch, ch 3, turn, sc in sc on top of next star, *ch 7, sc in next sl st, ch 3, turn, sk 3 ch of ch-7 sp, tr in next ch, ch 3, turn, sc in sc on top of next star; rep from * across, turn.

Row 6: Ch 4, tr in next tr, ch 7, tr2tog in top of prev tr and next ch (same ch as tr on prev row), ch 3, *sc in next sc, ch 3, tr in next tr, ch 7, tr2tog in top of prev tr and next ch (same ch as tr on prev row), ch 3; rep from * to last ch-10 sp, sc in last ch-sp, turn.

Rep rows 3–6 to desired length.

Last row: Turn work 90 degrees and beg work on sides of rows, *sc in next ch, hdc in next ch, dc in next ch, tr in top of next tr, ch 3, tr in same ch as base of tr, dc in next ch, hdc in next ch, sc in next ch, sl st in next 2 sc; rep from * across to foundation row, fasten off.

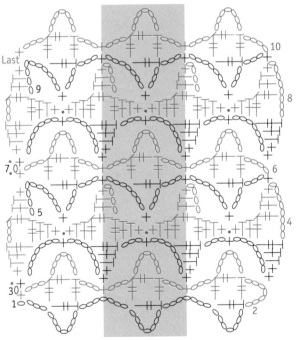

Drika

This basic Brussels lace fills in the space between the rows with double crochet stitches to make it look like a seamless fabric.

First Column

Row 1 (RS): Ch 4, dc in 4th ch from hook, turn.

Row 2: Ch 5, dc in dc, dc in top of t-ch from row 1, turn—2 dc.

Row 3: Ch 5, dc in next 2 dc, turn.

Rep row 3 to desired length.

Bottom Turning

Row 1: Ch 2, sl st to ch-5 sp above (2 rows prev), ch 2, dc in next 2 dc, turn.

Row 2: Ch 5, dc in next 2 dc, turn.

Rep rows 1 and 2 twice more, working sl st in same ch-5 sp as row 1.

Next Column

Row 1: Ch 2, dc2tog in ch-sp below (in prev row) and in ch-sp to the left (in prev column), sl st to next ch-5 sp above (in prev column), ch 2, dc in next 2 dc, turn.

Row 2: Ch 5, dc in next 2 dc, turn.

Rep rows 1 and 2 to row 3 of prev column; rep row 1.

Rep Bottom Turning.

Rep Next Column and Bottom Turning to desired width.

> **TIP**
>
> Brussels or Belgium lace is a technique that uses multiple short rows connected as you crochet. You can do this vertically, serpentine, or in a square or circle. The beauty comes from the trick of the eye being drawn in by the solid stitches in the backdrop of the chain connections. When planning your project, be sure to account for the extra height created by turning from column to column.

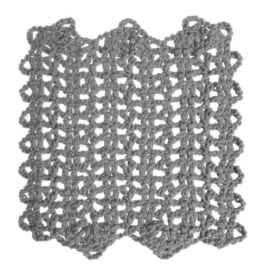

Annaleise

Combining the double crochet stitches in the center of each group sets up columns of Vs and lattice that will look impressive in any project.

First Column

Row 1 (RS): Ch 4, 3 dc in 4th ch from hook, turn.

Row 2: Ch 5, sk 1 dc, 4 dc btw next 2 dc, turn.

Rep row 2 to desired length.

Bottom Turning

Row 1: Ch 2, sl st to ch-5 sp above (2 rows prev), ch 2, sk 1 dc, 4 dc btw next 2 dc, turn.

Row 2: Ch 5, sk 1 dc, 4 dc btw next 2 dc, turn.

Rep rows 1 and 2 twice more, working sl st in same ch-5 sp as row 1.

Next Column

Row 1: Ch 2, sl st to next ch-5 sp above (in prev column), ch 2, sk 1 dc, 4 dc btw next 2 dc, turn.

Row 2: Ch 5, sk 1 dc, 4 dc btw next 2 dc, turn.

Rep rows 1 and 2 to row 3 on prev column; rep row 1.

Rep Bottom Turning.

Rep Next Column and Bottom Turning to desired width.

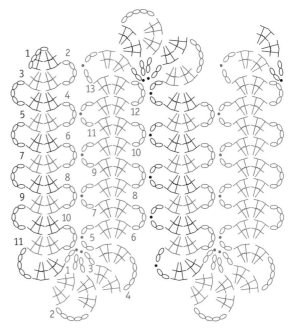

Lotte

The lattice stitches in this fabric create quite an eye-grabbing pattern with columns of crossed lines racing up the center.

Lattice Stitch (lat st): Yo 4 times, insert hk into ch-5 sp 2 rows below and pull up lp, [yo, pull through 2 lps] twice, yo twice, insert hk into ch-sp across from same ch-5 sp on prev column and pull up lp, [yo, pull through 2 lps] twice, insert hk into ch-5 sp above on prev column and pull up lp, [yo, pull through 2 lps on hk] twice, yo, pull through 4 lps on hk, [yo, pull through 2 lps on hk] twice.

First Column

Row 1 (RS): Ch 6, dc in 4th ch from hook, dc in next 2 ch, turn.

Row 2: Ch 5, dc in ea dc, dc in 3rd ch of ch 6 from row 1, turn—4 dc.

Row 3: Ch 5, dc in ea dc across, turn.

Rep row 3 to desired length.

Bottom Turning

Row 1: Ch 2, sl st to ch-5 sp above (2 rows prev), ch 2, dc in next 4 dc, turn.

Row 2: Ch 5, dc in next 4 dc, turn.

Rep rows 1 and 2 three more times, working sl st in same ch-5 sp as row 1.

Next Column

Row 1: Ch 2, lat st in ch-5 sp below (in prev row), in ch-sp to the left (in prev column) and ch-sp above (on prev column), ch 2, dc in next 4 dc, turn.

Row 2: Ch 5, dc in next 2 dc, turn.

Rep rows 1 and 2 to row 3 of prev column; rep row 1.

Rep Bottom Turning.

Rep Next Column and Bottom Turning to desired width.

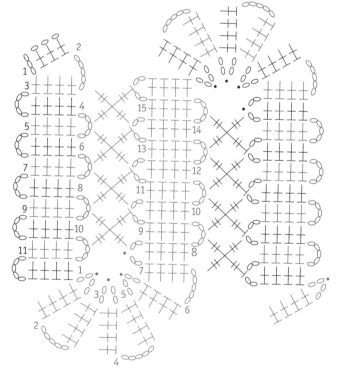

Jacintha

This version of Brussels lace shows how easily the pattern can be adapted to serpentine shapes and unique joinings in its wake.

Quad Treble (quadtr): Yo 5 times, insert hk into st and pull up lp, [yo, and pull through 2 lps on hk] 6 times.

Double Treble Together (dtrtog): Yo 3 times, insert hk into st indicated and pull up lp, [yo, pull through 2 lps on hk] twice, yo twice, insert hk into next st indicated and pull up lp, [yo, pull through 2 lps on hk] twice, yo and pull through 3 lps on hk, yo and pull through 2 lps on hk.

First Column

Row 1 (RS): Ch 8, dc in 6th ch from hk, dc in next 2 ch, turn.

Row 2: Ch 5, dc in next 3 dc, turn.

Rep row 2—29 times.

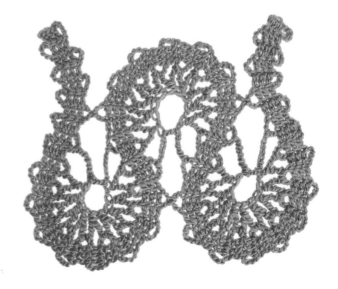

Next Column

Row 1: Ch 2, sk last 25 rows, sl st to next ch-5 sp, ch 2, dc in next 3 dc, turn.

Row 2: Ch 5, dc in next 2 dc, turn.

Rep row 2—17 times.

Rep Next Column to desired length.

Oval Void

Row a: Sl st to 1st inner ch-5 sp above column join, ch 7, dtrtog in next 2 ch-sps, ch 1, (dtrtog in prev ch-sp and next ch-sp) around to last 3 ch-sps, ch 1, dtrtog in prev and next ch-sp, quadtr in next ch-sp, dc in top of ch 7 sp to close, fasten off.

Fill in all oval voids with a row a.

Fleur Brussels Motif

Brussels lace can wrap around any shape to border it. This motif shows just one way you can use Brussels lace.

Picot: Ch 3, sl st in 1st ch.

Fleur Motif

Make an adjustable ring.

Rnd a: Ch 1, *[sc, ch 3, tr] in ring, picot, ch 4, sl st in 1st ch, picot, [tr, ch 3, 2 sc] in ring, ch 7, sc in ring; rep from * 3 more times, sl st to 1st sc, fasten off.

Brussels Edging

Row 1 (RS): Ch 9, dc in 6th ch from hk, dc in next 3 ch, turn.

Row 2: Ch 2, tr in ch-7 sp on fleur, ch 2, dc in next 4 dc, turn.

Row 3: Ch 5, dc in next 4 dc, turn.

Row 4: Ch 2, sc in next ch-4 sp on fleur, ch 2, dc in next 4 dc, turn.

Rep row 3 on all odd rows.

Row 6: Ch 2, tr in next ch-7 sp on fleur, ch 2, dc in next 4 dc, turn.

Row 8: Ch 2, dtr in same ch-7 sp on fleur, ch 2, dc in next 4 dc, turn.

Row 10: Ch 2, sl st to prev dtr, ch 2, dc in next 4 dc, turn.

Rep rows 2–11 around fleur, end with a row 10, fasten off whipstitch foundation chain and last row together.

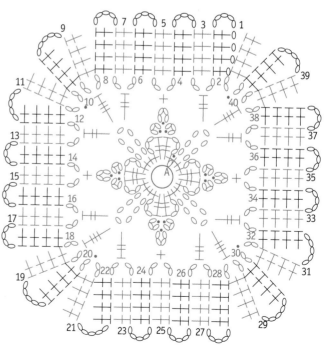

Solomon's Knot Stitch

This classic stitch pattern can be super lacy or not at all, depending on the length of your main Solomon's Knot. Try swatching first to determine your favorite length.

Main Solomon's Knot (msk): Draw up long lp on hk, ch 1 through the long lp, sc in blp of msk.

Edge Solomon's Knot (esk): Draw up long lp on hk to about one-half length of the msk, yo, and draw the lp through the long lp, sc in blp of esk.

Back Loop (blp): The back loop is the single strand of the Solomon's knot made from the ch 1, (the double strand is the front lp).

Ch 2.

Row 1 (WS): Sc in 2nd ch from hk, esk across to desired length.

Row 2: Esk, msk, turn, sk 1 esk, sc in next sc of esk, *work 2 msk, sk 1 sc, sc in next sc of esk; rep from * across.

Row 3: Esk twice, msk, turn, sk 1st msk of row below, sc in next sc of msk, *msk twice, sk 2 msk, sc in next sc of esk; rep from * across.

Rep row 3 to desired length.

TIP

Stitch patterns made from lacy loops can make the most unique fabrics. The key to a great pattern is to make the same loop stitch over and over. I like to mark off a spot on a piece of paper so I can double-check to make sure the loop is the same size each time.

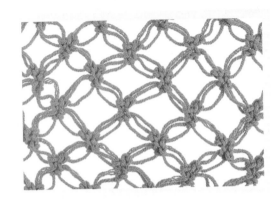

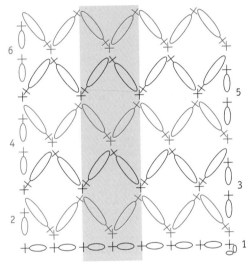

Bathsheba Knot Stitch

Slightly more organized and advanced pattern based on the basic Solomon's Knot, Bathsheba Knot Stitch is perfect for lovely shawls.

Main Solomon's Knot (msk): Draw up long lp on hk, ch 1 through the long lp, sc in blp of msk.

Edge Solomon's Knot (esk): Draw up long lp on hk to about two-thirds length (about 3 ch lengths) of the msk, ch 1 through the long lp, sc in blp of esk.

Back Loop (blp): The back loop is the single strand of the Solomon's Knot made from the ch 1 (the double strand is the front lp).

Stitch pattern is a multiple of 16 sts plus 2.

Row 1 (RS): Sc in 2nd ch from hk, *esk, sk 3 ch, sc in next ch; rep from * across, turn.

Row 2: Ch 1, sc in 1st sc, *msk, sk next esk, tr in next sc, msk, sk next esk, ttr in next sc, msk, sk next esk, tr in next sc, msk, sk next esk, sc in next sc; rep from * across, turn.

Row 3: Ch 3, *msk, sk msk, dc in next st; rep from * across, turn.

Row 4: Ch 6, *esk, tr in next dc, esk, sc in next dc, esk, tr in next dc, esk, ttr in next dc; rep from * across, turn.

Row 5: Ch 1, sc in 1st st, sk esk, *esk, sk esk, sc in next st; rep from * across to t-ch, sc in top of t-ch, turn.

Row 6: Ch 6, sk 1st sc, sk esk, *msk, tr in next sc, sk next esk, msk, sc in next sc, sk next esk, msk, tr in next sc, sk next esk, msk, ttr in next sc, sk next esk; rep from * across, turn.

Row 7: Rep row 3.

Row 8: Ch 1, sc in 1st dc, *esk, tr in next dc, esk, ttr in next dc, esk, tr in next dc, esk, sc in next dc; rep from * across, turn.

Row 9: Rep row 5.

Rep rows 2–9 to desired length.

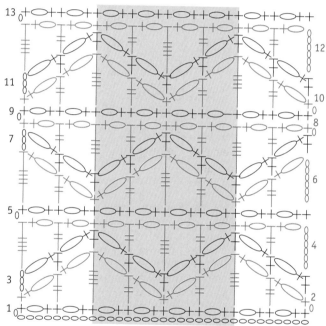

Abishag Cluster Knot

This is a slightly different take on the classic Solomon's Knot with clusters dotted throughout the pattern.

Main Solomon's Knot (msk): Draw up long lp on hk, ch 1 through the long lp, sc in blp of msk.

Edge Solomon's Knot (esk): Draw long lp on hk to about one-half length of the msk, ch 1 through the long lp, sc in blp of esk.

Back Loop (blp): The back loop is the single strand of the Solomon's Knot made from the ch 1 (the double strand is the front lp).

Ch 2.

Row 1 (WS): Sc in 2nd ch from hk, esk, in a multiple of 2 to desired length, turn.

Row 2: Ch 1, sc in 1st sc of esk, *msk twice, sk 1 esk, sc in next sc of esk; rep from * across, turn.

Row 3: Ch 6, esk, *sk 1 sc, sk 1 msk, 3 dc-cl in next sc of msk, msk,; rep from * across to last sc, esk, ttr in last sc, turn.

Row 4: Ch 4, msk, *sc in next dc-cl, msk twice; rep from * to last dc-cl, sc in last dc-cl, msk, tr in top of t-ch, turn.

Row 5: Ch 2, dc in tr, *msk, sk 2 msk, 3 dc-cl in next sc of msk; rep from * across to t-ch, 2 dc-cl in top of t-ch, turn.

Row 6: Ch 1, sc in 1st dc-cl, *msk twice, sc in next dc-cl; rep from * across, turn.

Rep rows 3–6 to desired length.

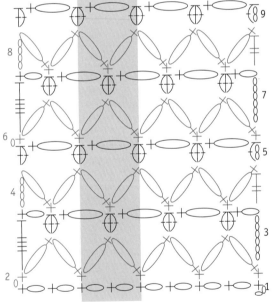

Classic Broomstick Lace

Classic broomstick lace highlights the strands of yarn encased in rows of single crochet.

Ch a multiple of 4 sts plus 1.

Row 1 (RS): Sc in 2nd ch from hk and ea ch across, turn.

Row 2: Ch 1, sc in ea sc across, turn.

Row 3: Pull up lp in ea sc across, moving lps to broomstick holder, ch 1 in last lp to lock st, turn.

Row 4: Ch 1, working from right to left, *insert hook in first 4 loops at once, 4 sc in group; rep from * in groups of 4 lps across, turn.

Row 5: Rep row 2.

Rep rows 2–5 to desired length.

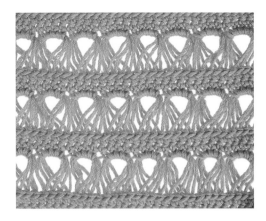

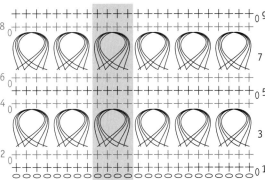

Broomstick Lace Flower

Using the lace loops as petals makes this motif perfect for alternative fibers like wire or plastic bags.

Ch 25.

Rnd 1 (RS): Sc in 2nd ch from hk and ea ch across, sl st to 1st sc, do not turn— 24 sc.

Rnd 2: Pull up lp in blp and flp of each sc around, remove all but last loop from hook, sl st back to foundation ch, turn work 180 degrees—48 loops.

Rnd 3: Ch 1, *sc in next ch, sc2tog over next 2 ch; rep from * around, sl st to 1st sc, do not turn—16 sc.

Rnd 4: Ch 1, (sc2tog over next 2 sc) across, do not turn—8 sc.

Rnd 5: Rep rnd 4, fasten off, weave tail through center of motif—4 sc.

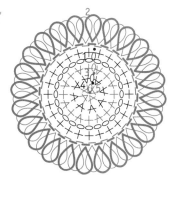

Madena Lace

Teardrops are combined with picot edgings for a pretty paisley design.

Ch 5, sl st to 1st ch to form ring.

Row 1: Ch 4 (counts as dc, ch 1), [dc, ch 1, dc] in ring, turn.

Row 2: Ch 5, 2 sc in ch-1 sp, ch 4, 2 sc in last ch-sp, ch 2, dc in 3rd ch of t-ch, turn.

Row 3: Ch 3, dc in ch-2 sp, ch 7, sk ch-4 sp, 2 dc in last ch-sp, turn.

Row 4: Ch 1, sc in 1st dc, [2 sc, 2 hdc, 6 dc, 2 hdc, 2 sc] in ch-7 sp, sc in top of t-ch, turn.

Row 5: Ch 2, sk 2 sc, sk 1 hdc, [dc in next st, ch 1] 7 times, dc2tog in next hdc and last sc, turn.

Row 6: Ch 1, sc in 1st st, [sc, ch 4, sc] in ea ch-1 sp across, sc in last st, turn.

Next Motif

Row 7: Ch 3, dc in last sc of prev row, ch 4 (counts as dc, ch 1), [dc, ch 1, dc] around post of dc, sl st to edge of prev motif, turn.

Row 8: Ch 5, 2 sc in ch-1 sp, ch 4, 2 sc in last ch-sp, ch 2, dc in 3rd ch of t-ch, turn.

Row 9: Ch 3, dc in ch-2 sp, ch 7, sk ch-4 sp, 2 dc in last ch-sp, sl st to edge of prev motif, turn.

Row 10: Sc in 1st dc, [2 sc, 2 hdc, 6 dc, 2 hdc, 2 sc] in ch-7 sp, sc in top of t-ch, turn.

Row 11: Ch 2, sk 2 sc, sk 1 hdc, [dc in next st, ch 1] 7 times, dc2tog in next hdc and last sc, sl st to edge of prev motif, turn.

Row 12: Sc in 1st st, [sc, ch 4, sc] in ea ch-1 sp across, sc in last st, turn.

Rep Next Motif to desired length.

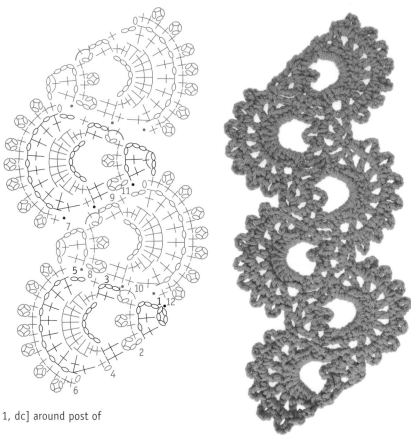

TIP

Partial motifs are a half or quarter or another fraction of a full motif that are all crocheted together to form strips. The strips can be combined to make an incredible fabric.

Anesha Lace

Flowers are combined off-center for a petal-like wave pattern.

Four Double Crochet Cluster (4 dc-cl): *Yo, insert hk into st indicated and pull up lp, yo, pull through 2 lps on hk; rep from * once in same st and twice in next st indicated, yo and pull through all lps on hk.

Three Double Crochet Cluster (3 dc-cl): *Yo, insert hk into st indicated and pull up lp, yo, pull through 2 lps on hk; rep from * once in same st and once in next st indicated, yo and pull through all lps on hk.

Ch 9, sl st to 1st ch to form ring.

Row 1 (RS): Ch 3, 11 dc in ring, turn.

Row 2: Ch 4, [dc, ch 1] in ea dc across to t-ch, dc in top of t-ch, turn.

Row 3: Ch 2, sk 1 ch-1 sp, 2 dc-cl in next ch-1 sp, *ch 5, 4 dc-cl over prev ch-1 sp and ch-1 sp 2 away (skipping 1 ch-1 sp); rep from * across to last ch-1 sp, ch 5, 3 dc-cl in prev ch-1 sp and 3rd ch of t-ch, turn.

Row 4: Ch 1, [Sc, hdc, 6 dc, hdc, sc] in ea ch-5 sp across.

Next Motif

Row 5: Ch 7, tr in 5th ch from hk, ch 3, 11 dc in ring, sl st to edge of prev motif, turn.

Row 6: Ch 2, sl st to edge of prev motif, ch 1, [dc, ch 1] in ea dc across to t-ch, dc in top of t-ch, turn.

Row 7: Ch 2, sk 1 ch-1 sp, 2 dc-cl in next ch-1 sp, *ch 5, 4 dc-cl over prev ch-1 sp and ch-1 sp 2 away (skipping 1 ch-1 sp); rep from * across to last ch-1 sp, ch 5, 3 dc-cl in prev ch-1 sp and 3rd ch of t-ch, sl st to edge of prev motif, turn.

Row 8: Ch 1, [Sc, hdc, 6 dc, hdc, sc] in ea ch-5 sp across.

Rep Next Motif to desired length.

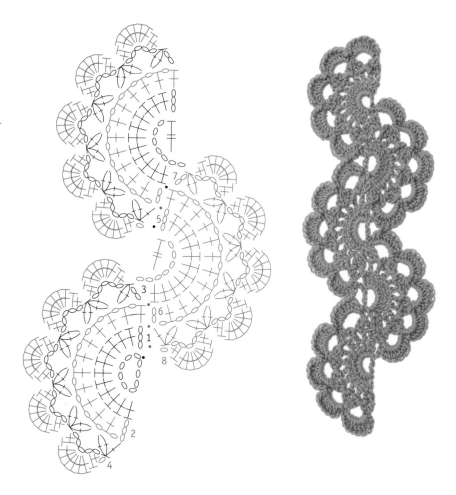

Zaria Lace

Partial snowflakes are combined along a petal seam to look like the rows are continuous between motifs.

Picot: Ch 3, sl st in 1st ch from hk.

First Motif

Ch 8, sl st to 1st ch to form ring.

Row 1 (WS): Ch 3 (counts as dc), 11 dc in ring, turn—12 dc.

Row 2: Ch 3 (counts as dc), dc in next dc, *ch 3, dc in next 4 dc; rep from * once, ch 3, dc in next dc, dc in top of t-ch, turn—12 dc.

Row 3: Ch 3 (counts as dc), dc in next dc, *ch 4, dc in next 4 dc; rep from * once, ch 4, dc in next dc, dc in top of t-ch, turn—12 dc.

Row 4: Ch 3 (counts as dc), dc in next dc, *ch 5, dc in next 4 dc; rep from * once, ch 5, dc in next dc, dc in top of t-ch, turn—12 dc.

Row 5: Ch 3 (counts as dc), dc in next dc, *ch 7, dc in next 4 dc; rep from * once, ch 7, dc in next dc, dc in top of t-ch, turn—12 dc.

Row 6: Ch 1, *sc in next dc, [2 dc, picot, 3 dc, picot, 3 dc, picot, 2 dc] in next ch-7 sp, sk next dc, sc in next dc; rep from * across, ch 5, dc in last sc, turn—30 dc.

Next Motif

Row 7 (RS): Ch 3 (counts as dc), 11 dc in ch-5 sp, sl st to top of t-ch on prev motif's row 5, turn—12 dc.

Row 8: Ch 3 (counts as dc), dc in next dc, *ch 3, dc in next 4 dc; rep from * once, ch 3, dc in next dc, dc in top of t-ch, turn—12 dc.

Row 9: Ch 3 (counts as dc), dc in next dc, *ch 4, dc in next 4 dc; rep from * once, ch 4, dc in next dc, dc in top of t-ch, sl st to top of t-ch on prev motif's row 3, turn—12 dc.

Row 10: Ch 3 (counts as dc), dc in next dc, *ch 5, dc in next 4 dc; rep from * once, ch 5, dc in next dc, dc in top of t-ch, turn—12 dc.

Row 11: Ch 3 (counts as dc), dc in next dc, *ch 7, dc in next 4 dc; rep from * once, ch 7, dc in next dc, dc in top of t-ch, sl st to top of t-ch on prev motif's row 1, turn—12 dc.

Row 12: Ch 1, *sc in next dc, [2 dc, picot, 3 dc, picot, 3 dc, picot, 2 dc] in next ch-7 sp, sk next dc, sc in next dc; rep from * across, ch 5, dc in last sc, turn—30 dc.

Rep Next Motif to desired length.

Innya Lace

Half doilies are stacked on top of each other at angles for a layered look.

First Motif

Ch 8, sl st to 1st ch to form ring.

Row 1 (RS): Ch 4, [dc, ch 1] 6 times in ring, dc in ring, turn.

Row 2: Ch 4, [2 dc-cl, ch 2] in ea ch-1 sp around, [2 dc-cl, ch 1, dc] in t-ch, turn.

Row 3: Ch 2, [dc, ch 3, dc] in ea dc-cl to last, dc in last dc-cl, ch 3, dc2tog in last dc-cl and 3rd ch of t-ch, turn.

Row 4: Ch 6, *dc2tog over next 2 dc, ch 5, rep from * around to last 2 dc, dc2tog over last 2 dc, ch 3, dc in last dc, turn.

Second Motif

Row 5 (RS): Ch 7, dc in 1st dc2tog, ch 4, [dc, ch 1] 6 times in ring, dc in ring, turn.

Row 6: Ch 4, [2 dc-cl, ch 2] in ea ch-1 sp around, [2 dc-cl, ch 1, dc] in t-ch, sl st to top edge of prev motif, turn.

Row 7: Ch 2, [dc, ch 3, dc] in ea dc-cl to last, dc in last dc-cl, ch 3, dc2tog in last dc-cl and 3rd ch of t-ch, turn.

Row 8: Ch 6, *dc2tog over next 2 dc, ch 5, rep from * around to last 2 dc, dc2tog over last 2 dc, turn.

Next Motif

Row 9 (RS): Dtr in 3rd ch-sp from end of 2nd prev motif, ch 4, [dc, ch 1] 6 times in ring, dc in ring, turn.

Row 10: Ch 2, sc in ch-sp of 2nd prev motif, ch 1, [2 dc-cl, ch 2] in ea ch-1 sp around, [2 dc-cl, ch 1, dc] in t-ch, sc to top edge of prev motif, turn.

Row 11: Ch 2, [dc, ch 3, dc] in ea dc-cl to last, dc in last dc-cl, ch 3, dc2tog in last dc-cl and 3rd ch of t-ch, turn.

Row 12: Ch 2, sc in next ch-sp of 2nd prev motif, ch 3, [dc2tog, ch 5] in ea ch-3 sp around to last, dc2tog in last ch-3 sp, turn.

Rep Next Motif to desired length.

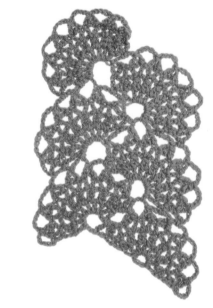

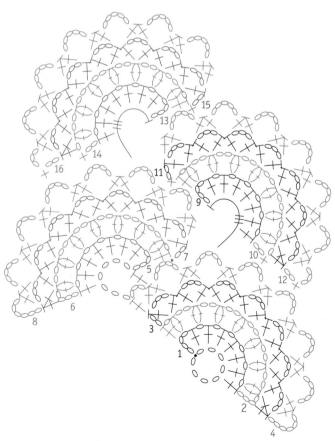

Nadja Lace

Combining one petal along its seam makes a triangular motif with teardrop voids.

Trefoil: Ch 4, sl st to 2nd ch, ch 3, sl st to 1st ch, ch 4, sl st to 2nd ch.

First Motif

Ch 5, sl st to 1st ch to form ring.

Row 1: Ch 5, dc2tog in ring, ch 2, dc in ring, turn.

Row 2: Ch 3, 3 dc in ch-2 sp, 4 dc in t-ch sp, turn.

Row 3: Ch 3, dc in next 3 dc, FPdtr, ch 4, FPquadtr, ch 4, FPdtr around dc2tog on row 1, dc in next 3 dc, dc in top of t-ch, turn.

Row 4: Ch 1, sc in 1st dc, [2 dc, ch 3, 2 dc] in ch-4 sp, ch 3, turn, dtr in 1st sc, ch 1, turn, 3 sc in ch-3 sp, ch 1, [2 dc, ch 3, 2 dc] in same ch-4 sp, , trefoil, [(2 dc, ch 3) 3 times, 2 dc] in ch-4 sp, sc in top of t-ch, ch 8, turn, sk 1 ch-3 sp, sl st to next ch-3 sp, turn, 3 sc in ch-3 sp, do not turn.

Next Motif

Ch 3, dc in 1st ch.

Row 1: Ch 5, [dc2tog, ch 2, dc] around post of dc, sl st to edge of prev motif, turn.

Row 2: Ch 3, 3 dc in ch-2 sp, 4 dc in t-ch sp, turn.

Row 3: Ch 3, dc in next 3 dc, [BPdtr, ch 4, BPquadtr, ch 4, BPdtr] around dc2tog on row 1, dc in next 3 dc, dc in top of t-ch, sl st to edge of prev motif, turn.

Row 4: Sc in 1st dc, [2 dc, ch 3, 2 dc] in ch-4 sp, ch 3, turn, dtr in 1st sc, sl st in edge of prev motif, ch 1, turn, 3 sc in ch-3 sp, ch 1, [2 dc, ch 3, 2 dc] in same ch-4 sp, trefoil, [(2 dc, ch 3) 3 times, 2 dc] in ch-4 sp, sc in top of t-ch, ch 8, turn, sk 1 ch-3 sp, sl st to next ch-3 sp, turn, 3 sc in ch-3 sp, do not turn.

Rep Next Motif, alternating front and back post stitch on row 3 for every new motif.

CHAPTER 5

Colorwork Stitch Patterns

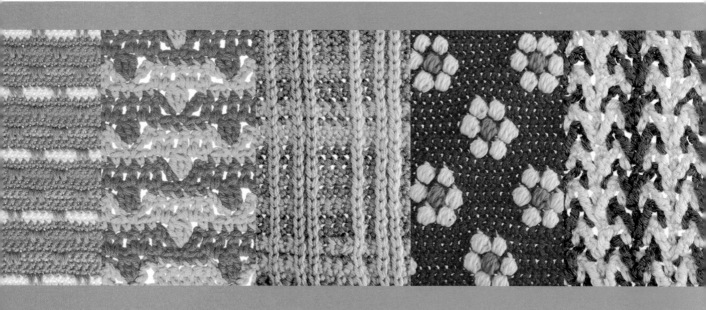

Popsicle Spike

This simple pattern just drops a stitch down every so often to give the look of bricks. Using bold colors for the rows of single crochet and a muted color for the spike stitches, you get an eye-catching fabric.

Single Crochet Spike (sc spike): Insert hk into next st 3 rows below and pull up a lp, yo and pull through all the lps on the hk.

Ch a multiple of 6 sts plus 5.

Row 1 (WS): Sc in the 2nd ch from hk and ea ch across, change color, turn.

Rows 2 and 3: Ch 1, sc in ea sc across, turn.

Row 4: Change color, ch 1, sc in 1st sc, *sc spike over next 2 sc, sc in next 4 sc; rep from * across to last 3 sts, sc over next 2 sc, sc in last sc, turn.

Row 5: Ch 1, sc in ea sc across, change color, turn.

Rows 6 and 7: Rep rows 2 and 3.

Row 8: Change color, ch 1, *sc in next 4 sc, sc spike over next 2 sc; rep from * across to last 4 sts, sc in last 4 sc, turn.

Row 9: Ch 1, sc in ea sc across, change color, turn.

Rep rows 2–9 to desired length.

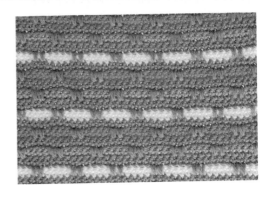

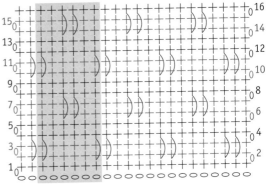

TIP

Color patterns are great for their bold look, but it can get hard to hold so many strands at once. All of the patterns in this section ease you into colorwork by changing the color at the end of each row. You work the pattern by crocheting into a stitch that is a row or two below the one you are working in. In most cases, the back of the work looks clean and neat, making these patterns great for projects in which you see both sides, such as scarves.

Ridge Diagonal

Dropping a stitch every few post stitches creates the look of the stitch falling down, while the post gives a bit of texture to the whole fabric. Using an odd number of colors makes changes a breeze.

Ch a multiple of 4 sts plus 1.

Row 1 (WS): Dc in 4th ch from hk (sk ch counts as dc), dc in next ch and ea ch across, change color, turn.

Row 2: Ch 3 (counts as dc), dc in next 2 dc, *FPtr in next dc, dc in next 3 dc; rep from * across, dc in t-ch, change color, turn.

Row 3: Ch 3 (counts as dc), *dc in next 3 dc, BPtr in next dc; rep from * across to last 2 dc, dc in next dc, dc in t-ch, change color, turn.

Row 4: Ch 3 (counts as dc), *FPtr in next dc, dc in next 3 dc; rep from * across to last 2 dc, FPtr in next dc, dc in t-ch, change color, turn.

Row 5: Ch 3 (counts as dc), dc in next dc, *BPtr in next dc, dc in next 3 dc; rep from * across to t-ch, dc in t-ch, change colors, turn.

Rep rows 2–5 to desired length.

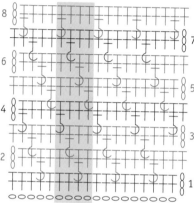

Dotted Frieze

The dropped stitches in this pattern make squares in the rows appear from thin air.

Ch a multiple of 4 sts plus 3.

Row 1 (WS): Sc in 2nd ch from hk and ea ch across, change color, turn.

Row 2: Ch 3 (counts as dc), dc in next dc, *ch 2, sk 2 sc, dc in next 2 sc; rep from * across, turn.

Row 3: Ch 1, sc in 1st 2 sc, *ch 2, sk ch-sp, sc in next 2 dc; rep from * across to end, change color, turn.

Row 4: Ch 1, sc in 1st 2 sc, *dtr in next 2 sts 3 rows below (in front of ch-sps), sc in next 2 sc; rep from * across, change color, turn.

Row 5: Ch 1, sc in ea sc across, turn.

Row 6: Sl st in ea sc across, change color, turn.

Row 7: Ch 1, sc in ea sc 2 rows below, change color, turn.

Rep rows 2–7 to desired length.

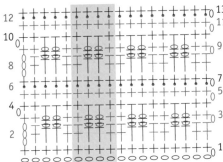

TIP

Do you have a hank of beautiful variegated yarn wasting away in your yarn stash? If so, these mosaic patterns are great for any variegated yarn—whether they are pooling on you or not. Since you are only crocheting one row at a time, mixing a variegated with a solid will tone down the variegated while still letting the stitch pattern shine.

Wave Tote

When you vary stitch heights, a bold wave pops into your project.

Single Crochet Spike (sc spike): Insert hk into next st 3 rows below and pull up a lp, yo and pull through all the lps on the hk.

Ch a multiple of 10 sts plus 2.

Row 1 (RS): Sc in 2nd ch, and ea ch across, change color, turn.

Row 2: Ch 1, sc in 1st sc, *sc in next sc, hdc in next sc, dc in next 5 sc, hdc in next sc, sc in next sc, ch 1, sk 1 sc; rep from * across to last sc, sc in last sc, turn.

Row 3: Ch 1, sc in 1st sc, *sc in next sc, hdc in next hdc, dc in next 5 dc, hdc in next hdc, sc in next sc, ch 1, sk ch-sp; rep from * across to last sc, sc in last sc, change color, turn.

Row 4: Ch 1, sc in 1st sc, *sc in next 9 sc, sc spike over ch-sp in sc 2 rows below; rep from * across to last 10 sts, sc in last 10 sts, turn.

Row 5: Ch 1, sc in ea sc across, change color, turn.

Row 6: Ch 3 (counts as dc), *dc in next 2 sc, hdc in next sc, sc in next sc, ch 1, sk 1 sc, sc in next sc, hdc in next sc, dc in next 3 sc; rep from * across, turn.

Row 7: Ch 1, sc in 1st sc, *dc in next 2 dc, hdc in next hdc, sc in next sc, ch 1, sk ch-sp, sc in next sc, hdc in next hdc, dc in next 3 dc; rep from * across, change color, turn.

Row 8: Ch 1, sc in 1st sc, *sc in next 4 sc, sc spike over ch-sp in sc 2 rows below, sc in next 5 sc; rep from * across, turn.

Row 9: Ch 1, sc in ea sc across, change color, turn.

Rep rows 2–9 to desired length.

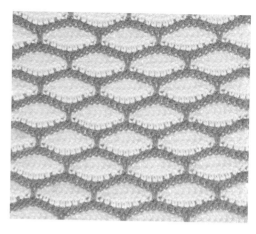

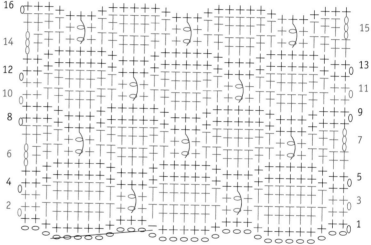

Gentle Wave

The gentle waves are highlighted in this pattern, separated by rows of single crochet.

Ch a multiple of 14 sts plus 2.

Row 1 (WS): Sc in 2nd ch from hk and ea ch across, change color, turn.

Row 2: Ch 1, sc in 1st sc, *sc in next sc, hdc in next 2 sc, dc in next 2 sc, tr in next 3 sc, dc in next 2 sc, hdc in next 2 sc, sc in next 2 sc; rep from * across, do not turn.

Row 3: Pick up yarn from 2 rows below, with right side facing, sc in 1st sc and ea across, change color, turn.

Row 4: Ch 4 (counts as tr), *tr in next sc, dc in next 2 sc, hdc in next 2 sc, sc in next 3 sc, hdc in next 2 sc, dc in next 2 sc, tr in next 2 sc; rep from * across, do not turn.

Row 5: Rep row 3 with WS facing do not turn.

Row 6: Pick up yarn from 2 rows below, rep row 2, turn.

Row 7: Rep Row 3, do not turn.

Row 8: Pick up yarn, Rep Row 4, turn.

Row 9: Ch 1, Rep Row 3 with WS facing, turn.

Rep rows 2–9 to desired length.

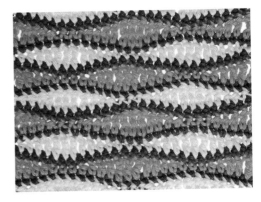

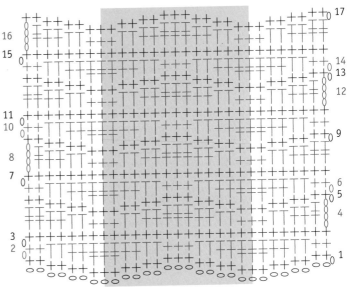

Twilight

The stars in this pattern bring a smile to the fabric with the night sky effect that emerges.

Star Spike: Insert hk into 2nd prev st 1 row below and pull up a lp, insert hk into prev st 2 rows below and pull up a lp, insert hk into next st 3 rows below and pull up a lp, insert hk into st 1 away and 2 rows below and pull up a lp, insert hk into st 2 away and 1 row below and pull up a lp, yo and pull through all lps on hk.

Ch a multiple of 8 sts.

Row 1 (WS): Sc in 2nd ch from hk and ea ch across, turn.

Rows 2 and 3: Ch 1, sc in ea sc across, turn.

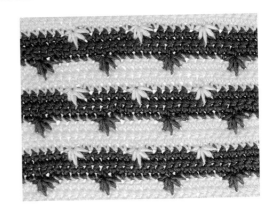

Row 4: Change color, ch 1, sc in 1st 3 sc, *star spike over next st (sk st behind), sc in next 7 sc; rep from * across to last 4 sts, star spike over next st, sc in last 3 sc, turn.

Rows 5–7: Ch 1, sc in ea sc across, turn.

Row 8: Change color, ch 1, sc in 1st 7 sc, star spike over next st (sk st behind), sc in next 7 sc; rep from * across, turn.

Row 9: Ch 1, sc in ea sc across, turn.

Rep rows 2–9 to desired length.

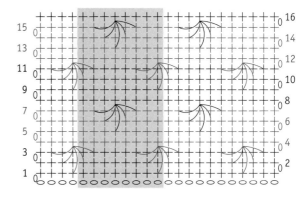

Gambia

This stitch pattern really does not have a right or wrong side, making it perfect for scarves or blankets.

Ch a multiple of 8 sts plus 7.

Row 1 (WS): Dc in 4th ch from hk, dc in next 3 ch, *ch 3, sk 1 ch, sc in next ch, ch 3, sk 1 ch, dc in next 5 ch, rep from * across, change color, turn.

Row 2: Ch 1, sc in 1st 5 dc, *ch 1, 3 dc-cl in sc, ch 1, sc in next 5 dc; rep from * across, turn.

Row 3: Ch 6 (counts as dc, ch 3), sk 2 sc, sc in next sc, ch 3, sk next sc, *dc in next sc, dc in next ch-1 sp, dc in next dc-cl, dc in next ch-1 sp, dc in next sc, ch 3, sk 1 sc, sc in next sc, ch 3, sk 1 sc; rep from * across to last sc, dc in last sc, change color, turn.

Row 4: Ch 1, sc in dc, *ch 1, 3 dc-cl in sc, ch 1, sc in next 5 dc; rep from * across to last sc, ch 1, 3 dc-cl in next sc, ch 1, sc in 3rd ch of t-ch, turn.

Row 5: Ch 3 (counts as dc), dc in next ch-1 sp, dc in next dc-cl, dc in next ch-1 sp, dc in next sc, *ch 3, sk 1 sc, sc in next sc, ch 3, sk 1 sc, dc in next sc, dc in next ch-1 sp, dc in next dc-cl, dc in next ch-1 sp, dc in next sc; rep from * across, change color, turn.

Rep rows 2–5 to desired length.

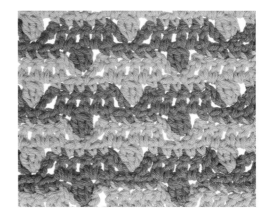

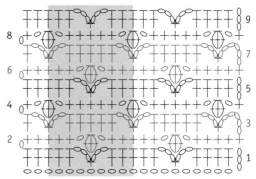

Cameroon

This pattern crosses itself to create a three-dimensional lattice look, making it great for kids' toys so they can cuddle and hold it by the crosses.

Ch a multiple of 8 sts plus 1.

Row 1 (WS): Sc in 2nd ch from hk and ea ch across, change color, turn.

Row 2: Ch 1, sc in 1st sc, *ch 1, sk 1 sc, sc in next 2 sc, ch 1, sk 1 sc, sc in next 4 sc; rep from * across to last 2 sc, sc in last 2 sc, turn.

Row 3: Ch 3 (counts as dc), dc in each sc and ch across, change color, turn.

Row 4: Ch 1, sc in 1st 2 sc, *sk 3 sc 3 rows below, dtr in next sc 3 rows below (under 2nd ch-sp in front of fabric), sc in next 2 dc, dtr in 1st sk sc 3 rows below (under 1st ch-sp in front of prev dtr), sc in next 4 dc; rep from * across to last 2 dc, sc in last 2 dc, turn.

Row 5: Ch 1, sc in ea st across, change color, turn.

Row 6: Ch 1, sc in 1st 6 sc, *ch 1, sk 1 sc, sc in next 2 sc, ch 1, sk 1 sc, sc in next 4 sc; rep from * across to last 2 sc, sc in last 2 sc, turn.

Row 7: Rep row 3.

Row 8: Ch 1, sc in 1st 4 dc, *sc in next 2 dc, sk 3 sc 3 rows below, dtr in next sc 3 rows below (under 2nd ch-sp in front of fabric), sc in next 2 dc, dtr in 1st sk sc 3 rows below (under 1st ch-sp in front of prev dtr), sc in next 2 dc; rep from * across to last 4 sts, sc in last 4 sts, turn.

Row 9: Ch 1, sc in ea st across, change color, turn.

Rep rows 2–9 to desired length.

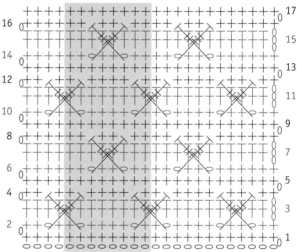

Malawi

Repeating dropped stitches over and over creates a woven fabric that looks quite impressive and makes great warm hats.

Ch a multiple of 4 sts.

Row 1 (RS): Sc in 2nd ch from hk, sc in next 2 ch, *ch 1, sk 1 ch, sc in next 3 sc; rep from * to end, turn.

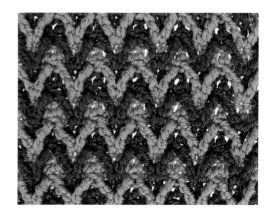

Row 2: Ch 3 (counts as dc), dc in ea st across, change color, turn.

Row 3: Ch 1, sc in 1st sc, dtr in st below next ch-1 sp 3 rows below (in front of prev sts), sc in next dc, *ch 1, sk next dc, sc in next dc, dtr2tog in st below prev ch-1 sp and next ch-1 sp 3 rows below, sc in next dc; rep from * across to last 4 sts, ch 1, sk next dc, sc in next dc, dtr in prev st below prev ch-1 sp 3 rows below, sc in top of t-ch, turn.

Rep rows 2 and 3 to desired length.

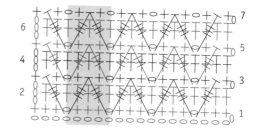

Congo

The bright pattern of this fabric looks great from either side and is almost three-dimensional in nature.

Ch a multiple of 7 sts plus 2.

Row 1 (RS): Sc in 2nd ch from hk, *sc in next sc, ch 7, sk 4 ch, sc in next 2 sc; rep from * across, change color, turn.

Row 2: Ch 1, sc in 1st sc, *sc in next sc, hdc in next 4 ch on foundation (sk ch-sps), sc in next 2 sc; rep from * across, turn.

Row 3: Ch 1, sc in ea sc and hdc across (sk ch-sps), change color, turn.

Row 4: Ch 3 (counts as dc), *dc in next dc, ch 3, sc in ch-7 sp, ch 3, sk 4 sc, dc in next 2 sc; rep from * across, turn.

Row 5: Ch 1, sc in 1st dc, *sc in next dc, ch 7, sk ch-sps, sc in next 2 dc; rep from * across, change color, turn.

Row 6: Ch 1, sc in 1st sc, *sc in next sc, tr in next 4 sc 3 rows below (in front of ch-sps), sc in next 2 sc; rep from * across, turn.

Rep rows 3–6 to desired length. End with a row 4, change color.

Last row: Ch 1, sc in 1st sc, *sc in next sc, dc in next 4 sc 2 rows below (in front of ch-sps), sc in next 2 sc; rep from * across, fasten off.

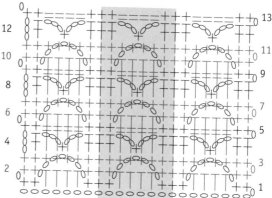

Kenitra

This classic shell pattern is given new life with dashes of color in the fabric to transform it into something new.

Ch a multiple of 4 sts plus 3.

Row 1 (RS): 3 dc in 4th ch from hk, sk 2 ch, sc in next ch, *ch 2, 3 dc in next ch, sk 2 ch, sc in next ch; rep from * across, do not turn, drop color.

Row 2: Join new color to start of prev row at t-ch, sc in top of t-ch, *sc in next 3 dc, sc in next sc, ch 3; rep from * across, change color, turn.

Row 3: Ch 3 (counts as dc), 3 dc in 1st ch, [sc, ch 2, 3 dc] in ea ch-3 sp across, sc in last sc, do not turn, drop color.

Row 4: Join next color to top of t-ch, sc in t-ch, sc in next 3 dc, *sc in sc, ch 3, sc in next 3 dc; rep from * across, sc in last sc, change color, turn.

Rep rows 3 and 4 to desired length.

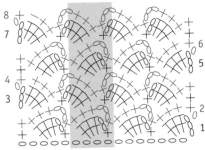

Azilal

This two-color repeat brings to mind ancestral patterns that get more defined as the contrast in color increases.

V-Stitch (v-st): [Dc, ch 1, dc] in st indicated.

Ch a multiple of 6 sts plus 4.

Row 1 (RS): Dc in 4th ch from hk, *sk 1 ch, dc in next 3 ch, sk 1 ch, v-st in next ch; rep from * across to last ch, 2 dc in last ch, do not turn.

Row 2: Join new color to top of t-ch on prev row, ch 3, dc in next dc, *sk 1 dc, dc btw next 2 dc, ch 1, dc btw next 2 dc, dtr in same ch as v-st on foundation, dc in ch-1 sp, dtr in same ch as last dtr; rep from * across to last 5 dc, sk 1 dc, dc btw next 2 dc, ch 1, dc btw next 2 dc, dc in last 2 dc, change color, turn.

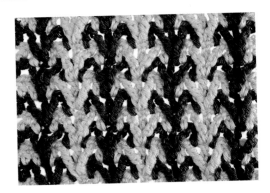

Row 3: Ch 3 (counts as dc), dc in 1st dc, *dtr in dc below ch-1 sp 2 rows below, dc in ch-1 sp, dtr in same dc below ch-1 sp, sk 1 st, dc btw next 2 sts, ch 1, dc btw next 2 sts; rep from * across to last ch-1 sp, dtr in dc below ch-1 sp 2 rows below, dc in ch-1 sp, dtr in same dc below ch-1 sp, 2 dc in top of t-ch, do not turn.

Row 4: Join color to top of t-ch, ch 3 (counts as dc), dc in next dc, *sk 1 st, dc btw next 2 sts, ch 1, dc btw next 2 sts, dtr in dc below ch-1 sp 2 rows below, dc in ch-1 sp, dtr in same dc below ch-1 sp; rep from * across to 5 sts, sk 1 st, dc btw next 2 sts, ch 1, dc btw next 2 sts, dc in last 2 dc, change color, turn.

Rep rows 3 and 4 to desired length. End with a row 3.

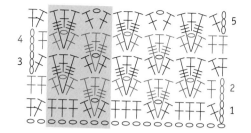

Zagora

The filet lace in this stitch pattern offsets the bulkiness of the double crochet shells. By using an odd number of colors, you will always have the color you need at the end of each row.

Shell (sh): [2 dc, ch 1, 2 dc] in ch-sp indicated.

Stitch pattern is a multiple of 10 sts plus 3.

Row 1 (WS): Dc in 6th ch from hk, ch 5, sk 5 ch, dc in next ch, ch 1, sk 1 ch, *dc in next ch, ch 1, sk 1 ch, dc in next ch, ch 5, sk 5 ch, dc in next ch, ch 1, sk 1 ch; rep from * across, dc in last ch, change color, turn.

Row 2: Ch 1, sc in 1st dc, *sc in ch-1 sp, sc in next dc, sk 2 ch on foundation row, sh in next ch on foundation (in front of ch-5 sp), sc in next dc, sc in next ch-1 sp, sc in next dc; rep from * across to t-ch, sc in 4th and 5th ch of t-ch, change color, turn.

Row 3: Ch 4 (counts as dc, ch 1), sk 2 sc, dc in next sc, *ch 5, sk sh, [dc in next sc, ch 1, sk next sc] twice, dc in next sc; rep from * across; to last sh, ch 5, sk sh, dc in next sc, ch 1, sk next sc, dc in last sc, change color, turn.

Row 4: Ch 1, sc in 1st dc, * sc in ch-1 sp, sc in next dc, sh in next ch-1 sp on sh below (in front of ch-5 sp), sc in next dc, sc in next ch-1 sp, sc in next dc; rep from * across to t-ch, sc in 3rd and 4th ch of t-ch, change color, turn.

Rep rows 3 and 4 to desired length.

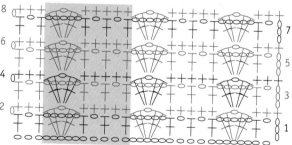

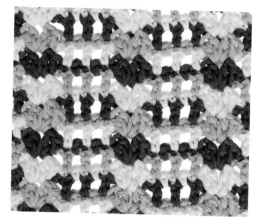

Tarfaya

When you use one color for all the double crochet rows and another for the rest, the resulting fabric looks like the second color is bursting out of the first in little curls.

Ch a multiple of 4 sts plus 2.

Row 1 (RS): Dc in 4th ch from hk and ea ch across, change color, turn.

Row 2: Ch 1, sc in ea dc across to t-ch, sc in top of t-ch, turn.

Row 3: Ch 3 (counts as dc), sk 1st 2 sc, dc in next sc, dc in 1st sk sc, ch 3, turn, sl st to 1st dc, turn, 5 sc in ch-3 sp, *[sk next sc, dc in next sc, dc in sk sc] twice, ch 3, turn, sl st in 2nd prev dc, turn, 5 sc in ch-3 sp; rep from * across to last sc, dc in last sc, change color, turn.

Row 4: Ch 3 (counts as dc), 2 dc btw ea set of crossed dc across (working in front of the sc), dc in top of t-ch, turn.

Row 5: Ch 3 (counts as dc), dc in ea dc across, change color, turn.

Rep rows 2–5 to desired length.

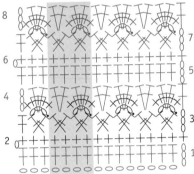

Oujda

This pattern's biggest challenge is in keeping the colors straight. The stitches are simple—either a shell or a single crochet and chains. After a main color row, you always turn, and after the contrasting color row, you never turn.

Shell (sh): [(Dc, ch 1) 3 times, dc] in st indicated.

Ch a multiple of 8 sts plus 2.

Row 1 (RS): Sc in 2nd ch from hk, *sk 3 ch, sh in next ch, sk 3 ch, sc in next ch; rep from * across, turn.

Row 2: Join new color to 1st ch-1 sp with sl st, *[sc, ch 5, sc] in ch-1 sp, ch 5, sk next ch-sp, [sc, ch 5, sc] in next ch-1 sp, ch 1, sk next ch-1 sp, sh in next ch-1 sp, ch 1, sk next ch-1 sp; rep from * across, dc in last sc, do not turn.

Row 3: Ch 5 with prev color, *sk 1 ch-1 sp on sh 2 rows below, sh in next ch-1 sp on sh below, ch 1, [sc, ch 5, sc] in next ch-1 sp on next sh, ch 5, sk next ch-1 sp, [sc, ch 5, sc] in next ch-1 sp, ch 1; rep from * across, turn.

Row 4: Rep row 3 with next color, do not turn.

Row 5: Ch 4 with prev color, *[sc, ch 5, sc] in next ch-1 sp on next sh, ch 5, sk next ch-1 sp, [sc, ch 5, sc] in next ch-1 sp, ch 1, sk 1 ch-1 sp on sh 2 rows below, sh in next ch-1 sp on sh below, ch 1; rep from * across, tr in 4th ch of t-ch 2 rows below, turn.

Row 6: Rep row 5 with next color, do not turn.

Rep rows 3–6 to desired length.

Rutherglen

This simple plaid pattern comes from changing colors on alternating rows and embroidering on the vertical lines. It may be time consuming, but the results are worth it.

Ch a multiple of 7 sts plus 1.

Row 1 (RS): Sc in 2nd ch from hk and ea ch across, turn.

Row 2: Ch 1, sc in ea sc across, turn.

Rep row 2 to desired length, changing colors on rows 2, 3, 5; then 9, 10, 12; and 16, 17, 19 and so on.

Join yarn to edge at foundation ch, sl st up fabric with 1 sl st in ea row going up the fabric by holding the working yarn to the back of the fabric and inserting your hk into the fabric from the front. Sl st up next st over, then sk 1 sc, sl st up next sc, sk 3 sc, and sl st up next; rep sl st embroidery across fabric.

TIP

Embroidery and crochet can go hand in hand. Color patterns, especially charted, can look a bit mottled in crochet. But by simply slip stitching around the graphics in the chart, you can get a smooth, polished finish. These are only a few patterns to wet your whistle; try mixing the bevy of embroidery stitches with your crochet. I promise the results will not disappoint.

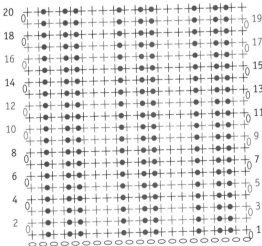

Bearsden

Using extended single crochet in this pattern lengthens the plaid design and makes a fabric that is thin enough for garments.

Extended Single Crochet (esc): Insert hk into next st and pull up a lp, yo and pull through 1 lp on hk, yo and pull through last 2 lps on hk.

Ch a multiple of 4 sts plus 3.

Row 1 (RS): Esc in 3rd ch from hk and ea ch across, turn.

Row 2: Ch 2 (counts as esc), esc in ea st across, change color, turn.

Row 3: Ch 1, sc in ea st across, change color, turn.

Rows 4 and 5: Ch 2 (counts as esc), esc in ea st across, turn.

Row 6: Change color, ch 1, sc in ea st across, change color, turn.

Row 7: Ch 2 (counts as esc), esc in ea st across, change color, turn.

Rows 8–13: Ch 2 (counts as esc), esc in ea st across, turn.

Rep rows 2–13 to desired length.

Join yarn to edge at foundation ch, sl st up fabric with 1 sl st in ea row going up the fabric by holding the working yarn to the back of the fabric and inserting your hk into the fabric from the front. Change color, sk 3 sts, sl st up next st, change color, sl st up next st, sk 7 sts, and sl st up next; rep sl st embroidery across fabric.

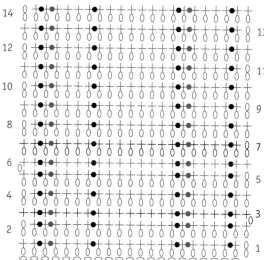

Glasgow

This pattern takes a new twist on an old technique with a mod, print-inspired fabric.

Ch a multiple of 10 sts plus 4.

Row 1 (RS): Dc in 4th ch from hk and ea ch across, turn.

Row 2: Ch 1, sc in ea st across, change color, turn.

Rows 3 and 4: Rep row 2, do not change color after row 4.

Row 5: Ch 3 (counts as dc), dc in ea st across, turn.

Rep rows 2–5 to desired length.

Join color to 4th st on row 5, sl st btw the next 5 sts, turn 90 degrees, sl st btw the next 4 rows, turn 90 degrees, sl st btw the next 5 sts, turn 90 degrees, sl st btw the rows to join (making a rectangle). Using chart as a guide, sl st crochet rectangles 4 sts away or 4 rows up.

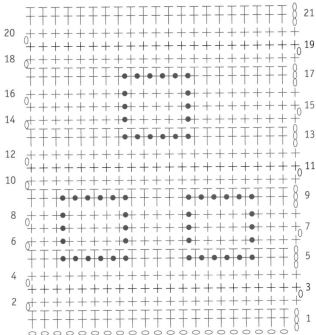

Larkhall

Using chain spaces as guidelines can make for a great slip stitch embroidery pattern. Here the spaces make a cable-like fabric.

Ch a multiple of 8 sts plus 1.

Row 1 (RS): Sc in 2nd ch, sc in next ch, *ch 1, sk 1 ch, sc in next 2 ch, ch 1, sk 1 ch, sc in next 4 ch; rep from * across to last 6 ch, ch 1, sk 1 ch, sc in next 2 ch, ch 1, sk 1 ch, sc in last 2 ch, turn.

Rows 2 and 3: Ch 1, sc in 1st 2 sc, *[ch 1, sk ch-1 sp, sc in next 4 sc] twice; rep from * across to last 2 sc, sc in last 2 sc, turn.

Row 4: Ch 1, sc in 1st 2 sc, *sc in next ch-1 sp, ch 2, sk 2 sc, sc in next ch-1 sp, sc in next 4 sc; rep from * across to last 2 sc, sc in last 2 sc, turn.

Row 5: Ch 1, sc in 1st 3 sc, *ch 2, sk ch-sp, sc in next 6 sc; rep from * across to last 3 sc, sc in last 3 sc, turn.

Row 6: Ch 1, sc in 1st 2 sc, *ch 1, sk 1 sc, 2 sc in next ch-2 sp, ch 1, sk 1 sc, sc in next 4 sc; rep from * across to last 2 sc, sc in last 2 sc, turn.

Rows 7–9: Rep row 2.

Rep rows 2–9 to desired length.

Join new color to foundation row, sl st up fabric rows in each ch-sp by inserting the hk from the front of the fabric and pulling up a lp from the back.

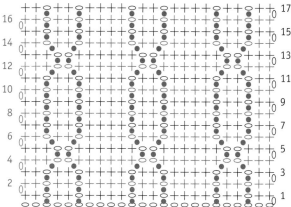

Alloa

This use of slip stitch embroidery combines with standard chains for a loop-d-loop edging.

Stitch pattern is a multiple of 8 sts.

Crochet an edging of at least 6 rows of sc.

Join new color to edge with sl st, ch 7, turn work 180 degrees, sl st to same spot, *using chart as a guide, sl st from right to left: 1 st over and 1 row down, 1 row down below last sl st, [1 st over and 1 row down] twice, 1 st over, [1 st over and 1 row up] twice, 1 st up, 1 st over and 1 row up, ch 7, turn work 180 degrees around, sl st to same spot; rep from * across.

For a stronger edge, work another row of sl st in ea sl st and chain around.

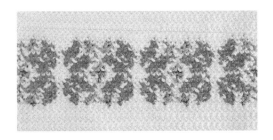

CHARTED COLOR STITCH PATTERNS

Snowflake

Who says ski sweaters are for knitters only? This charted pattern looks great as a band of color in any crocheted ski sweater.

Stitch pattern is a multiple of 15 sts.

Crochet 15 rows of single crochet following the chart for color changes.

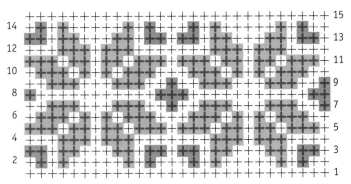

Jumping Beans

Adding polka dots to any kid or baby project just makes it even cuter. Watch that all the odd rows are right sides and the evens are wrong. The way crochet stitches sit will naturally give you the dot.

Stitch pattern is a multiple of 7 sts.

Crochet a multiple of 10 rows of single crochet, following the chart for color changes.

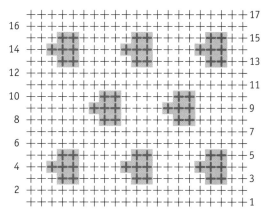

Tapestry vs. Stranded Tips

Deciding whether to carry your yarn strands (stranded) or crochet around them (tapestry) depends on how you like to crochet, but there are some benefits to each technique. When using tapestry crochet and crocheting around your yarn ends, you get a nearly reversible fabric which can make projects where you see both sides (like afghans) really special. When stranding your yarn ends, you can get a less dense fabric since you do not have to crochet over every yarn end and just need to carry along your end on the wrong side, as you work. For me, it comes down to numbers: if there are only two colors in my chart, I use tapestry; if there are more, I strand; if there are more than four colors, I use a yarn bobbin of each color so I do not have four hanks hanging off of one project.

TIP

Diamond Jacquard

Using taller stitches in charts gives an extended look to the pattern, as in our example here with half doubles.

Stitch pattern is a multiple of 8 sts.

Crochet a multiple of 8 rows of half double crochet, following the chart for color changes.

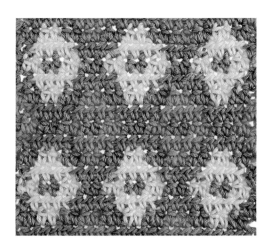

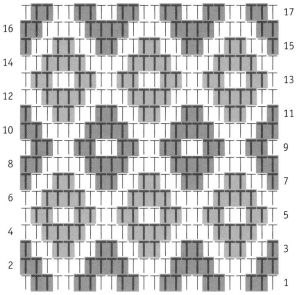

Bright Daisy

When you change the color of the bobbles from the background color, the stitches appear to burst from the fabric.

Ch a multiple of 12 sts plus 10.

Row 1 (RS): Sc in 2nd ch from hk and ea ch across, turn.

Row 2: Ch 1, sc in ea sc across, turn.

Row 3: Ch 1, sc in 1st 3 sc, *[change color, 4 hdc-cl in next sc, change color, sc in next sc] twice sc in next 8 sc; rep from * across to last 6 sts, change color, 4 hdc-cl in next sc, change color, sc in next sc, change color, 4 hdc-cl in next sc, change color, sc in last 3 sc, turn.

Row 4: Ch 1, sc in ea sc and hdc-cl across, turn.

Row 5: Ch 1, sc in 1st 2 sc, *[change color, 4 hdc-cl in next sc, change color, sc in next sc] 3 times, sc in next 6 sc; rep from * across to last 7 sts, [change color, 4 hdc-cl in next sc, change color, sc in next sc] 3 times, sc in last sc, turn.

Rows 6–10: Rep row 4, rep row 3; rep row 4; rep row 2 twice.

Row 11: Ch 1, sc in 1st 9 sc, *[change color, 4 hdc-cl in next sc, change color, sc in next sc] twice, sc in next 8 sc; rep from * across, turn.

Row 12: Rep row 4.

Row 13: Ch 1, sc in 1st 8 sc, *[change color, 4 hdc-cl in next sc, change color, sc in next sc] 3 times, sc in next 6 sc; rep from * across to last sc, sc in last sc, turn.

Rows 14–17: Rep row 4; rep row 11; rep row 4; rep row 2.

Rep rows 2–17 to desired length.

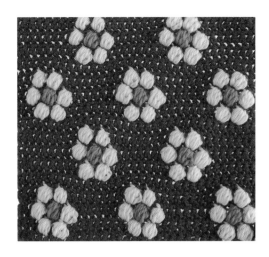

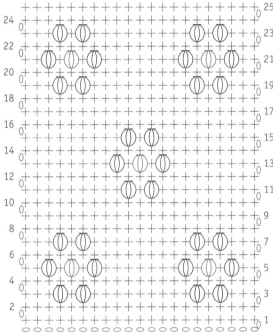

Carnation Wallpaper

Combining bobbles and charted flowers brings this pattern to life, making it pretty enough to frame.

Stitch pattern is a multiple of 27 sts.

Working in rows of single crochet, follow the chart for color changes to rows 7, 11, 21, 25, and so on.

Rows 7, 11, 21, 25, and so on: Substitute 4 hdc-cl bobbles in 8th and 11th sc from edge of carnation in new color, continue to follow chart for color changes in single crochet.

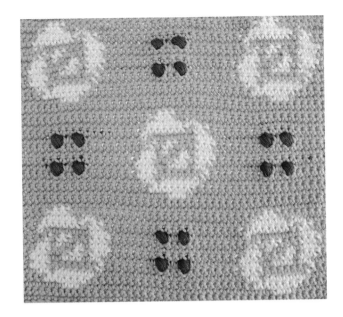

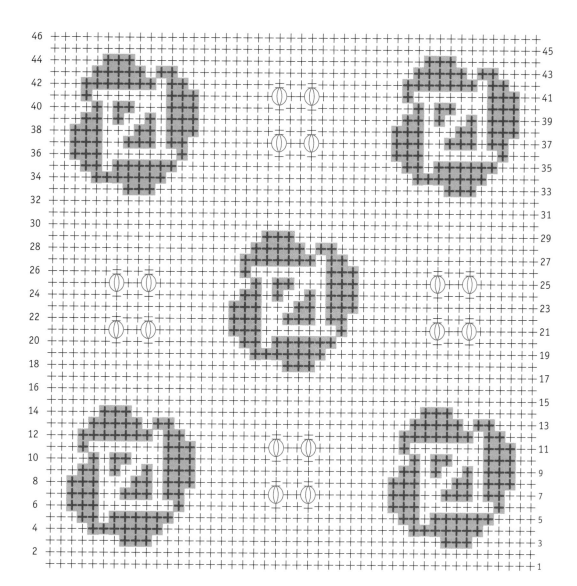

CHAPTER 6

Tunisian Stitch Patterns

Tunisian Simple Stitch

Referred to as Tss for short, this stitch is the basis for all Tunisian stitch patterns. Used alone, it makes for a great fabric to embellish with embroidery or cross stitches in the vertical bar.

Tunisian Simple Stitch (Tss): Insert hk, from right to left, into front vert bar of next st and pull up a lp.

Ch any number of sts.

Row 1 (RS) Fwd: Pull up lp in 2nd ch from hk and ea ch across. **Rtn:** Yo, pull through 1 lp on hk, *yo, pull through 2 lps on hk; rep from * to end.

Row 2 Fwd: (Lp on hk counts as 1st st.) Tss across row. **Rtn:** Yo, pull through 1 lp on hk, *yo, pull through 2 lps on hk; rep from * to end.

Rep row 2 to desired length.

Last row: *Tss in next st and pull through lp on hk; rep from * to end, fasten off.

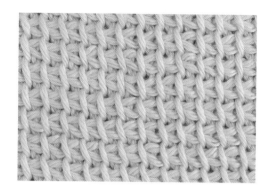

TIP

Unlike typical crochet projects, the recommended hook size on the yarn ball band will be too small for Tunisian crochet, which generally makes a dense fabric. When you use a hook that is sized for the yarn, it will make an incredibly dense fabric. To start your swatch, try a hook that is two sizes larger and decide if you like the resulting fabric.

Tunisian Purl Stitch

By simply moving the yarn to the front of the project before inserting your hook, you create an entirely different fabric. This stitch, which mimics purling in knitting, is usually referred to as Tps.

Tunisian Purl Stitch (Tps): Move yarn to front of work, insert hk, from right to left, into front vert bar of next st, yo, pull up a lp.

Ch any number of sts.

Row 1 (RS) Fwd: Pull up lp in 2nd ch from hk and ea ch across. **Rtn:** Yo, pull through 1 lp on hk, *yo, pull through 2 lps on hk; rep from * to end.

Row 2 Fwd: (Lp on hk counts as 1st st.) Tps in each st across row. **Rtn:** Yo, pull through 1 lp on hk, *yo, pull through 2 lps on hk; rep from * to end.

Rep row 2 to desired length.

Last row: *Tps in next st and pull through lp on hk; rep from * to end, fasten off.

Tunisian Knit Stitch

This stitch mimics stockinette stitch in knitting almost perfectly, except that Tunisian fabric is thicker than knitting. It makes for great, sturdy bags. The stitch is often referred to as Tks.

Tunisian Knit Stitch (Tks): Insert hk, from front to back, btw front and back vert bars and under all horiz bars of next st, yo, pull up a lp.

Ch any number of sts.

Row 1 (RS) Fwd: Pull up lp in 2nd ch from hk and ea ch across. **Rtn:** Yo, pull through 1 lp on hk, *yo, pull through 2 lps on hk; rep from * to end.

Row 2 Fwd: (Lp on hk counts as 1st st.) Tks across row. **Rtn:** Yo, pull through 1 lp on hk, *yo, pull through 2 lps on hk; rep from * to end.

Rep row 2 to desired length.

Last row: *Tks in next st and pull through lp on hk; rep from * to end, fasten off.

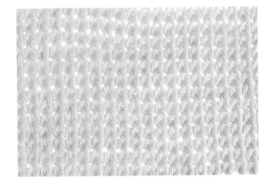

Tunisian Extended Stitch

By adding a simple chain stitch at the end of each standard Tunisian simple stitch, you get a lovely thin fabric perfect for any stylish garment.

Ch any number of sts.

Row 1 (RS) Fwd: Pull up lp in 3rd ch from hk, ch 1, *pull up lp in next ch, ch 1; rep from * across. **Rtn:** Yo, pull through 1 lp on hk, *yo, pull through 2 lps on hk; rep from * to end.

Row 2 Fwd: Ch 1, *Tss in next st, ch 1; rep from * across row. **Rtn:** Yo, pull through 1 lp on hk, *yo, pull through 2 lps on hk; rep from * to end.

Rep row 2 to desired length.

Last row: *Tss in next st, ch 1 and pull through lp on hk; rep from * to end, fasten off.

Tire Tread Stitch

By simply changing the yarn position on each stitch in the row, you produce a gentle, geometric texture.

Work off lps as normal: Yo, pull through 1 lp on hk, *yo, pull through 2 lps on hk; rep from * to end

Ch an odd number of sts.

Row 1 (RS) Fwd: Pull up lp in 2nd ch from hk and ea ch across. **Rtn:** Work off lps as normal.

Row 2 Fwd: (Lp on hk counts as 1 st.) *Tps in next st, Tss in next st; rep from * across to end. **Rtn:** Work off lps as normal.

Row 3 Fwd: (Lp on hk counts as 1 st.) *Tss in next st, Tps in next st; rep from * across to last 2 sts, Tss in last 2 sts. **Rtn:** Work off lps as normal.

Rep rows 2 and 3 to desired length.

Last row: *Tps in next st and pull through lp on hk, Tss in next st and pull through lp on hk; rep from * to end, fasten off.

Griddle Stitch

Tunisian double crochet stitches add a touch of texture to this simple pattern and produce a soft, bobbly fabric.

Tunisian Double Crochet (Tdc): Yo, insert hk into vert bar of next st, yo and pull lp through st, yo and pull through 2 lps, leaving last lp on hk.

Ch an even number of sts.

Row 1 (RS) Fwd: Pull up lp in 2nd ch from hk and ea ch across. **Rtn:** Yo, pull through 1 lp on hk, *yo, pull through 2 lps on hk; rep from * to end.

Row 2 Fwd: (Lp on hk counts as 1st st.) *Tdc in next st, Tps in next st; rep from * across to last st, Tss in last st. **Rtn:** Work off lps as normal.

Row 3 Fwd: (Lp on hk counts as 1st st.) *Tps in next st, Tdc in next st; rep from * across to last st, Tss in last st. **Rtn:** Work off lps as normal.

Rep rows 2 and 3 to desired length.

Last row: *Tdc in next st and pull through lp on hk, Tps in next st and pull through lp on hk; rep from * across to last st, Tss in last st and pull through lp on hk. Fasten off.

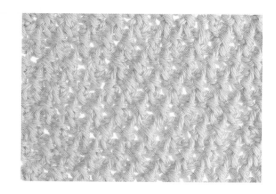

Twisted Simple Stitch

The columns of twisted stitches make a great simple fabric that works for projects from scarves to vests. Because you are inserting the hook from left to right, the opposite direction from Tss, the twisted stitch will slant, or twist, the vertical bar to the right. When combined with Tss, the two bars almost look like they are grouped together. This stitch is commonly referred to as Twtss.

Twisted Simple Stitch (Twtss): Insert hk from left to right into front vert bar of next st and pull up a lp.

Ch an odd number of sts.

Row 1 (RS) Fwd: Pull up lp in 2nd ch from hk and ea ch across. **Rtn:** Yo, pull through 1 lp on hk, *yo, pull through 2 lps on hk; rep from * to end.

Row 2 Fwd: (Lp on hk counts as 1 st.) *Twtss in next st, Tss in next st; rep from * across to end. **Rtn:** Work off lps as normal.

Rep row 2 to desired length.

Last row: *Twtss in next st and pull through lp on hk, Tss in next st and pull through lp on hk; rep from * to end, fasten off.

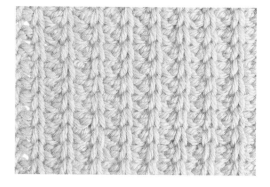

Ribbed Simple Stitch

The beauty of simple stitches is highlighted in this pattern.

Ch a multiple of 5 sts plus 4.

Row 1 (RS) Fwd: Pull up lp in 2nd ch from hk and ea ch across. **Rtn:** Yo, pull through 1 lp on hk, *yo, pull through 2 lps on hk; rep from * to end.

Row 2 Fwd: (Lp on hk counts as 1 st.) *Tks in next 2 sts, Tss in next st, Tps in next st, Tss in next st; rep from * across to last 3 sts, Tks in next 2 sts, Tss in last st. **Rtn:** Work off lps as normal.

Rep row 2 to desired length.

Last row: *Tks in next st and pull through lp on hk, Tks in next st and pull through lp on hk, Tss in next st and pull through lp on hk, Tps in next st and pull through lp on hk, Tss in next st and pull through lp on hk; rep from * to end, fasten off.

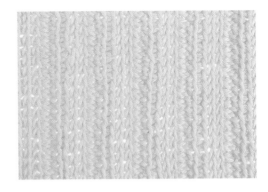

Dropped Simple Stitch

This simple lace stitch pattern can be challenging if you don't watch the number of stitches on each forward row. Be careful not to add stitches to the beginning or end of the row.

Ch any number of sts.

Row 1 (RS) Fwd: Pull up lp in 2nd ch from hk and ea ch across. **Rtn:** Yo, pull through 1 lp on hk, *yo, pull through 2 lps on hk; rep from * to end.

Row 2 Fwd: (Lp on hk counts as 1st st throughout.) Insert hk between 2nd and 3rd sts (around horiz bars) and pull up a lp, *insert hk btw next 2 sts and pull up a lp; rep from * across to last st, Tss in last st. **Rtn:** Yo, pull through 1 lp on hk, *yo, pull through 2 lps on hk; rep from * to end.

Row 3 Fwd: (Lp on hk counts as 1st st throughout.) Insert hk between 1st and 2nd sts and pull up a lp, *insert hk btw next 2 sts and pull up a lp; rep from * across to last 2 sts, sk 2nd to last st, Tss in last st. **Rtn:** Yo, pull through 1 lp on hk, *yo, pull through 2 lps on hk; rep from * to end.

Rep rows 2 and 3 to desired length.

Last row: *Insert hk btw next 2 sts, pull up a lp and through lp on hk; rep from * across to last st, Tss in last st and pull through lp on hk; fasten off.

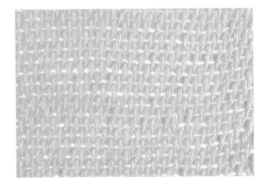

Crossed Simple Stitch

This pretty crisscross stitch pattern looks fantastic as a background to afghan projects.

Ch an even number of sts.

Row 1 (RS) Fwd: Pull up lp in 2nd ch from hk and ea ch across. **Rtn:** Yo, pull through 1 lp on hk, *yo, pull through 2 lps on hk; rep from * to end.

Row 2 Fwd: (Lp on hk counts as 1st st.) *Sk next st, Tss in next st, Tss in skipped st and pull up a lp; rep from * across to last st, Tss in last st. **Rtn:** Yo, pull through 1 lp on hk, *yo, pull through 2 lps on hk; rep from * to end.

Row 3 Fwd: (Lp on hk counts as 1st st.) Tss in next st, *sk next st, Tss in next st, Tss in skipped st and pull up a lp; rep from * across to last 2 sts, Tss in last 2 sts. **Rtn:** Yo, pull through 1 lp on hk, *yo, pull through 2 lps on hk; rep from * to end.

Rep rows 2 and 3 to desired length.

Last row: *Sk next st, Tss in next st and pull through lp on hk, Tss in skipped st, and pull through lp on hk; rep from * across to last st, Tss in last st and pull through lp on hk, fasten off.

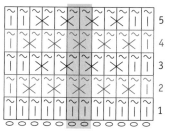

TEXTURED STITCH PATTERNS

Basketweave Stitch

This basketweave stitch greatly mimics knitting with the blocks of changing stitches.

Ch a multiple of 10 sts plus 2.

Row 1 (RS) Fwd: Pull up lp in 2nd ch from hk and ea ch across. **Rtn:** Yo, pull through 1 lp on hk, *yo, pull through 2 lps on hk; rep from * to end.

Row 2 Fwd: (Lp on hk counts as 1 st.) *Tss in next 5 sts, Tps in next 5 sts; rep from * across to last st, Tss in last st. **Rtn:** Work off lps as normal.

Rows 3 and 4: Rep row 2 twice.

Row 5 Fwd: (Lp on hk counts as 1 st.) *Tps in next 5 sts, Tss in next 5 sts; rep from * across to last st, Tss in last st. **Rtn:** Work off lps as normal.

Rows 6–8: Rep row 5 three times.

Row 9 Fwd: (Lp on hk counts as 1 st.) *Tss in next 5 sts, Tps in next 5 sts; rep from * across to last st, Tss in last st. **Rtn:** Work off lps as normal.

Rows 10–12: Rep row 9 three times.

Rep rows 5–12 to desired length.

Last row: *[Tss in next st and pull through lp on hk] 5 times, [Tps in next st and pull through lp on hk] 5 times; rep from * to last st, Tss and pull through lp on hk, fasten off.

Ocean

The alternating shells in the overall pattern look like waves in the ocean.

Ch a multiple of 3 sts plus 1.

Row 1 (RS) Fwd: Pull up lp in 2nd ch from hk and ea ch across. **Rtn:** Yo, pull through 2 lps on hk (half sh made), *ch 2, yo, pull through 4 lps on hk (ch 3, sh made); rep from * across to last 3 lps on hk, ch 2, yo, pull through last 3 lps on hk (half sh made).

Row 2 Fwd: Ch 1, sk half sh, *pull up lp in next ch, pull up lp in ch btw shells on foundation ch, sk next ch, pull up lp in next ch, sk next sh; rep from * across to end, pull up lp in top of half sh. **Rtn:** Yo, pull through 1 lp on hk, ch 1, *yo, pull through 4 lps on hk, ch 2; rep from * across to last 5 lps on hk, yo, pull through 4 lps on hk, ch 1, pull through last 2 lps on hk.

Row 3 Fwd: Ch 1, sk 1st vert bar, pull up lp in next ch, *sk next sh, pull up lp in next ch, pull up lp on top of sh 1 row below, sk next ch, pull up lp in next ch; rep from * across to end, sk next sh, pull up lp in next ch, sk next ch, pull up lp in last vert bar. **Rtn:** Yo, pull through 2 lps on hk, *ch 2, yo, pull through 4 lps on hk; rep from * across to last 3 lps on hk, ch 2, yo, pull through last 3 lps on hk.

Row 4 Fwd: Ch 1, sk half sh, *pull up lp in next ch, pull up lp on top of sh 1 row below, sk next ch, pull up lp in next ch, sk next sh; rep from * across to end, pull up lp in top of half sh. **Rtn:** Yo, pull through 1 lp on hk, ch 1, *yo, pull through 4 lps on hk, ch 2; rep from * across to last 5 lps on hk, yo, pull through 4 lps on hk, ch 1, pull through last 2 lps on hk.

Rep rows 3 and 4 to desired length.

Last row: *Insert hk into vert bar of next st, and pull through lp on hk; rep from * to end, fasten off.

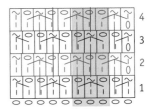

Neom

The crossed stitches in this pattern create a diagonal feel to the fabric.

Ch a multiple of 4 sts plus 2.

Row 1 (RS) Fwd: Pull up lp in 2nd ch from hk and ea ch across. **Rtn:** Yo, pull through 1 lp on hk, *yo, pull through 2 lps on hk; rep from * to end.

Row 2 Fwd: (Lp on hk counts as 1st st.) *Tps in next 2 sts, sk next st, Tss in next st, Tss in skipped st; rep from * across to last st, Tss in last st. **Rtn:** Yo, pull through 1 lp on hk, *yo, pull through 2 lps on hk; rep from * to end.

Row 3 Fwd: (Lp on hk counts as 1st st.) Tps in next st, *sk next st, Tss in next st, Tss in skipped st, Tps in next 2 sts; rep from * across to last 4 sts, sk next st, Tss in next st, Tss in skipped st, Tps in next st, Tss in last st. **Rtn:** Yo, pull through 1 lp on hk, *yo, pull through 2 lps on hk; rep from * to end.

Row 4 Fwd: (Lp on hk counts as 1st st.) *Sk next st, Tss in next st, Tss in skipped st, Tps in next 2 sts; rep from * across to last st, Tss in last st. **Rtn:** Yo, pull through 1 lp on hk, *yo, pull through 2 lps on hk; rep from * to end.

Row 5 Fwd: (Lp on hk counts as 1st st.) Tps in next 3 sts, *sk next st, Tss in next st, Tss in skipped st, Tps in next 2 sts; rep from * across to last 2 sts, Tps in next st, Tss in last st. **Rtn:** Yo, pull through 1 lp on hk, *yo, pull through 2 lps on hk; rep from * to end.

Rep rows 2–5 to desired length.

Last row: *Tps in next st and pull through lp on hk; rep from * to end, fasten off.

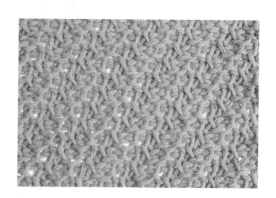

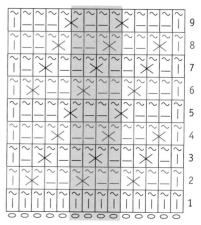

Knotted Cross Stitch

The purl stitches in this pattern give a knotted look to the fabric, which can be soft enough for pillows and afghans.

Ch an even number of sts.

Row 1 (RS) Fwd: Pull up lp in 2nd ch from hk and each ch across. **Rtn:** Yo, pull through 1 lp on hk, *yo, pull through 2 lps on hk; rep from * to end.

Row 2 Fwd: (Lp on hk counts as 1st st.) *Move yarn to front, insert hk into next 2 sts and pull up a lp, move yarn to front, insert hk into top horiz bar of 2nd st; rep from * across to last st, Tss in last st. **Rtn:** Work off lps as normal.

Row 3 Fwd: Tss in ea st across. **Rtn:** Work lp off as normal.

Rep rows 2 and 3 to desired length.

Last row: *Tps in next st and pull through lp on hk; rep from * across, fasten off.

Cordon Stitch

This textured stitch pattern with long double crochet stitches makes for great accessories such as scarves and mittens.

Tunisian Double Crochet (Tdc): Yo, insert hk, from right to left, into front vert bar of next st, yo and pull lp through st, yo and pull through 2 lps, leaving last lp on hk.

Ch a multiple of 3 sts plus 2.

Row 1 (RS) Fwd: Pull up lp in 2nd ch from hk and ea ch across. **Rtn:** Yo, pull through 1 lp on hk, *yo, pull through 2 lps on hk; rep from * to end.

Row 2 Fwd: Tss in ea st across. **Rtn:** Work off lps as normal.

Row 3 Fwd: (Lp on hk counts as 1 st.) *Tss in next st, Tdc in next st 2 rows below, Tss in next st; rep from * across to last st, Tss in last st. **Rtn:** Work off lps as normal.

Row 4 Fwd: (Lp on hk counts as 1 st.) *Tss in next 2 sts, Tdc in next st 2 rows below; rep from * across to last st, Tss in last st. **Rtn:** Work off lps as normal.

Row 5 Fwd: (Lp on hk counts as 1 st.) *Tdc in next st 2 rows below, Tss in next 2 sts; rep from * across to last st, Tss in last st. **Rtn:** Work off lps as normal.

Rep rows 3–5 to desired length.

Last row: *Tss in next st and pull through lp on hk; rep from * across, fasten off.

In Tunisian crochet you often use double and treble crochet in a number of rows below the row you are working in. To make even stitches, when pulling up a loop in the stitch indicated, pull up the loop even with the row you are working in. When complete, the stitch will extend to the height of the row and not pucker the rows together.

Single Rib Stitch

This cabled fabric is thicker than ribbing and makes for great hats and cowls.

Tunisian Extended Double Crochet (Tedc): Yo, insert hk, from right to left, into front vert bar of st indicated, pull up a lp, yo and pull through 1 lp on hk, yo and pull through 2 lps, leaving last lp on hk.

Ch an odd number of sts.

Row 1 (RS) Fwd: Pull up lp in 2nd ch from hk and ea ch across. **Rtn:** Yo, pull through 1 lp on hk, *yo, pull through 2 lps on hk; rep from * to end.

Row 2 Fwd: Tss across. **Rtn:** Work off lps as normal.

Row 3 Fwd: (Lp on hk counts as 1st st.) *Tedc in bottom of next st 2 rows below, Tss in next st; rep from * across. **Rtn:** Work off lps as normal.

Rep rows 2 and 3 to desired length.

Last row: *Tss next st, and pull through lp on hk; rep from * across, fasten off.

Starburst Stitch

Double crochet clusters dominate this stitch pattern, which makes for great afghans.

Tunisian Double Crochet (Tdc): Yo, insert hk, from right to left, into front vert bar of indicated st, yo and pull lp through st, yo and pull through 2 lps.

Starburst: Tdc in st 2 sts to the right and 2 rows below, Tdc in st 1 st to the right and 3 rows below, Tdc in st 4 rows below, Tdc in st 1 st to the left and 3 rows below, Tdc in st 2 sts to the left and 2 rows below, yo and pull through 5 lps on hk.

Ch a multiple of 10 sts plus 2.

Row 1 (RS) Fwd: Pull up lp in 2nd ch from hk and ea ch across. **Rtn:** Yo, pull through 1 lp on hk, *yo, pull through 2 lps on hk; rep from * to end.

Rows 2–4 Fwd: Tss in ea st across. **Rtn:** Work off lps as normal.

Row 5 Fwd: (Lp on hk counts as 1 st.) *Tss in next 7 sts, starburst, sk st behind starburst, Tss in next 2 sts; rep from * across to last st, Tss in last st. **Rtn:** Work off lps as normal.

Rows 6–8 Fwd: Tss in ea st across. **Rtn:** Work off lps as normal.

Row 9 Fwd: (Lp on hk counts as 1 st.) *Tss in next 2 sts, starburst, sk st behind starburst, Tss in next 7 sts; rep from * across to last st, Tss in last st. **Rtn:** Work off lps as normal.

Rep rows 2–9 to desired length.

Last row: *Tss in next st, and pull through lp on hk; rep from * to end, fasten off.

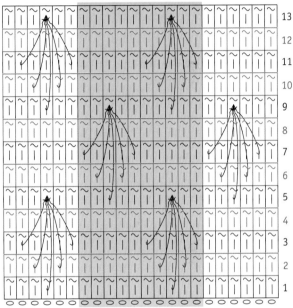

Borla Ripple Stitch

Alternating the cable stitches makes the fabric ripple in a wonderfully textured pattern.

Tunisian Treble Crochet (Ttc): Yo twice, insert hk, from right to left, into front vert bar of next st, yo and pull lp through st, [yo and pull through 2 lps] twice, leaving last lp on hk.

Ch an odd number of sts.

Row 1 (RS) Fwd: Pull up lp in 2nd ch from hk and ea ch across. **Rtn:** Yo, pull through 1 lp on hk, *yo, pull through 2 lps on hk; rep from * to end.

Row 2 Fwd: Tss in ea st across. **Rtn:** Work off lps as normal.

Row 3 Fwd: (Lp on hk counts as 1 st.) *Ttc in next st 2 rows below, Tss in next st; rep from * across. **Rtn:** Work off lps as normal.

Row 4 Fwd: Tss in ea st across. **Rtn:** Work off lps as normal.

Row 5 Fwd: (Lp on hk counts as 1 st.) Tss in next st, *Ttc in next st 2 rows below, Tss in next st; rep from * across to last st, Tss in last st. **Rtn:** Work off lps as normal.

Rep rows 2–5 to desired length.

Last row: Tss in next st and pull through lp on hk, rep to end, fasten off.

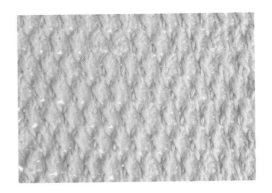

Diamond Knit Stitch

The double crochet clusters make diamond bobbles in the knitted fabric that look great in simple rectangular projects.

Three Double Crochet Cluster (3 dc-cl): *Yo, insert hk btw vert bar of next st, yo and pull lp through st, yo and pull through 2 lps; rep from * twice more in same st, yo and pull through 3 lps on hk.

Ch a multiple of 10 sts plus 7.

Row 1 (RS) Fwd: Pull up lp in 2nd ch from hk and ea ch across. **Rtn:** Yo, pull through 1 lp on hk, *yo, pull through 2 lps on hk; rep from * to end.

Row 2 Fwd: (Lp on hk counts as 1st st throughout.) *Tks in next 2 sts, 3 dc-cl in next st, Tks in next 7 sts; rep from * across to last 6 sts, Tks in next 2 sts, 3 dc-cl in next st, Tks in next 2 sts, Tss in last st. **Rtn:** Work off lps as normal.

Row 3 Fwd: (Lp on hk counts as 1st st throughout.) *3 dc-cl in next st, Tks in next 3 sts, 3 dc-cl in next st, Tks in next 5 sts; rep from * across to last 6 sts, 3 dc-cl in next st, Tks in next 3 sts, 3 dc-cl in next st, Tss in last st. **Rtn:** Work off lps as normal.

Row 4: Rep row 2.

Row 5 Fwd: Tks in ea st across to last, Tss in last st. **Rtn:** Work off lps as normal.

Row 6 Fwd: (Lp on hk counts as 1st st throughout.) *Tks in next 7 sts, 3 dc-cl in next st, Tks in next 2 sts; rep from * across to last 6 sts, Tks in next 5 sts, Tss in last st. **Rtn:** Work off lps as normal.

Row 7 Fwd: (Lp on hk counts as 1st st throughout.) *Tks in next 5 sts, 3 dc-cl in next st, Tks in next 3 sts, 3 dc-cl in next st; rep from * across to last 6 sts, Tks in next 5 sts, Tss in last st. **Rtn:** Work off lps as normal.

Row 8: Rep Row 6

Row 9 Fwd: Tks in ea st across to last, Tss in last st. **Rtn:** Work off lps as normal.

Rep rows 2–9 to desired length.

Last row: *Tks in next st and pull through lp on hk; rep from * across to last st, Tss in last st and pull through lp on hk; fasten off.

Cable Column Stitch

The cable in this stitch pattern almost pops off the fabric to draw interest to it. The pattern makes a great edge on lacier projects.

Tunisian Treble Crochet (Ttc): Yo twice, insert hk, from right to left, into front vert bar of next st, yo and pull lp through st, [yo and pull through 2 lps] twice, leaving last lp on hk.

Tunisian Triple Treble Crochet (Tttc): Yo 4 times, insert hk, from right to left, into front vert bar of next st, yo and pull lp through st, [yo and pull through 2 lps] 4 times, leaving last lp on hk.

Ch a multiple of 8 sts plus 3.

Row 1 (RS) Fwd: Pull up lp in 2nd ch from hk and ea ch across. **Rtn:** Yo, pull through 1 lp on hk, *yo, pull through 2 lps on hk; rep from * to end.

Row 2 Fwd: Tss in ea st across. **Rtn:** Work off lps as normal.

Row 3 Fwd: (Lp on hk counts as 1st st.) Tss in next st, *Tss in next st, Ttc in next st 2 rows below, Tss in next 3 sts, Ttc in next st 2 rows below, Tss in next 2 sts; rep from * across to last st, Tss in last st. **Rtn:** Work off lps as normal.

Row 4 Fwd: Tss in ea st across. **Rtn:** Work off lps as normal.

Row 5 Fwd: (Lp on hk counts as 1st st.) Tss in next st, *Tss in next st, sk next Ttc, Tttc around post of next Ttc 2 rows below, Tss in next 3 sts, Tttc around post of skipped Ttc 2 rows below, Tss in next 2 sts; rep from * across to last st, Tss in last st. **Rtn:** Work off lps as normal.

Row 6 Fwd: Tss in ea st across. **Rtn:** Work off lps as normal.

Row 7 Fwd: (Lp on hk counts as 1st st.) Tss in next st, *Tss in next st, Ttc around post of next Tttc 2 rows below, Tss in next 3 sts, Ttc around post of next Tttc 2 rows below, Tss in next 2 sts; rep from * across to last st, Tss in last st. **Rtn:** Work off lps as normal.

Rep rows 4–7 to desired length.

Last row: *Tss in next st and pull through lp on hk; rep from * across, fasten off.

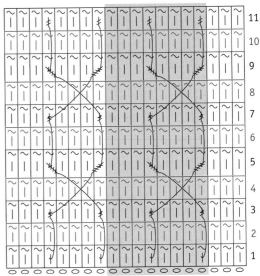

LACE STITCH PATTERNS

Esme Lace

Shells and chain spaces make a lovely lace fabric in the overall simple lines of the Tunisian simple stitch.

Ch a multiple of 5 sts plus 2.

Row 1 (RS) Fwd: Pull up lp in 2nd ch from hk and ea ch across.
Rtn: Yo, pull through 1 lp on hk, *yo, pull through 2 lps on hk, ch 1, yo, pull through 4 lps on hk (gathers the next 3 sts, making a sh), ch 1, yo, pull through 2 lps on hk; rep from * to last st, pull through 2 lps on hk.

Row 2 Fwd: (Lp on hk counts as 1 st.) Tss in next st, *insert hk in next ch-sp, pull up a lp, insert hk in top of sh, pull up lp, insert hk in next ch-sp and pull up a lp, Tss in each of next 2 sts; rep from * across. **Rtn:** Yo, pull through 1 lp on hk, *yo, pull through 2 lps on hk, ch 1, yo, pull through 4 lps on hk (gathers the next 3 sts, making a sh), ch 1, yo, pull through 2 lps on hk; rep from * to last st, pull through 2 lps on hk.

Rep row 2 to desired length.

Last row: *Insert hk into vert bar of next st, yo and pull up a lp and through lp on hk, insert hk in next ch-sp, yo and pull up a lp and through lp on hk, insert hk in top bar on top of sh, yo and pull up a lp and through lp on hk, insert hk in next ch-sp, yo and pull up a lp and through lp on hk, insert hk into vert bar of next st, yo and pull up a lp and through lp on hk; rep from * to last st, Tss and pull through lp on hk, fasten off.

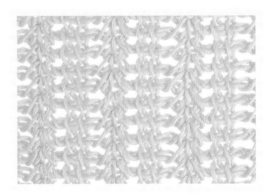

Julianna Lace

The diagonal lines of chain spaces make an enchanting fabric that is great for wraps.

Ch a multiple of 10 sts plus 7.

Row 1 (RS) Fwd: Pull up lp in 2nd ch from hk and ea ch across. **Rtn:** Yo, pull through 1 lp on hk, *yo, pull through 2 lps on hk; rep from * to end.

Row 2 Fwd: (Lp on hk counts as 1st st.) *Insert hk btw next 2 sts (around top bars) and pull up a lp, [yo, insert hk into next 2 sts together and pull up a lp] twice, Tss in next 5 sts; rep from * across to last 6 sts, insert hk btw next 2 sts (around top bars) and pull up a lp, [yo, insert hk into next 2 sts together and pull up a lp] twice, Tss in last st. **Rtn:** Work off lps as normal.

Row 3 Fwd: (Lp on hk counts as 1st st.) *Tss in next st, insert hk btw next 2 sts (around top bars) and pull up a lp, [yo, insert hk into next 2 sts together and pull up a lp] twice, Tss in next 4 sts; rep from * across to last 6 sts, Tss in next st, insert hk btw next 2 sts (around top bars) and pull up a lp, [yo, insert hk into next 2 sts together and pull up a lp] twice. **Rtn:** Work off lps as normal.

Row 4 Fwd: (Lp on hk counts as 1st st.) *Tss in next 2 sts, insert hk btw next 2 sts (around top bars) and pull up a lp, [yo, insert hk into next 2 sts together and pull up a lp] twice, Tss in next 3 sts; rep from * across to last 6 sts, Tss in next 2 sts, insert hk btw next 2 sts (around top bars) and pull up a lp, yo, insert hk into next 2 sts together and pull up a lp, Tss in last st. **Rtn:** Work off lps as normal.

Row 5 Fwd: (Lp on hk counts as 1st st.) *Tss in next 3 sts, insert hk btw next 2 sts (around top bars) and pull up a lp, [yo, insert hk into next 2 sts together and pull up a lp] twice, Tss in next 2 sts; rep from * across to last 6 sts, Tss in next 3 sts, insert hk btw next 2 sts (around top bars) and pull up a lp, yo, insert hk into next 2 sts together and pull up a lp. **Rtn:** Work off lps as normal.

Row 6 Fwd: (Lp on hk counts as 1st st.) *Tss in next 4 sts, insert hk btw next 2 sts (around top bars) and pull up a lp, [yo, insert hk into next 2 sts together and pull up a lp] twice, Tss in next st; rep from * across to last 6 sts, Tss in next 4 sts, insert hk btw next 2 sts (around top bars) and pull up a lp, Tss in last st. **Rtn:** Work off lps as normal.

Row 7 Fwd: (Lp on hk counts as 1st st.) *Tss in next 5 sts, insert hk btw next 2 sts (around top bars) and pull up a lp, [yo, insert hk into next 2 sts and pull up a lp] twice; rep from * across to last 6 sts, Tss in next 6 sts. **Rtn:** Work off lps as normal.

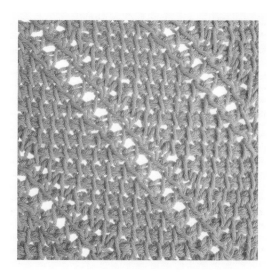

Row 8 Fwd: (Lp on hk counts as 1st st.) Tss in next st, *Tss in next 5 sts, insert hk btw next 2 sts (around top bars) and pull up a lp, [yo, insert hk into next 2 sts together and pull up a lp] twice; rep from * across to last 5 sts, Tss in next 5 sts. **Rtn:** Work off lps as normal.

Row 9 Fwd: (Lp on hk counts as 1st st.) Ch 1, insert hk into next 2 sts and pull up a lp, *Tss in next 5 sts, insert hk btw next 2 sts (around top bars) and pull up a lp, [yo, insert hk into next 2 sts together and pull up a lp] twice; rep from * across to last 4 sts, Tss in next 4 sts. **Rtn:** Work off lps as normal.

Row 10 Fwd: (Lp on hk counts as 1st st.) Insert hk btw next 2 sts (around top bars) and pull up a lp, yo, insert hk into next 2 sts together and pull up a lp, *Tss in next 5 sts, insert

hk btw next 2 sts (around top bars) and pull up a lp, [yo, insert hk into next 2 sts together and pull up a lp] twice; rep from * across to last 3 sts, Tss in next 3 sts. **Rtn:** Work off lps as normal.

Row 11 Fwd: (Lp on hk counts as 1st st.) [Yo, insert hk into next 2 sts together and pull up a lp] twice, *Tss in next 5 sts, insert hk btw next 2 sts (around top bars) and pull up a lp, [yo, insert hk into next 2 sts together and pull up a lp] twice; rep from * across to last 2 sts, Tss in next 2 sts. **Rtn:** Work off lps as normal.

Rep rows 2–11 to desired length.

Last row: *Tss in next st and pull through lp on hk; rep from * to end, fasten off.

Mildred Lace

The tall stitches in the lace make for a long, flowing fabric.

Ch an even number of sts.

Row 1 (RS) Fwd: Pull up lp in 2nd ch from hk and ea ch across. **Rtn:** Yo, pull through 1 lp on hk, *yo, pull through 2 lps on hk; rep from * to end.

Row 2 Fwd: Ch 2 (counts as 1st st.) *Tks in next st, ch 2, sk next st; rep from * across. **Rtn:** Yo, pull through 1 lp on hk, *ch 1, yo, pull through 2 lps on hk; rep from * to last 2 sts, [yo, pull through 2 lps on hk] twice.

Rep row 2 to desired length.

Last row: *Tks in next st and pull through lp on hk, insert hk in next ch-sp (around top 2 bars), yo and pull up a lp and through lp on hk; rep from * to last st. Tks in last st and pull through lp on hk, fasten off.

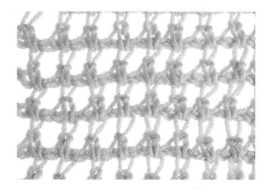

Cedany Lace

When you gather two stitches together, the resulting fabric mimics a diamond lattice.

Tunisian Double Crochet (Tdc): Yo, insert hk, from right to left, into front vert bar of next st, yo and pull lp through st, yo and pull through 2 lps, leaving last lp on hk.

Ch a multiple of 4 sts.

Row 1 (RS) Fwd: Pull up lp in 2nd ch from hk, ch 1, *pull up lp in next ch, ch 1; rep from * across. **Rtn:** Yo, pull through 1 lp on hk, *yo, pull through 2 lps on hk; rep from * to end.

Row 2 Fwd: Ch 1 (counts as 1st st), *sk next 2 sts, yo, insert hk into front vert bar of next 2 sts at once and pull up a lp, yo, pull through 2 lps on hk, yo twice, insert hk into vert bar of 2 skipped sts at once and pull up a lp, yo, pull through 2 lps on hk, yo; rep from * across to last 3 sts, Tdc in last 3 sts. **Rtn:** Work off lps as normal.

Row 3 Fwd: Ch 1 (counts as 1st st), Tdc in next 2 sts, *sk next 2 sts, yo, insert hk into vert bar of next 2 sts at once and pull up a lp, yo, pull through 2 lps on hk, yo twice, insert hk into vert bar of last 2 skipped sts and pull up a lp, yo, [pull through 2 lps on hk] twice, yo; rep from * across to last st, Tdc in last st. **Rtn:** Work off lps as normal.

Rep rows 2 and 3 to desired length.

Last row: Ch 1, *sk next 2 sts, yo, insert hk into vert bar of next 2 sts at once and pull up a lp, [yo, pull through 2 lps on hk] twice, ch 1, insert hk into vert bar of last 2 skipped sts and pull up a lp, [yo, pull through 2 lps on hk] twice; rep from * across, Tdc in next st and pull through lp on hk to end, fasten off.

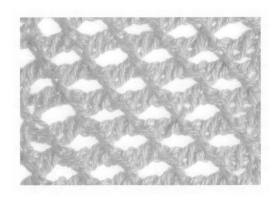

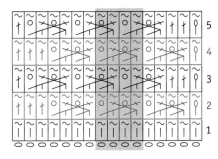

Adelaide Lace

The crossed stitches add both texture and lace to this pretty fabric.

Tunisian Double Crochet (Tdc): Yo, insert hk into vert bar of next st, yo and pull lp through st, yo and pull through 2 lps, leaving lp on hk.

Ch an odd number of sts.

Row 1 (RS) Fwd: Pull up lp in 2nd ch from hk and ea ch across. **Rtn:** Yo, pull through 1 lp on hk, *yo, pull through 2 lps on hk; rep from * to end.

Row 2 Fwd: Ch 1 (counts as 1st sc), *sk 1 st, Tdc in next st, Tdc in skipped st; rep from * across to last 2 sts, Tdc in next st, Tss in next st, ch 1. **Rtn:** Work off lps as normal.

Row 3 Fwd: Ch 1 (counts as 1st sc), Tdc in next st, *sk 1 st, Tdc in next st, Tdc in skipped st; rep from * across to last st, Tss in next st, ch 1. **Rtn:** Work off lps as normal.

Rep rows 2 and 3 to desired length.

Last row: *Tss in next st and pull through lp on hk; rep from * across, fasten off.

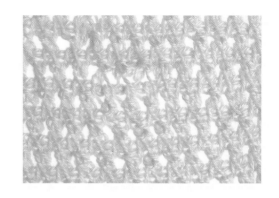

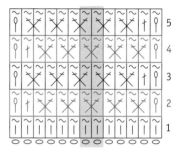

> **TIP**
>
> As you will notice, to fasten off properly in Tunisian, you start the row as normal but instead of leaving the loop on the hook, you pull the loop off. The fastening-off row can be a bit looser than the rest; if so, drop a hook size for the last row only.

Emeline Lace

This lace is thicker than most lace fabric with its alternating shells and spaces; it makes for great garments.

Tunisian Simple Stitch (Tss): Insert hk, from right to left, into front vert bar of next st and pull up a lp.

Ch a multiple of 6 sts plus 5.

Row 1 (RS) Fwd: Pull up lp in 2nd ch from hk and ea ch across. **Rtn:** Yo, pull through 1 lp on hk, *yo, pull through 2 lps on hk; rep from * to end.

Row 2 Fwd: Tss in ea st across. **Rtn:** Yo, pull through 1 lp on hk, *ch 1, yo, pull through 4 lps on hk (sh made), ch 1, [yo, pull through 2 lps on hk] 3 times; rep from * to end.

Row 3 Fwd: (Lp on hk counts as 1st st.) *Insert hk into top horiz bar of sh and pull up a lp, yo, insert hk into same horiz bar and pull up a lp, Tss in next 3 sts; rep from * across, Tss in last st. **Rtn:** Yo, pull through 1 lp on hk, *[yo, pull through 2 lps on hk] 3 times, ch 1, yo, pull through 4 lps on hk (sh made), ch 1; rep from * to end.

Row 4 Fwd: (Lp on hk counts as 1st st.) * Tss in next 3 sts, Insert hk into top horiz bar of sh and pull up a lp, yo, insert hk into same horiz bar and pull up a lp; rep from * across, Tss in last 4 sts. **Rtn:** Yo, pull through 1 lp on hk, *ch 1, yo, pull through 4 lps on hk (sh made), ch 1, [yo, pull through 2 lps on hk] 3 times; rep from * to end.

Rep rows 3 and 4 to desired length.

Last row: *Tss in next st and pull through lp on hk; rep from * across, fasten off.

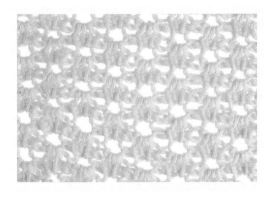

Catrain Lace

The columns of shells create a very linear pattern, which makes great scarves.

Ch a multiple of 5 sts plus 2.

Row 1 (RS) Fwd: Pull up lp in 2nd ch from hk and ea ch across. **Rtn:** Yo, pull through 1 lp on hk, ch 1, *yo, pull through 6 lps on hk (sh made), ch 3; rep from * to last 6 sts, yo, pull through 6 lps on hk, ch 1, yo, pull through last 2 lps on hk.

Row 2 Fwd: (Lp on hk counts as 1st st.) *[Insert hk into top horiz bar of next st and pull up a lp] twice, insert hk into horiz bar on top of next sh and pull up a lp, [insert hk into top horiz bar of next st and pull up a lp] twice; rep from * across to last st, Tss in last st. **Rtn:** Yo, pull through 1 lp on hk, ch 1, *yo, pull through 6 lps on hk (sh made), ch 3; rep from * to last 6 sts, yo, pull through 6 lps on hk, ch 1, yo, pull through last 2 lps on hk.

Rep row 2 to desired length.

Last row: *[Insert hk into top horiz bar of next st, pull up a lp and through lp on hk] twice, insert hk into horiz bar on top of next sh, pull up a lp and through lp on hk, [insert hk into top horiz bar of next st, pull up a lp and through lp on hk] twice; rep from * to last st, Tss in last st and pull through lp on hk, fasten off.

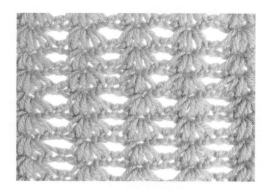

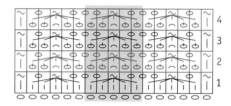

Alianor Lace

Rows of clusters separated by rows of vertical lines give a very structured lace pattern that works nicely for wraps.

Two Extended Double Crochet Cluster (2 edc-cl): *Yo, insert hk into vert bar of next st, yo and pull up a lp, yo and pull through 2 lps on hk; rep from * once in same st, yo and pull through 2 lps, ch 1.

Ch an odd number of sts.

Row 1 (RS) Fwd: Pull up lp in 2nd ch from hk and ea ch across. **Rtn:** Yo, pull through 1 lp on hk, *yo, pull through 2 lps on hk; rep from * to end.

Row 2 Fwd: Ch 2 (counts as 1st st), *2 edc-cl in next st, sk next st; rep from * across to last st, Tss in last st, ch 2. **Rtn:** Yo, pull through 1 lp on hk, *yo, pull through 2 lps on hk, ch 1; rep from * last 2 sts, [yo, pull through 2 lps on hk] twice.

Row 3 Fwd: (Lp on hk counts as 1 st.) *Tss in next st, insert hk into top horiz bar of next st and pull up a lp; rep from * across to last 2 sts, Tss in last 2 sts. **Rtn:** Work off lps as normal.

Rep rows 2 and 3 to desired length.

Last row: *Tss in next st and pull through lp on hk; rep * to end, fasten off.

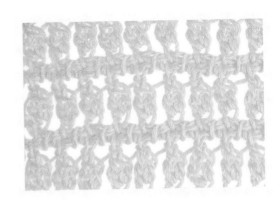

Peronell Lace

When you change the position of the yarn, the strands create a lattice look with clusters under the bars.

Two Double Crochet Cluster (2 dc-cl): *Yo, insert hk into vert bar of next st, yo and pull up a lp, yo and pull through 2 lps; rep from * once more in same st, yo and pull through 2 lps on hk.

Ch a multiple of 4 sts plus 3.

Row 1 (RS) Fwd: Pull up lp in 2nd ch from hk and ea ch across. **Rtn:** Yo, pull through 1 lp on hk, *yo, pull through 2 lps on hk; rep from * to end.

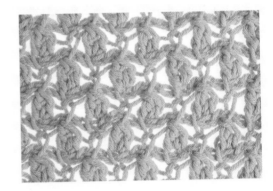

Row 2 Fwd: Ch 1 (counts as 1st st), *2 dc-cl in next st, sk next st, Tps in next st, sk next st; rep from * across to last 2 sts, 2 dc-cl in next st, Tss in last st, ch 1. **Rtn:** Yo, pull through 1 lp on hk, *yo, pull through 2 lps on hk, ch 1; rep from * to last 2 sts, [yo, pull through 2 lps on hk] twice.

Row 3 Fwd: Ch 1 (counts as 1st st), *Tps in next st, sk next st, 2 dc-cl in next st, sk next st; rep from * across to last 2 sts, Tps in next st, Tss in last st, ch 1. **Rtn:** Yo, pull through 1 lp on hk, *yo, pull through 2 lps on hk, ch 1; rep from * to last 2 sts, [yo, pull through 2 lps on hk] twice.

Rep rows 2 and 3 to desired length.

Last row: *Tss in next st and pull through lp on hk, insert hk in next ch-s, pull up a lp and through lp on hk; rep from * across, fasten off.

Cleves Lace

This simple lace pattern is strong enough for beautiful, flowing skirts and tops.

Ch an even number of sts.

Row 1 (RS) Fwd: Pull up lp in 2nd ch from hk and ea ch across. **Rtn:** Yo, pull through 1 lp on hk, *yo, pull through 2 lps on hk; rep from * to end.

Row 2 Fwd: (Lp on hk counts as 1st st on hk.) *Tss in next 2 sts at once, yo and pull up a lp, yo; rep from * across to last st, Tss in last st. **Rtn:** Work off lps as normal.

Row 3 Fwd: (Lp on hk counts as 1st st.) *Tss in next st, insert hk around horiz bars of next st, yo and pull up a lp; rep from * across to last st, Tss in last st. **Rtn:** Work off lps as normal.

Rep rows 2 and 3 to desired length.

Last row: * Tss in next st and pull up a lp and through lp on hk; rep from * across, fasten off.

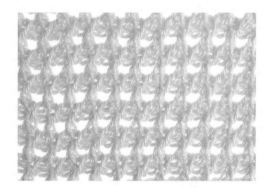

Fendrel

The dropped-stitch look makes a great zigzag fabric that can work great for kids' or adults' projects. The stitch pattern does tend to lean, so blocking is necessary.

Ch an odd number of sts.

Row 1 (RS) Fwd: Pull up lp in 2nd ch from hk and ea ch across. **Rtn:** Yo, pull through 2 lps on hk, *ch 1, yo, pull through 3 lps on hk (dec made); rep from * to last st (last 2 lps on hk), ch 1 with new color, yo and pull through last 2 lps on hk.

Row 2 Fwd: Ch 1 (counts as 1st st), *insert hk around next ch-sp and pull up a lp, ch 2, Tss in next st; rep from * across. **Rtn:** Yo, pull through 2 lps on hk, ch 1, *yo, pull through 3 lps on hk (dec made), ch 1; rep from * to last st (last 2 lps on hk), change color, yo and pull through last 2 lps on hk.

Rep row 2 to desired length.

Last row: *Insert hk around next ch-sp, yo and pull up a lp and through lp on hk, Tss in next st and pull through lp on hk; rep from * across, fasten off.

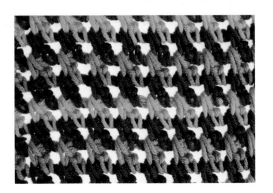

Cartwright

Staggering of mitered corners gives an appealing pattern to the slightly textured fabric.

Tunisian Double Crochet (Tdc): Yo, insert hk into vert bar of next st 2 rows below, yo and pull lp through st, yo and pull through 2 lps, leaving last lp on hk.

Ch a multiple of 4 sts plus 1.

Row 1 (RS) Fwd: Pull up lp in 2nd ch from hk and ea ch across. **Rtn:** Yo, pull through 1 lp on hk, *yo, pull through 2 lps on hk; rep from * to end, change color before last st (last 2 lps).

Row 2 Fwd: (Lp on hk counts as 1st st.) *Tss in next 3 sts, sk next st; rep from * across to last 4 sts, Tss in last 4 sts. **Rtn:** Yo, pull through 1 lp on hk, *[yo, pull through 2 lps on hk] 3 times, ch 1; rep from * to last 4 sts (last 5 lps on hk), [yo, pull through 2 lps on hk] 3 times, change color, yo, pull through 2 lps on hk.

Row 3 Fwd: (Lp on hk counts as 1st st.) *Tss in next 2 sts, sk next st, Tdc in next st; rep from * across to last 4 sts, Tss in next 2 sts, sk next st, Tss in last st. **Rtn:** Yo, pull through 1 lp on hk, *ch 1, [yo, pull through 2 lps on hk] 3 times; rep from * to end, change color before last st (last 2 lps).

Row 4 Fwd: (Lp on hk counts as 1st st.) *Tss in next st, sk next st, Tdc in next st, Tss in next st; rep from * across. **Rtn:** Yo, pull through 1 lp on hk, yo, pull through 2 lps on hk, *ch 1, [yo, pull through 2 lps on hk] 3 times; rep from * to last 2 sts (3 lps on hk), ch 1, yo, pull through 2 lps on hk, change color, yo, pull through 2 lps on hk.

Row 5 Fwd: (Lp on hk counts as 1st st.) *Sk next st, Tdc in next st, Tss in next 2 sts; rep from * across. **Rtn:** Yo, pull through 1 lp on hk, [yo, pull through 2 lps on hk] twice, *ch 1, [yo, pull through 2 lps on hk] 3 times; rep from * to last st (last 2 lps on hk), ch 1, change color, yo, pull through last 2 lps on hk.

Row 6 Fwd: (Lp on hk counts as 1st st.) *Tdc in next st, Tss in next 2 sts, sk next st; rep from * across to last 4 sts, Tdc in next st, Tss in last 3 sts. **Rtn:** Yo, pull through 1 lp on hk, *[yo, pull through 2 lps on hk] 3 times, ch 1; rep from * to last 4 sts (last 5 lps on hk), [yo, pull through 2 lps on hk] 3 times, change color, yo, pull through 2 lps on hk.

Rep rows 3–6 to desired length.

Last row: *[Tss in next st and pull lp through lp on hk] 3 times, Tdc in next st and pull lp through lp on hk; rep from * to end, fasten off.

Wykeham

This woven-looking fabric makes great projects that need a sturdy fabric with a tweedish look.

Ch an odd number of sts.

Row 1 (RS) Fwd: Pull up lp in 2nd ch from hk and ea ch across. **Rtn:** Yo, pull through 1 lp on hk, *yo, pull through 2 lps on hk; rep from * to end, change color in last st (last 2 lps).

Row 2 Fwd: (Lp on hk counts as 1st st.) *Move yarn to front, insert hk into vert bar of next st (do not pull up a lp), Tss in next st; rep from * across. **Rtn:** Work off lps as normal, change color in last st.

Row 3 Fwd: (Lp on hk counts as 1st st.) *Tss in next st, move yarn to front, insert hk into vert bar of next st (do not pull up a lp); rep from * across to last 2 sts, Tss in last 2 sts. **Rtn:** Work off lps as normal, change color in last st.

Rep rows 2 and 3 to desired length.

Last row: *Tss in next st and pull through lp on hk; rep from * to end, fasten off.

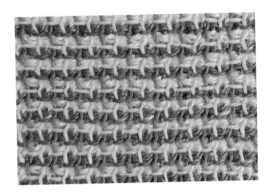

Bolbec

This slipped-stitch pattern brings the color from below up to the current row to add little parallel lines throughout the fabric. The slipped stitches may tend to scrunch the fabric, so plan to use larger hook sizes.

Twisted Simple Stitch (Twtss): Move yarn to front, insert hk from left to right into front vert bar of next st and pull up a lp (opp direction from Tss and twists bar).

Ch a multiple of 4 sts.

Row 1 (RS) Fwd: Pull up lp in 2nd ch from hk and ea ch across. **Rtn:** Change color, yo, pull through 1 lp on hk, *yo, pull through 2 lps on hk; rep from * to end.

Row 2 Fwd: (Lp on hk counts as 1st st.) *Insert hk into vert bar of next 2 sts (do not pull up a lp), Twtss in next st and pull up a lp, Tps in next st; rep from * across to last 3 sts, insert hk into vert bar of next 2 sts (do not pull up a lp), Tss in last st. **Rtn:** Change color, work off lps as normal.

Row 3 Fwd: (Lp on hk counts as 1st st.) *Tss in next 2 sts, insert hk into vert bar of next 2 sts (do not pull up a lp); rep from * across to last 3 sts, Tss in last 3 sts. **Rtn:** Work off lps as normal.

Row 4 Fwd: Tss in ea st across. **Rtn:** Change color, work off lps as normal.

Row 5 Fwd: (Lp on hk counts as 1st st.) *Twtss in next st, Tps in next st, insert hk into vert bar of next 2 sts (do not pull up a lp); rep from * across to last 3 sts, Twtss in next st, Tps in next st, Tss in last st. **Rtn:** Change color, work off lps as normal.

Row 6 Fwd: (Lp on hk counts as 1st st.) *Insert hk into vert bar of next 2 sts (do not pull up a lp), Tss in next 2 sts; rep from * across to last 3 sts, insert hk into vert bar of next 2 sts (do not pull up a lp), Tss in last st. **Rtn:** Work off lps as normal.

Row 7: Rep Row 4

Rep rows 2–7 to desired length, ending on a Row 6.

Last row: *Tss in next st and pull through lp on hk; rep from * to end, fasten off.

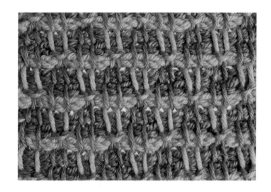

Terryn

When you change colors in each direction and slowly gather stitches, a beautiful wave fabric emerges.

Ch a multiple of 6 sts plus 1.

Row 1 (RS) Fwd: Pull up lp in 2nd ch from hk and ea ch across. **Rtn:** Change color, yo, pull through 1 lp on hk, *yo, pull through 2 lps on hk; rep from * to end, change color at last st.

Row 2 Fwd: (Lp on hk counts as 1st sc.) Yo, *Tps in next st, move yarn to front, insert hk in vert bar of next 3 sts at once, yo and pull up a lp, Tps in next st, yo, Tps in next st, yo; rep from * across to last 6 sts, Tps in next st, move yarn to front, insert hk in vert bar of next 3 sts at once, yo and pull up a lp, Tps in next st, yo, sk next st, Tps in last st. **Rtn:** Change color, work off lps as normal, change color at last st.

Row 3 Fwd: (Lp on hk counts as 1st sc.) Yo, *Tss in back vert bar of next st, insert hk in back vert bar of next 3 sts at once, yo and pull up a lp, Tss in back vert bar of next st, yo, Tss in back vert bar of next st, yo; rep from * across to last 6 sts, Tss in back vert bar of next st, insert hk in back vert bar of next 3 sts at once, yo and pull up a lp, Tss in back vert bar of next st, yo, Tss in back vert bar of last st. **Rtn:** Change color, work off lps as normal, change color at last st.

Rep rows 2 and 3 to desired length.

Last row: *Insert hk around horiz bar of next st, pull up a lp and through lp on hk, insert hk into vert bar of next st, pull up a lp and through lp on hk, insert hk into vert bar of next 3 sts at once, pull up a lp and through lp on hk, insert hk into vert bar of next st, pull up a lp and through lp on hk, insert hk around horiz bar of next st, pull up a lp and through lp on hk, insert hk into vert bar of next st, pull up a lp and through lp on hk; rep from * across, fasten off.

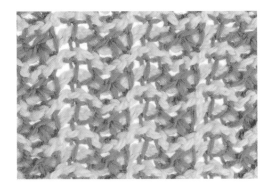

TIP

Changing color in Tunisian crochet is as simple as folding the new color strand over the hook and continuing as the pattern directs. When the color changes at the beginning of a row, add the new color when there are two loops left on the previous row. When the color changes at the end of the row, you can change the color on the first yarn over.

CHAPTER 7

Square and Hexagonal Granny Squares

Traditional Granny Square

This is the most classic of all the granny squares, and what some consider the definition of a granny square.

Ch 4, sl st to 1st ch to form a ring.

Rnd 1 (RS): Ch 3 (counts as dc), 2 dc in ring, [ch 3, 3 dc in ring] 3 times, ch 1, hdc in top of t-ch, do not turn—12 dc.

Rnd 2: Ch 3 (counts as dc), 2 dc around post of hdc, *ch 1, [3 dc, ch 3, 3 dc] in ch-3 sp; rep from * around to last ch-3 sp, ch 1, 3 dc in ch-1 sp, ch 1, hdc in top of t-ch, do not turn—24 dc.

Rnd 3: Ch 3 (counts as dc), 2 dc around post of hdc, *ch 1, 3 dc in ch-1 sp, ch 1, [3 dc, ch 3, 3 dc] in ch-3 sp; rep from * around to last ch-3 sp, ch 1, 3 dc in ch-1 sp, ch 1, 3 dc in ch-1 sp, ch 1, hdc in top of t-ch, do not turn—36 dc.

Rnd 4: Ch 3 (counts as dc), 2 dc around post of hdc, *[ch 1, 3 dc in ch-1 sp] twice, ch 1, [3 dc, ch 3, 3 dc] in ch-3 sp; rep from * around to last ch-3 sp, [ch 1, 3 dc in ch-1 sp] twice, ch 1, 3 dc in ch-1 sp, ch 1, hdc in top of t-ch, fasten off—48 dc.

> **TIP**
>
> Granny square patterns are easy to follow because they are mainly the same pattern on each side of the motif. The only difference is in the beginning and ending of each round. If the pattern wants the next stitch to be at the bottom of the arch made from a chain space, then it will end in a slip stitch to the first stitch of the round. If the pattern wants the next stitch on the next round to be at the top of the arch of the chain space, then it will break up the last chain space with a chain and a stitch to the first stitch. It can be confusing, so instead of thinking of these last stitches as stitches, look at them as just additional chain spaces.

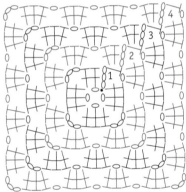

Double Crochet Granny Square

The simple construction of this square highlights the chain spaces more than the solid fabric.

Ch 4, sl st to 1st ch to form a ring.

Rnd 1 (RS): Ch 3 (counts as dc), dc in ring, [ch 3, 3 dc in ring] 3 times, ch 3, dc in ring, sl st to top of t-ch, do not turn—12 dc.

Rnd 2: Ch 3 (counts as dc), dc in dc, *[2 dc, ch 3, 2 dc] in ch-3 sp, dc in next 3 dc; rep from * around to last ch-3 sp, [2 dc, ch 3, 2 dc] in last ch-3 sp, dc in last dc, sl st to top of t-ch, do not turn—28 dc.

Rnd 3: Ch 3 (counts as dc), dc in next 3 dc, *[2 dc, ch 3, 2 dc] in ch-3 sp, dc in next 7 dc; rep from * around to last ch-3 sp, [2 dc, ch 3, 2 dc] in last ch-3 sp, dc in last 3 dc, sl st to top of t-ch, do not turn—44 dc.

Rnd 4: Ch 3 (counts as dc), dc in next 5 dc, *[2 dc, ch 3, 2 dc] in ch-3 sp, dc in next 11 dc; rep from * around to last ch-3 sp, [2 dc, ch 3, 2 dc] in last ch-3 sp, dc in last 5 dc, sl st to top of t-ch, fasten off—60 dc.

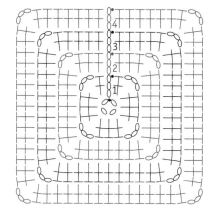

Brick Granny Square

You can make this simple granny come alive by changing color on every other round to highlight the small stitches on the wrong-side rounds.

Ch 4, sl st to 1st ch to form a ring.

Rnd 1 (RS): Ch 3 (counts as dc), 2 dc in ring, [ch 3, 3 dc in ring] 3 times, ch 3, sl st to top of t-ch, turn, fasten off—12 dc.

Rnd 2: Join new color, ch 1, *[sc, ch 3, sc] in ch-3 sp, ch 3; rep from * around, sl st to 1st sc, turn, fasten off—8 sc.

Rnd 3: Join new color, ch 3 (counts as dc), 2 dc in ch-3 sp, *[3 dc, ch 3, 3 dc] in next ch-3 sp, 3 dc in next ch-3 sp; rep from * around to last ch-3 sp, [3 dc, ch 3, 3 dc] in last ch-3 sp, sl st to top of t-ch, fasten off, turn—36 dc.

Rnd 4: Join new color, ch 1, sc btw t-ch and dc, *ch 3, [sc, ch 3, sc] in next ch-3 sp, [ch 3, sk 3 dc, sc btw prev and next dc] twice; rep from * around, sl st to 1st sc, fasten off, turn—16 sc.

Rnd 5: Join new color, ch 3 (counts as dc), 2 dc in ch-3 sp, *3 dc in next ch-3 sp, [3 dc, ch 3, 3 dc] in next ch-3 sp, 3 dc in next 2 ch-3 sps; rep from * around to last ch-3 sp, 3 dc in last ch-3 sp, sl st to top of t-ch, fasten off, turn—60 dc.

Rnd 6: Join new color, ch 1, sc btw t-ch and dc, *ch 3, sk 3 dc, sc btw prev and next dc, ch 3, [sc, ch 3, sc] in next ch-3 sp, [ch 3, sk 3 dc, sc btw prev and next dc] 3 times; rep from * around, sl st to 1st sc, fasten off, turn—24 sc.

Rnd 7: Join new color, ch 3 (counts as dc), 2 dc in ch-3 sp, *3 dc in next 2 ch-3 sps, [3 dc, ch 3, 3 dc] in next ch-3 sp, 3 dc in next 3 ch-3 sps; rep from * around to last ch-3 sp, 3 dc in last ch-3 sp, sl st to top of t-ch, fasten off, turn—84 dc.

Rnd 8: Join new color, ch 1, sc btw t-ch and dc, *[ch 3, sk 3 dc, sc btw prev and next dc] twice, ch 3, [sc, ch 3, sc] in next ch-3 sp, [ch 3, sk 3 dc, sc btw prev and next dc] 4 times; rep from * around, sl st to 1st sc, fasten off, turn—32 sc.

Rnd 9: Join new color, ch 1, *3 sc in next 4 ch-3 sps, 5 sc in next ch-3 sp, 3 dc in next 3 ch-3 sps; rep from * around, sl st to 1st sc, fasten off—104 sc.

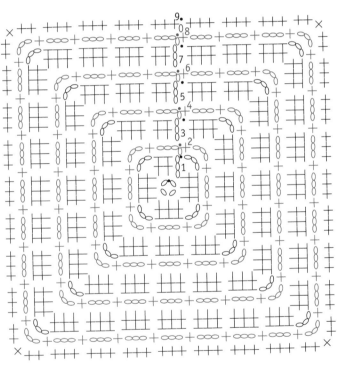

Open Cross Granny Square

The voids created by the chain spaces create a visible cross that you can use as a design feature when you combine it all together.

Ch 7, sl st to 1st ch to form a ring.

Rnd 1 (RS): Ch 3 (counts as dc), 15 dc in ring, sl st to top of t-ch, do not turn.

Rnd 2: Ch 5 (counts as dc, ch-2 sp), sk 1 dc, *3 dc in next dc, ch 2, sk 1 dc, dc in next dc, ch 2, sk 1 dc; rep from * 3 times total, 3 dc in next dc, ch 2, sl st to 3rd ch of t-ch, do not turn—16 dc.

Rnd 3: Ch 5 (counts as dc, ch-2 sp), sk ch-sp, *dc in next dc, 5 dc in next dc, dc in next dc, ch 2, dc in dc, ch 2; rep from * 3 times total, dc in next dc, 5 dc in next dc, dc in next dc, ch 2, sl st to 3rd ch of t-ch, do not turn—32 dc.

Rnd 4: Ch 5 (counts as dc, ch-2 sp), sk ch-sp, *dc in next 3 dc, 5 dc in next dc, dc in next 3 dc, ch 2, dc in dc, ch 2; rep from * 3 times total, dc in next 3 dc, 5 dc in next dc, dc in next 3 dc, ch 2, sl st to 3rd ch of t-ch, do not turn—48 dc.

Rnd 5: Ch 5 (counts as dc, ch-2 sp), sk ch-sp, *dc in next 5 dc, 5 dc in next dc, dc in next 5 dc, ch 2, dc in dc, ch 2; rep from * 3 times total, dc in next 5 dc, 5 dc in next dc, dc in next 5 dc, ch 2, sl st to 3rd ch of t-ch, do not turn—68 dc.

Rnd 6: Ch 5 (counts as dc, ch-2 sp), sk ch-sp, *dc in next 7 dc, 5 dc in next dc, dc in next 7 dc, ch 2, dc in dc, ch 2; rep from * 3 times total, dc in next 7 dc, 5 dc in next dc, dc in next 7 dc, ch 2, sl st to 3rd ch of t-ch, do not turn—80 dc.

Rnd 7: Ch 3 (counts as dc), 2 dc in next ch-sp, *dc in next 9 dc, 5 dc in next dc, dc in next 9 dc, 2 dc in next ch-sp, dc in dc, 2 dc in next ch-sp; rep from * 3 times total, dc in next 9 dc, 5 dc in next dc, dc in next 9 dc, 2 dc in ch-sp, sl st to top of t-ch, fasten off—112 dc.

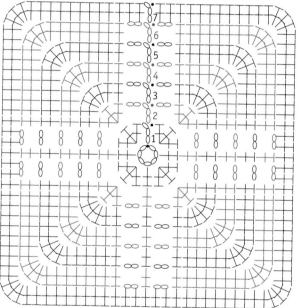

Window Granny Square

The middle round of chain spaces combines with the voids on the corners to create quite an architectural motif.

Make an adjustable ring.

Rnd 1 (RS): Ch 3 (counts as dc), 15 dc in ring, sl st to top of t-ch, do not turn.

Rnd 2: Ch 2 (counts as hdc), *hdc in next dc, [2 dc, ch 2, 2 dc] in next dc, hdc in next 2 dc; rep from * around, sl st to top of t-ch, do not turn—16 dc.

Rnd 3: Ch 4 (counts as dc, ch-1 sp), *sk hdc, dc in next dc, ch 1, [2 dc, ch 2, 2 dc] in next ch-2 sp, ch 1, sk dc, dc in next dc, ch 1, dc in next hdc; rep from * around, sl st to 3rd ch of t-ch, do not turn—28 dc.

Rnd 4: Ch 3 (counts as dc), *[dc in ch-1 sp, dc in next dc] twice, dc in next dc, [2 dc, ch 2, 2 dc] in next ch-2 sp, dc in next 2 dc, [dc in ch-1 sp, dc in next dc] twice; rep from * around, sl st to top of t-ch, do not turn—60 dc.

Rnd 5: Ch 3 (counts as dc), *dc in ea dc across to ch-sp, [2 dc, ch 2, 2 dc] in ch-2 sp; rep from * around, dc in ea dc across to t-ch, sl st to top of t-ch, fasten off—76 dc.

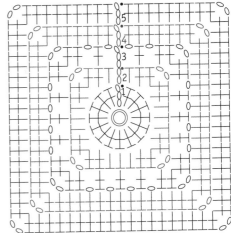

Crossed Clusters Granny Square

This classic afghan granny square makes a great impact with the simple clusters in the corners.

Ch 6, sl st to 1st ch to form a ring.

Rnd 1 (RS): Ch 2, 2 dc-cl in ring, *ch 4, 3 dc-cl in ring, ch 2, 3 dc-cl; rep from * 3 times total, ch 4, 3 dc-cl in ring, ch 2, sl st to 2 dc-cl, do not turn—8 dc-cl.

Rnd 2: Ch 5 (counts as dc, ch-2 sp), *[3 dc-cl, ch 2, 3 dc-cl] in ch-4 sp, ch 2, 3 dc in next ch-2 sp, ch 2; rep from * 3 times total, [3 dc-cl, ch 2, 3 dc-cl] in ch-4 sp, ch 2, 2 dc in last ch-2 sp, sl st to 3rd ch of t-ch, do not turn—12 dc.

Rnd 3: Ch 3 (counts as dc), *2 dc in next ch-2 sp, ch 2, [3 dc-cl, ch 2, 3 dc-cl] in next ch-2 sp, ch 2, 2 dc in next ch-2 sp, dc in next 3 dc; rep from * around, sl st to top of t-ch, do not turn—28 dc.

Rnd 4: Ch 3 (counts as dc), *dc in next 2 dc, 2 dc in next ch-2 sp, ch 2, [3 dc-cl, ch 2, 3 dc-cl] in next ch-2 sp, ch 2, 2 dc in next ch-2 sp, dc in next 5 dc; rep from * around, sl st to top of t-ch, do not turn—44 dc.

Rnd 5: Ch 3 (counts as dc), *dc in ea dc to ch-sp, 2 dc in next ch-2 sp, [3 dc, ch 2, 3 dc] in next ch-2 sp, 2 dc in next ch-2 sp; rep from * around, dc in ea dc to t-ch, sl st to top of t-ch, do not turn—84 dc.

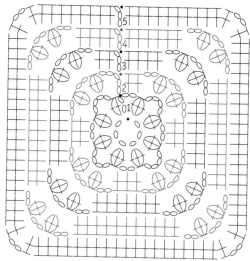

Gerber Daisy Granny Square

The beauty of the three-dimensional daisy in the center of the classic granny square is as lovely in two colors as in one solid square.

Ch 4, sl st to 1st ch to form a ring.

Rnd 1 (RS): Ch 1, 8 sc in ring, sl st to 1st sc, do not turn.

Rnd 2: Ch 3 (counts as dc), 4 dc in 1st sc, turn, ch 3, dc in next 4 dc, *ch 4, turn, 5 dc in next sc, turn, ch 3, dc in next 4 dc (petal made); rep from * in ea sc around, ch 2, hdc in top of t-ch, do not turn—8 petals.

Rnd 3: Ch 3 (counts as dc), 2 dc around post of hdc, *ch 1, sc in next ch-4 sp, ch 1, [3 dc, ch 2, 3 dc] in next ch-4 sp; rep from * 2 times, ch 1, sc in next ch-4 sp, ch 1, 3 dc in last ch-sp, hdc in top of t-ch, do not turn—24 dc.

Rnd 4: Ch 3 (counts as dc), 2 dc around post of hdc, *[ch 1, 3 dc in next ch-1 sp] twice, ch 1, [3 dc, ch 2, 3 dc] in ch-2 sp; rep from * around to last ch-2 sp, [ch 1, 3 dc in next ch-1 sp] twice, ch 1, 3 dc in last ch-sp, hdc in top of t-ch, do not turn—48 dc.

Rnd 5: Ch 3 (counts as dc), 2 dc around post of hdc, *[ch 1, 3 dc in next ch-1 sp] 3 times, ch 1, [3 dc, ch 2, 3 dc] in ch-2 sp; rep from * around to last ch-2 sp, [ch 1, 3 dc in next ch-1 sp] 3 times, ch 1, 3 dc in last ch-sp, hdc in top of t-ch, do not turn—60 dc.

Rnd 6: Ch 3 (counts as dc), 2 dc around post of hdc, *[ch 1, 3 dc in next ch-1 sp] 4 times, ch 1, [3 dc, ch 2, 3 dc] in next ch-2 sp; rep from * around to last ch-2 sp, [ch 1, 3 dc in ch-1 sp] 4 times, ch 1, 3 dc in last ch-sp, hdc in top of t-ch, fasten off—72 dc.

Posy in the Granny

The flower in the center is almost three-dimensional and is even more highlighted by a color change on the flower.

Ch 7, sl st to 1st ch to form a ring.

Rnd 1 (RS): Ch 1, *[sc, ch 3, 3 dc, sk 3, sc] in ring, ch 5; rep from * twice, sc in ring, ch 3, 3 dc in ring, ch 3, sc in ring, ch 2, dc to 1st sc, do not turn, fasten off—12 dc.

Rnd 2: Join new color, ch 3 (counts as dc), 2 dc around post of dc, *ch 2, [3 dc, ch 3, 3 dc] in next ch-5 sp; rep from * around, ch 2, 3 dc in ch-2 sp, ch 1, hdc to top of t-ch, do not turn—24 dc.

Rnd 3: Ch 3 (counts as dc), 2 dc around post of hdc, *ch 2, dc in next ch-2 sp, ch 2, [3 dc, ch 3, 3 dc] in next ch-3 sp; rep from * around, ch 2, dc in ch-2 sp, ch 2, 3 dc in ch-1 sp, ch 3, sl st to top of t-ch, do not turn—28 dc.

Rnd 4: Ch 1, sc in ch-3 sp, *ch 4, sc in next ch-2 sp, ch 4, sc in next dc, ch 4, sc in next ch-2 sp, ch 4, [sc, ch 4, sc] in next ch-3 sp; rep from * around, ch 4, sc in next ch-2 sp, ch 4, sc in next dc, ch 4, sc in next ch-2 sp, ch 4, sc in next ch-3 sp, ch 4, sl st to 1st sc, fasten off—20 sc.

Gladiolus Granny Square

This simple square is transformed into a delicate motif by adding picots on the last round.

Picot: Ch 3, sl st to 1st ch.

Ch 5, sl st to 1st ch to form a ring.

Rnd 1 (RS): Ch 3 (counts as dc), [dc, ch 3, 2 dc] in ring, ch 1 *[2 dc, ch 3, 2 dc] in ring, ch 1; rep from * 3 times total, sl st to top of t-ch, do not turn—16 dc.

Rnd 2: Sl st to next dc, sl st to ch-3 sp, ch 3 (counts as dc), 6 dc in ch-3 sp, [sc, ch 3, sc] in ch-1 sp, *7 dc in ch-3 sp, [sc, ch 3, sc] in ch-1 sp; rep from * around, sl st to top of t-ch, do not turn—28 dc.

Rnd 3: Ch 3 (counts as dc), dc in next dc, picot, dc in next dc, [dc, picot, dc] in next dc, dc in next dc, picot, dc in next 2 dc, [sc, picot, sc] in ch-3 sp, *dc in next 2 dc, picot, dc in next dc, [dc, picot, dc] in next dc, dc in next dc, picot, dc in next 2 dc, [sc, picot, sc] in ch-3 sp; rep from * around, sl st to top of t-ch, fasten off—32 dc.

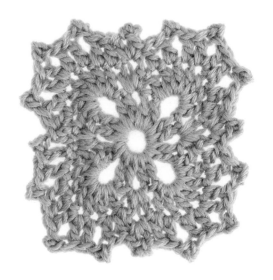

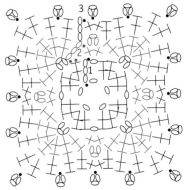

Beatrice Granny Square

The diamond pattern shines in this classic square by changing colors for the clusters.

Four Double Crochet Cluster (4 dc-cl): [Yo, insert hk into st indicated and pull up lp, yo, pull through 2 lps on hk] twice; rep from ( ) twice in next st, yo, pull through all lps on hk.

Begin Double Crochet Cluster (beg dc-cl): *Yo, insert hk into st indicated and pull up lp, yo, pull through 2 lps on hk; rep from * twice in next st, yo, pull through all lps on hk.

Ch 5, sl st to 1st ch to form a ring.

Rnd 1 (RS): Ch 3 (counts as dc), 15 dc in ring, sl st to top of t-ch, do not turn.

Rnd 2: Ch 2, 2 dc-cl in top of t-ch, *2 dc in next 2 dc, 3 dc-cl in next dc, ch 5, 3 dc-cl in next dc; rep from * around, sl st to 2 dc-cl, do not turn—8 dc-cl.

Rnd 3: Sl st in next dc, ch 2, 2 dc-cl in same dc, dc in next 2 dc, 3 dc-cl in next dc, *change color, ch 2, 5 dc in next ch-5 sp, ch 2, change color, 3 dc-cl in next dc, dc in next 2 dc, 3 dc-cl in next dc; rep from * around to last ch-5 sp, change color, ch 2, 5 dc in last ch-5 sp, ch 2, sl st to 2 dc-cl, do not turn—28 dc.

Rnd 4: Change color, sl st to next dc, ch 2, 2 dc-cl in same dc, 3 dc-cl in next dc, *change color, ch 2, dc in next ch-2 sp, dc in next dc, 2 dc in next dc, 3 dc in next dc, 2 dc in next dc, dc in next dc, dc in next ch-2 sp, ch 2, change color, 3 dc-cl in next dc; rep from * 3 times total, change color, ch 2, dc in next ch-2 sp, dc in next dc, 2 dc in next dc, 3 dc in next dc, 2 dc in next dc, dc in next dc, dc in next ch-2 sp, ch 2, sl st to 2 dc-cl, do not turn—44 dc.

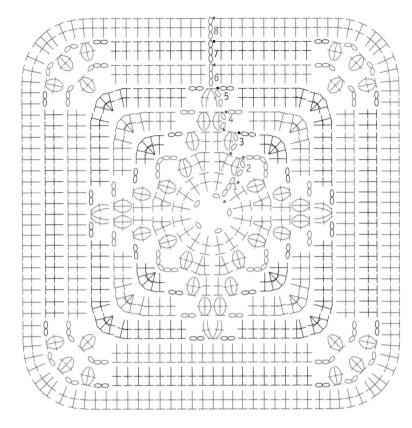

Rnd 5: Ch 2, beg dc-cl over next 2 sts, *change color, ch 2, dc in next ch-2 sp, dc in next 4 dc, 2 dc in next dc, 3 dc in next dc, 2 dc in next dc, dc in next 4 dc, dc in next ch-2 sp, ch 2, change color, 4 dc-cl over next 2 sts; rep from * 3 times total, change color, ch 2, dc in next ch-2 sp, dc in next 4 dc, 2 dc in next dc, 3 dc in next dc, 2 dc in next dc, dc in next 4 dc, dc in next ch-2 sp, ch 2, sl st to beg dc-cl, do not turn—68 dc.

Rnd 6: Change color, ch 3 (counts as dc), *2 dc in next ch-2 sp, dc in next 7 dc, ch 3, sk 1 dc, change color, 3 dc-cl in next dc, sk 1 dc, change color, ch 3, dc in ea dc across to ch-2 sp, 2 dc in next ch-2 sp, dc in next dc-cl; rep from * around, sl to top of t-ch, do not turn—76 dc.

Rnd 7: Ch 3 (counts as dc), *dc in ea dc to ch-sp, ch 2, change color, 3 dc-cl in ch-3 sp, ch 2, 3 dc-cl in next dc-cl, ch 2, 3 dc-cl in next ch-3 sp, change color, ch 2; rep from * around, dc in ea dc to t-ch, sl st to top of t-ch, do not turn—76 dc.

Rnd 8: Ch 3 (counts as dc), *dc in ea dc to ch-sp, 2 dc in ch-2 sp, dc in dc-cl, 2 dc in ch-2 sp, 3 dc in next dc-cl, 2 dc in ch-2 sp, dc in dc-cl, 2 dc in ch-2 sp; rep from * around, dc in ea dc to t-ch, sl st to top of t-ch, fasten off—128 dc.

Rose Granny Square

The clusters pop out in this classic square to create a unique fabric that you can use in fun projects from totes to blankets.

Ch 5, sl st to 1st ch to form a ring.

Rnd 1 (RS): Ch 2 (counts as hdc), 15 hdc in ring, sl st to top of t-ch, do not turn.

Rnd 2: Ch 3 (counts as dc), *dc in next hdc, 5 dc in next hdc, dc in next 2 hdc; rep from * around, sl st to top of t-ch, do not turn—32 dc.

Rnd 3: Ch 1, sc in top of t-ch, *change color, 4 dc-cl in next dc, change color, sc in next 3 dc, change color, 4 dc-cl in prev dc, change color, sc in prev dc, sc in next 2 dc, change color, 4 dc-cl in next dc, change color, sc in next dc; rep from * around, sl st to 1st sc, do not turn—12 dc-cl.

Rnd 4: Ch 3 (counts as dc), *dc in next 4 sts, 5 dc in next st, dc in next 5 sts; rep from * around, sl st to top of t-ch, do not turn—56 dc.

Rnd 5: Ch 1, sc in top of t-ch, *sc in next dc, change color, 4 dc-cl in next dc, change color, sc in next 3 dc, change color, 4 dc-cl in next dc, change color, 3 sc in next dc, change color, 4 dc-cl in next dc, change color, sc in next 3 dc, change color, 4 dc-cl in next dc, change color, sc in next 2 dc; rep from * around, sl st to 1st sc, do not turn—16 dc-cl.

Rnd 6: Ch 3 (counts as dc), *dc in next 7 sts, 5 dc in next st, dc in next 8 sts; rep from * around, sl st to top of t-ch, do not turn—80 dc.

Rnd 7: Ch 1, sc in top of t-ch, *sc in next 2 dc, [change color, 4 dc-cl in next dc, change color, sc in next 3 dc] twice, change color, 4 dc-cl in prev dc, change color, sc in prev dc, sc in next 2 dc, [change color, 4 dc-cl in next dc, change color, sc in next 3 dc] twice; rep from * around, sl st to 1st sc, do not turn—20 dc-cl.

Rnd 8: Ch 3 (counts as dc), *dc in next 10 sts, 5 dc in next st, dc in next 11 sts; rep from * around, sl st to top of t-ch, do not turn—104 dc.

Traditional Granny Square

Well known for its construction and simplicity, this traditional hexagon has graced many cherished afghans.

Ch 6, sl st to 1st ch to form a ring.

Rnd 1 (RS): Ch 2, 2 dc-cl in ring, [ch 3, 3 dc-cl] 5 times in ring, ch 1, hdc in top of 2 dc-cl, do not turn—6 dc-cl.

Rnd 2: Ch 2, 2 dc-cl around post of hdc, [(ch 3, 3 dc-cl) twice] in ea ch-3 sp around, ch 3, 3 dc-cl in last ch-1 sp, ch 1, hdc in top of 2 dc-cl, do not turn—12 dc-cl.

Rnd 3: Ch 2, 2 dc-cl around post of hdc, *ch 3, [3 dc-cl, ch 3, 3 dc-cl] in next ch-3 sp, ch 3, 3 dc-cl in next ch-3 sp; rep from * around to last ch-3 sp, ch 3, [3 dc-cl, ch 3, 3 dc-cl] in last ch-3 sp, ch 1, hdc in top of 2 dc-cl, do not turn—18 dc-cl.

Rnd 4: Ch 3 (counts as dc), dc around post of hdc, *3 dc in next ch-3 sp, [3 dc, ch 2, 3 dc] in next ch-3 sp, 3 dc in next ch-3 sp; rep from * around to last 2 ch-3 sps, 3 dc in next ch-3 sp, [3 dc, ch 2, 3 dc] in next ch-3 sp, dc in last ch-1 sp, sl st to top of t-ch, do not turn—72 dc.

Rnd 5: Ch 1, sc in top of t-ch, *sc in ea dc to ch-2 sp, 2 sc in ch-2 sp; rep from * around, sc in ea dc to end, sl st to 1st sc, fasten off—84 sc.

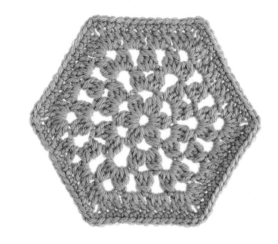

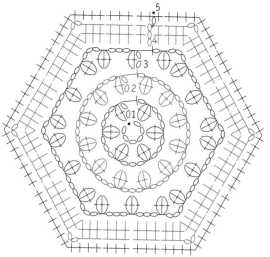

TIP

Whether you are hand sewing or crocheting hexagon motifs together, you have a great opportunity to play with their geometry for your benefit. For a ceramic tile look, match tiles together on their sides so that they nestle into the adjoining ones. By joining hexagons in columns and then joining the columns at the corners (keeping the motifs in line with adjoining ones), you gain a void between the motifs. Playing with other motifs to fill the void can be just as much fun as the beauty that unfolds.

Budding Hexagon

Turning the classic granny blossom square into a hexagon is not only pleasing to the eye but seems classic and fresh all at the same time.

Make an adjustable ring.

Rnd 1 (RS): Ch 1, 12 sc in ring, sl st to 1st sc, pull ring closed, do not turn—12 sc.

Rnd 2: Ch 2, 2 dc-cl in 1st sc, *ch 5, 3 dc-cl in next sc, ch 2, 3 dc-cl in next sc; rep from * around to last sc, ch 5, 3 dc-cl in last sc, hdc in top of 2 dc-cl, do not turn—12 dc-cl.

Rnd 3: Ch 3 (counts as dc), dc around post of hdc, ch 1, *[3 dc-cl, ch 3, 3 dc-cl] in next ch-5 sp, ch 1, 3 dc in ch-3 sp, ch 1; rep from * around to last ch-5 sp, [3 dc-cl, ch 3, 3 dc-cl] in last ch-5 sp, ch 1, dc around post of hdc, sl st to top of t-ch, do not turn—18 dc.

Rnd 4: Ch 3 (counts as dc), *dc in each dc and ch-1 sp across, ch 1, [3 dc-cl, ch 3, 3 dc-cl] in next ch-3 sp, ch 1; rep from * around, dc in last ch-1 sp, dc in last dc, sl st to top of t-ch, do not turn—30 dc.

Rnd 5: Ch 3 (counts as dc), *dc in each dc and ch-1 sp across, ch 1, [3 dc-cl, ch 3, 3 dc-cl] in next ch-3 sp, ch 1; rep from * around, dc in last ch-1 sp, dc in last 2 dc, sl st to top of t-ch, do not turn—42 dc.

Rnd 6: Ch 1, *sc in each dc and ch-1 sp across, [2 sc, ch 3, 2 sc] in next ch-3 sp; rep from * around, sc in last ch-1 sp, sc in last 3 dc, sl st to 1st sc, fasten off—78 sc.

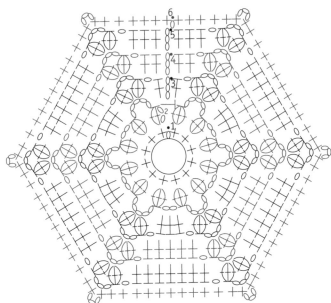

Ridged Hexagon

This stitch pattern is eye-catching not only for its raised rounds (perfect for kitchen scrubbies) but also for its color changing rounds.

V-Stitch (v-st): [Dc, ch 1, dc] in same sp.

Ch 6, sl st to 1st ch to form a ring.

Rnd 1 (RS): Ch 3 (counts as dc), v-st 5 times in ring, dc in ring, ch 1, sl st to top of t-ch, fasten off, do not turn—12 dc.

Rnd 2: Join new color to ch-1 sp with sl st, ch 3 (counts as dc), BPdc around t-ch, BPdc around next dc, *v-st in next ch-1 sp, BPdc around ea dc across to ch-1 sp; rep from * around to 1st ch-1 sp, dc in 1st ch-1 sp, ch 1, sl st to top of t-ch, fasten off, do not turn—24 dc.

Rnd 3: Join new color to ch-1 sp with sl st, ch 3 (counts as dc), BPdc around t-ch, BPdc around ea dc to ch-1 sp, *v-st in next ch-1 sp, BPdc around ea dc across to ch-1 sp; rep from * around to 1st ch-1 sp, dc in 1st ch-1 sp, ch 1, sl st to top of t-ch, fasten off color, do not turn—36 dc.

Rep rnd 3 to desired size. Each additional rnd adds 12 dc.

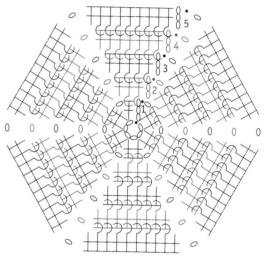

Spiral Hexagon

The simple repeating rounds that are not joined make the hexagon appear as if it is growing magically and twisting around itself.

Ch 5, sl st to 1st ch to form a ring.

Rnd 1 (RS): Ch 1, [sc, ch 5] 5 times in ring, sc in ring, ch 2, dc in 1st sc, do not turn—6 sc.

Rnd 2: *Ch 4, sc in next ch-5 sp; rep from * around to last ch-5 sp, ch 4, sc around post of dc, do not join, do not turn—6 sc.

Rnd 3: *Ch 4, 2 sc in ch-4 sp, sc in next sc; rep from * around, do not turn, do not join—18 sc.

Rnd 4: *Ch 4, 2 sc in ch-4 sp, sc in ea sc to last sc before ch-4 sp, sk last sc; rep from * around, do not turn, do not join—24 sc.

Rep rnd 4 to desired size. Each additional rnd adds 6 sc.

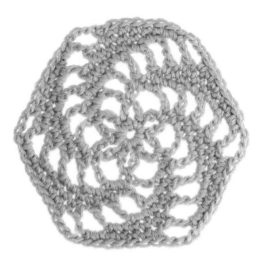

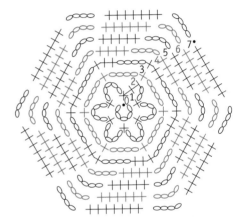

Peony Hexagon

You can punch up this simple motif with clusters of color separated by trebles, mimicking petals in a flower.

Make an adjustable lp.

Rnd 1 (RS): Ch 1, 12 sc in ring, sl st to 1st sc, pull lp closed, do not turn.

Rnd 2: Ch 1, sc in 1st sc, *ch 3, sk 1 sc, sc in next sc; rep from * around, omitting last sc, sl st to 1st sc, do not turn—6 ch-sps.

Rnd 3: Ch 7 (counts as tr, ch-3 sp), *change color, 5 dc-cl in next ch-3 sp, change color, ch 3, tr in next sc, ch 3; rep from * around, sl st to 4th ch of t-ch, do not turn—12 ch-sps.

Rnd 4: Ch 1, *3 sc in next ch-3 sp, sc in dc-cl, 3 sc in next ch-3 sp, ch 3, sk tr; rep from * around, sl st to 1st sc, do not turn—42 sc.

Rnd 5: Ch 3 (counts as dc), *dc in ea dc across to ch-sp, [dc, ch 2, dc] in ch-3 sp; rep from * around, sl st to top of t-ch, fasten off—54 dc.

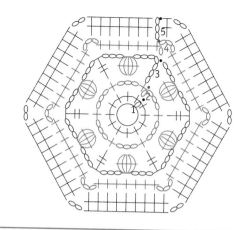

Crystal Hexagon

The flower trapped in the hexagon is similar to the shapes a crystal makes when the sun hits it and the reflections dance on the walls.

Make an adjustable lp.

Rnd 1 (RS): Ch 3 (counts as dc), 17 dc in lp, pull lp closed, do not turn—18 dc.

Rnd 2: Ch 1, sc in top of t-ch, *ch 3, sk 2 dc, sc in next dc; rep from * around to last 2 dc, ch 1, hdc in 1st sc, do not turn—6 ch-sps.

Rnd 3: Ch 3 (counts as dc), [dc, hdc, sc] around post of hdc, [sc, hdc, 3 dc, hdc, sc] in ea ch-3 sp around, [sc, hdc, dc] in last ch-sp, sl st to top of t-ch, fasten off, do not turn—6 petals.

Rnd 4: Join new color to t-ch, ch 1, sc in t-ch, *ch 2, [tr, ch 3, tr] in next sc on rnd 2, ch 2, sc in middle dc of petal; rep from * around, sl st to 1st sc, do not turn—18 ch-sps.

Rnd 5: Sl st to ch-2 sp, ch 3 (counts as dc), 2 dc in same ch-2 sp, *[2 dc, ch 2, 2 dc] in ch-3 sp, 3 dc in next 2 ch-2 sps; rep from * around, sl st to top of t-ch, do not turn—60 sc.

Rnd 6: Ch 1, sc in top of t-ch, *sc in ea dc to ch-2 sp, 2 sc in next ch-2 sp; rep from * around, sc in ea dc across to end, sl st to 1st sc, fasten off—72 sc.

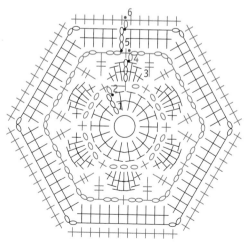

Gardenia Hexagon

Whether crocheted in different colors or all in one solid color, the gardenia center of this motif gives a shiny, fresh look to a classic hexagon.

Ch 5, sl st to 1st ch to form a ring.

Rnd 1 (RS): Ch 6 (counts as dc, ch-3 sp), [dc, ch 3] 4 times in ring, dc in ring, ch 1, hdc in 3rd ch of t-ch, do not turn—6 dc.

Rnd 2: Ch 4 (counts as tr), [tr, ch 3, sc] around post of hdc, [sc, ch 3, 3 tr, ch 3, sc] in ea ch-3 sp around, [sc, ch 3, tr] in 1st ch-sp, sl st to top of t-ch, do not turn—6 petals.

Rnd 3: Ch 5 (counts as dc, ch-2), dc in next ch-3 sp, *dc in next ch-3 sp, ch 2, sk 1 tr, [dc, ch 3, dc] in next tr, ch 2, dc in next ch-3 sp; rep from * around to 1st petal, dc in next ch-3 sp, ch 2, dc in top of t-ch from rnd 2, ch 1, hdc in 3rd ch of t-ch, do not turn—24 dc.

Rnd 4: Ch 3 (counts as dc), dc around post of hdc, *2 dc in next 2 ch-2 sps, [2 dc, ch 2, 2 dc] in next ch-3 sp; rep from * around to last 2 ch-2 sps, 2 dc in last 2 ch-2 sps, 2 dc in 1st ch-sp, ch 2, sl st to top of t-ch, fasten off—48 dc.

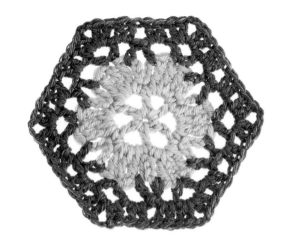

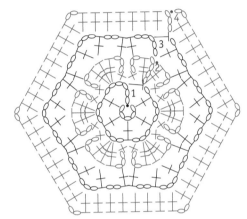

Dahlia Hexagon

The post stitches in this motif make the center flower literally pop out of its hexagon.

Ch 4, sl st to 1st ch to form a ring.

Rnd 1 (RS): Ch 6 (counts as dc, ch-3 sp), sl st in ring, [ch 3, dc, ch 3, sl st] 5 times in ring, ch 3, sl st to 3rd ch of t-ch, fasten off color, do not turn—6 dc.

Rnd 2: Join new color to top of t-ch, ch 4, *BPsc around next dc, ch 3; rep from * around, BPsc around ch-6 sp, sl st to 1st ch of t-ch, do not turn—6 ch-sps.

Rnd 3: Ch 3 (counts as dc), 2 dc in ch-sp, *[FPtr, ch 2, FPtr] around sc, 3 dc in ch-sp; rep from * around, [FPtr, ch 2, FPtr] around last sc, sl st to top of t-ch, do not turn—18 dc.

Rnd 4: Ch 3 (counts as dc), dc in next 2 dc, dc in tr, *3 dc in ch-sp, dc in tr, dc in next 3 dc, dc in tr; rep from * around, 3 dc in ch-sp, dc in last tr, sl st to top of t-ch, fasten off—48 dc.

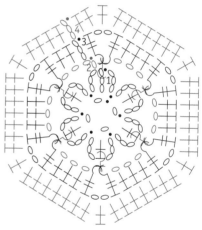

Kensington Hexagon

This hexagon mimics the lace of classic doilies with an overall flower design.

Ch 6, sl st to 1st ch to form a ring.

Rnd 1 (RS): Ch 1, 12 sc in ring, sl st to 1st sc, do not turn—12 sc.

Rnd 2: Ch 7 (counts as dc, ch-4 sp), *dc in next 2 sc, ch 4; rep from * around to last sc, dc in last sc, sl st to 3rd ch of t-ch, do not turn—12 dc.

Rnd 3: Sl st to next ch-4 sp, ch 3 (counts as dc), 3 dc in same ch-4 sp, [ch 5, 4 dc] in ea ch-4 sp, ch 2, dc in 3rd ch of t-ch, do not turn—24 dc.

Rnd 4: Ch 1, sc around post of dc, ch 4, 2 dc in top of t-ch, dc in next 2 dc, 2 dc in next dc, ch 4, *sc in next ch-5 sp, ch 4, 2 dc in next dc, dc in next 2 dc, 2 dc in next dc, ch 4; rep from * around to 1st sc, ch 2, hdc in 1st sc, do not turn—36 dc.

Rnd 5: Ch 1, sc around post of hdc, *ch 4, sc in next ch-4 sp, ch 4, 2 dc in next dc, dc in next 2 dc, ch 1, dc in next 2 dc, 2 dc in next dc, ch 4, sc in next ch-4 sp; rep from * around, ch 1, dc in 1st sc (counts as ch-sp), do not turn—48 dc.

Rnd 6: Ch 1, sc around post of dc, *[ch 5, sc in next ch-4 sp] twice, ch 4, [5 dc, ch 3, 5 dc] in ch-1 sp, ch 4, sc in next ch-4 sp; rep from * around, sl st to 1st sc, fasten off—60 dc.

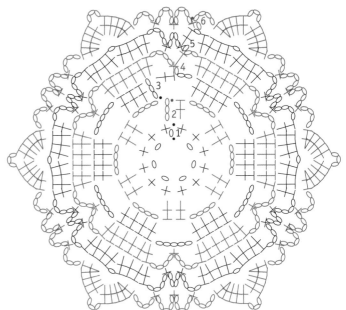

Beachwood Hexagon

This lacy hexagon can ruffle with the right yarn and with the clusters on the last round.

Ch 7, sl st to 1st ch to form a ring.

Rnd 1 (RS): Ch 3 (counts as dc), 23 dc in ring, sl st to top of t-ch, do not turn—24 dc.

Rnd 2: Ch 4 (counts as dc, ch-1 sp), [dc, ch 1] in ea dc around, sl st to 3rd ch of t-ch, do not turn—24 dc.

Rnd 3: Sl st in ch-1 sp, ch 2, 2 dc-cl in same ch-sp, [ch 2, 3 dc-cl] in ea ch-1 sp around, hdc in top of 2 dc-cl, do not turn—24 dc-cl.

Rnd 4: Ch 1, sc around post of hdc, [ch 5, sc] in ea ch-2 sp around, ch 2, dc in 1st sc, do not turn—24 ch-sps.

Rnd 5: Ch 1, sc around post of dc, *[ch 5, sc in next ch-5 sp] twice, ch 5, [4 dc-cl, ch 5, 4 dc-cl] in next ch-5 sp, ch 5, sc in next ch-5 sp; rep from * around, sl st to 1st sc, fasten off—30 ch-sps.

Winterburn Hexagon

This timeless hexagon is elegant and intricate. When combined together in a tile pattern, this motif makes a stunning fabric.

Ch 6, sl st to 1st ch to form a ring.

Rnd 1 (RS): Ch 1, 12 sc in ring, sl st to 1st sc, do not turn—12 sc.

Rnd 2: Ch 1, sc in 1st sc, *ch 7, sk 1 ch, sc in next sc; rep from * around to last sc, ch 2, sk last sc, dtr in 1st sc, do not turn—6 sc.

Rnd 3: Ch 3 (counts as dc), 4 dc around post of dtr, [ch 3, 5 dc] in ea ch-7 sp around, ch 3, sl st to top of t-ch, do not turn—30 dc.

Rnd 4: Ch 3 (counts as dc), dc in next 4 dc, *ch 3, sc in ch-3 sp, ch 3, dc in next 5 dc; rep from * around, ch 3, sc in last ch-3 sp, ch 3, sl st to top of t-ch, do not turn—30 dc.

Rnd 5: Ch 2, dc4tog over next 4 dc, *[ch 5, sc in next ch-3 sp] twice, ch 5, dc5tog over next 5 dc; rep from * around, [ch 5, sc in next ch-3 sp] twice, ch 3, hdc in top of dc4tog, do not turn—18 ch-5 sps.

Rnd 6: Ch 1, sc around post of hdc, [ch 5, sc] in ea ch-sp around, ch 5, sl st to 1st sc, do not turn—18 ch-sps.

Rnd 7: Sl st to ch-5 sp, ch 3 (counts as dc), [4 dc, ch 3, 5 dc] in same ch-sp, *ch 3, sc in next ch-5 sp, ch 5, sc in next ch-5 sp, ch 3, [5 dc, ch 3, 5 dc] in next ch-5 sp; rep from * around to last 2 ch-5 sps, ch 3, sc in next ch-5 sp, ch 5, sc in next ch-5 sp, ch 3, sl st to top of t-ch, fasten off—60 dc.

Brynwood Hexagon

This hexagon is like a stained glass design inside a beautiful window.

Make an adjustable ring.

Rnd 1 (RS): Ch 2, 2 dc-cl in ring, [ch 4, 3 dc-cl] 3 times in ring, ch 1, dc in top of 2 dc-cl, pull ring closed, do not turn.

Rnd 2: Ch 1, 4 sc around post of dc, 6 sc in ea ch-4 sp, 2 sc in 1st ch-sp, sl st to 1st sc, do not turn—24 sc.

Rnd 3: Ch 3 (counts as dc), dc in next 2 sc, [ch 5, sk 1 sc, dc in next 3 sc] 5 times, ch 2, dc in top of t-ch (counts as ch-sp), do not turn—18 dc.

Rnd 4: Ch 1, 5 sc around post of dc, sk t-ch, *sc in next dc, 9 sc in next ch-5 sp (arch made), sk 1 dc; rep from * around, sc in next dc, 4 sc in 1st ch-sp, sl st to 1st sc, do not turn—6 arches.

Rnd 5: Ch 6 (counts as dc, ch-3 sp), dc in 1st sc, *ch 4, dtr2tog over prev sc and middle sc of next arch, ch 4, [dc, ch 3, dc] in same sc; rep from * around, ch 4, dtr2tog over prev sc and middle sc of next arch, ch 4, sl st to 3rd ch of t-ch, do not turn—18 ch-sps.

Rnd 6: Ch 1, *5 sc in next ch-sp, 4 sc in next ch-4 sp, sc around dtr2tog, 4 sc in next ch-4 sp; rep from * around, sl st to 1st sc, do not turn—84 sc.

Rnd 7: Ch 3 (counts as dc), dc in next sc, *3 dc in next sc, dc in next 13 sc; rep from * around, sl st to top of t-ch, do not turn—96 dc.

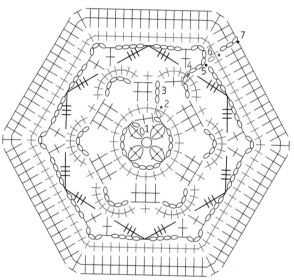

Crystal Lace Motif

The lace of this motif is spotted with clusters that can look like lattice with blossoms when combined with more crystal lace motifs.

Ch 6, sl st to 1st ch to form a ring.

Rnd 1 (RS): Ch 2, 2 dc-cl in ring, [ch 3, 3 dc-cl] 7 times in ring, ch 1, hdc in top of 2 dc-cl, do not turn—8 dc-cl.

Rnd 2: Ch 1, sc around post of hdc, [ch 5, sc] in ea ch-3 sp around, ch 2, dc in 1st sc, do not turn—8 sc.

Rnd 3: Ch 1, sc around post of dc, *ch 5, [3 dc-cl, ch 3, 3 dc-cl] in next ch-5 sp, ch 5, sc in next ch-5 sp; rep from * around to last ch-5 sp, ch 5, [3 dc-cl, ch 3, 3 dc-cl] in next ch-5 sp, ch 2, dc in 1st sc, do not turn—8 dc-cl.

Rnd 4: Ch 1, sc around post of dc, *ch 5, sc in next ch-5 sp, ch 5, [sc, ch 5, sc] in next ch-3 sp, ch 5, sc in next ch-5 sp; rep from * around, sl st to 1st sc, do not turn—16 ch-5 sps.

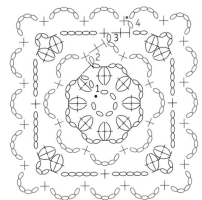

TIP

Yarn Choice

With all crochet projects, yarn choice can completely change the finished look. Yarns that are generally fluffy and bounce back when squeezed, as some wools do, pump up clusters and fill voids. Yarns that are generally slick and have a natural drape, as silk does, tend to lie down and spread out. Using a yarn's fiber to your benefit can completely change the look of many of these motifs. Swatching the same motif with different fibers is not only fun but quite educational as well.

RaeAnne Motif

The circle of clusters is highlighted on the last round with chain spaces.

Ch 6, sl st to 1st ch to form a ring.

Rnd 1 (RS): Ch 5 (counts as dc, ch-2 sp), [dc, ch 2] 7 times in ring, sl st to 3rd ch of t-ch, do not turn—8 dc.

Rnd 2: Ch 3, 3 dc-cl in ch-2 sp, [ch 4, 4 dc-cl] in ea ch-2 sp, ch 2, hdc in top of 3 dc-cl, do not turn—8 dc-cl.

Rnd 3: Ch 3 (counts as dc), 2 dc around post of hdc, *[ch 3, (sc, ch 5) twice, sc, ch 3] in next ch-4 sp, [3 dc, ch 5, 3 dc] in next ch-4 sp; rep from * to last ch-4 sp, [ch 3, (sc, ch 5) twice, sc, ch 3] in next ch-4 sp, 3 dc in last ch-sp, ch 5, sl st to top of t-ch, fasten off—20 ch-sps.

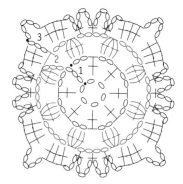

Moorish Motif

This bulky cross is encircled with a delicate line of picot chains. It's a beautiful motif that makes a delicate fabric when combined together.

Single Crochet Spike (sc spike): Insert hk into st indicated 1 rnd below, yo and pull up lp, yo, pull through lps on hk.

Picot: Ch 3, sl st to 1st ch.

Ch 6, sl st to 1st ch to form a ring.

Rnd 1 (RS): Ch 1, 16 sc in ring, sl st to top of t-ch, do not turn.

Rnd 2: Ch 1, *sc in next 2 sc, [sc, ch 9, sc] in next sc, sc in next sc; rep from * around, sl st to 1st sc, do not turn—20 sc.

Rnd 3: Ch 1, *sc in sc, [2 hdc, 17 dc, 2 hdc] in ch-9 sp, sk 2 sc; rep from * around, sl st to 1st sc, do not turn—68 dc.

Rnd 4: Ch 1, *sc spike in sc on rnd 2, ch 5, sk 5 sts, [sc in next dc, picot, ch 5, sk 4 dc] twice, sc in next dc, picot, ch 5; rep from * around, sl st to 1st sc, do not turn—16 ch-sps.

Zany Motif

In this quirky motif, the single crochet around the last round shows off the zigzag of the chain spaces perfectly.

Picot: Ch 3, sl st to 1st ch.

Ch 8, sl st to 1st ch to form a ring.

Rnd 1 (RS): Ch 3 (counts as dc), *dc in ring, picot, 2 dc in ring; rep from * 6 more times, [dc , picot, dc] in ring, sl st to top of t-ch, do not turn—24 dc.

Rnd 2: Ch 1, sc in top of t-ch, *ch 6, sk 2 dc, sc in next dc; rep from * around, ch 6, sl st to 1st sc, do not turn—8 ch-6 sps.

Rnd 3: *[3 sc, ch 3, sc, ch 3, 3 sc] in next ch-6 sp, ch 9, [3 sc, ch 3, sc, ch 3, 3 sc] in next ch-6 sp; rep from * around, sl st to 1st sc, fasten off—4 ch-9 sps.

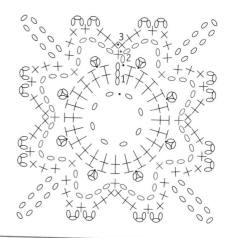

Hatsukoi Motif

The colorful flower trapped inside this motif can be sculptural with a thicker yarn and small hook, or lie flat with heavy blocking.

Ch 5, sl st to 1st ch to form a ring.

Rnd 1 (RS): Ch 1, 8 sc in ring, sl st to 1st sc, do not turn—8 sc.

Rnd 2: Ch 1, [sc, ch 4] in ea sc around, sl st to 1st sc, do not turn—8 sc.

Rnd 3: Ch 1, [sc, hdc, 3 dc, hdc, sc] in ea ch-4 sp around, sl st to 1st sc, fasten off color, do not turn—8 petals.

Rnd 4: Join new color to sl st, ch 1, *sc between next 2 sc on prev rnd, ch 6; rep from * around, sl st to 1st sc, do not turn—8 ch-sps.

Rnd 5: Ch 1, [sc, hdc, 5 dc, hdc, sc] in ea ch-6 sp around, sl st to 1st sc, fasten off color, do not turn—8 petals.

Rnd 6: Join new color with sl st btw 1st 2 dc on next petal, sc in same sp, *ch 5, sc btw 4th and 5th dc on petal, ch 5, sc btw 1st and 2nd dc on next petal; rep from * around to last petal, ch 5, sc btw 4th and 5th dc on last petal, ch 2, dc in 1st sc, do not turn—16 ch-sps.

Rnd 7: Ch 1, sc around post of dc, *ch 5, sc in next ch-5 sp, [ch 2, 4 dc, ch 3, 4 dc, ch 2] in next ch-5 sp, sc in next ch-5 sp, ch 5, sc in next ch-5 sp; rep from * around, sl st to 1st sc, fasten off—20 ch-sps.

Blomma Motif

This beautiful motif makes a great fabric when turned on its side into diamonds.

Ch 6, sl st to 1st ch to form a ring.

Rnd 1 (RS): Ch 4 (counts as dc, ch-1 sp), [dc, ch 1] 15 times in ring, sl st to 3rd ch in t-ch, do not turn—16 dc.

Rnd 2: Sl st in ch-1 sp, ch 2, 2 dc-cl in same ch-1 sp, ch 3, *3 dc-cl in next ch-1 sp, ch 5, [3 dc-cl in next ch-1 sp, ch 3] 3 times; rep from * around to last 3 ch-1 sps, 3 dc-cl in next ch-1 sp, ch 5, 3 dc-cl in next ch-1 sp, ch 3, 3 dc-cl in next ch-1 sp, ch 1, hdc in top of 2 dc-cl, do not turn—16 dc-cl.

Rnd 3: Ch 1, sc around post of hdc, *ch 5, sc in next ch-3 sp, [5 dc, ch 5, 5 dc] in next ch-5 sp, sc in next ch-3 sp, ch 5, sc in next ch-3 sp; rep from * around, sl st to 1st sc, fasten off—12 ch-sps.

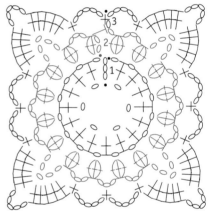

Calendula Motif

This fun motif mimics a sunflower with clusters that are turned on their sides to encircle the center.

Ch 7, sl st to 1st ch to form a ring.

Rnd 1 (RS): Ch 1, 12 sc in ring, sl st to 1st sc, do not turn—12 sc.

Rnd 2: Ch 2, dc in next sc, ch 3 (counts as dc2tog), *dc2tog in same sc and next sc, ch 3; rep from * 9 times, dc2tog in same sc and next sc, ch 1, hdc in top of 1st dc, do not turn—12 dc2tog.

Rnd 3: Ch 5 (counts as hdc), 2dc-cl in 3rd ch from hk, *hdc in next ch-3 sp, ch 3, 2dc-cl in 3rd ch from hk; rep from * around, sl st to 2nd ch of t-ch, do not turn—12 dc-cl.

Rnd 4: Ch 6 (counts as hdc, ch-4 sp), *hdc in next hdc, ch 4; rep from * around, sl st to 2nd ch of t-ch, do not turn—12 hdc.

Rnd 5: Sl st to ch-4 sp, ch 3 (counts as dc), [4 dc, ch 5, 5 dc] in same ch-4 sp, *sc in next ch-4 sp, ch 5, sc in next ch-4 sp, [5 dc, ch 5, 5 dc] in next ch-4 sp; rep from * twice, sc in next ch-4 sp, ch 5, sc in next ch-4 sp, sl st to t-ch, fasten off.

Glass Lace Motif

The Y-stitches in this motif bring it to life in the voids they leave behind, almost like the lead in stained glass.

Y-Stitch (y-st): Dtr in next sc, ch 3, dc in center of post of the same dtr.

Ch 10, sl st to 1st ch to form a ring.

Rnd 1 (RS): Ch 1, sc in ring 24 times, sl st to 1st sc, do not turn—24 sc.

Rnd 2: Ch 6, *[sk next sc, y-st in next sc] twice, sk next sc, dtr in next sc, ch 5, dc in center of post of prev dtr; rep from * twice, [sk next sc, y-st in next sc] twice, dc in 3rd ch of t-ch, ch 2, dc in 6th ch of t-ch, do not turn—12 ch-sps.

Rnd 3: Ch 5 (counts as tr, ch-1 sp), [dc, ch 1, hdc, sc] around post of dc, *[sc, hdc, (ch 1, dc) twice, ch 1, hdc, sc] in next 2 ch-3 sps, [sc, hdc, ch 1, dc, (ch 1, tr) twice, ch 1, dc, ch 1, hdc, sc] in next ch-5 sp; rep from * twice, [sc, hdc, (ch 1, dc) twice, ch 1, hdc, sc] in next 2 ch-3 sps, [sc, hdc, ch 1, dc, ch 1, tr, ch 1] in ch-2 sp, sl st to 4th ch of t-ch, fasten off.

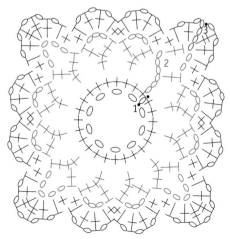

Rouz Motif

A large flower blooms out of the center of this granny square, and the color changes highlight the dramatic bloom.

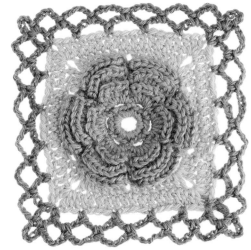

Ch 10, sl st to 1st ch to form a ring.

Rnd 1 (RS): Ch 1, 18 sc in ring, sl st to 1st sc, do not turn—18 sc.

Rnd 2: Ch 1, *sc in next sc, ch 3, sk 2 sc; rep from * around, sl st to 1st sc, do not turn—6 ch-sps.

Rnd 3: [Sc, ch 2, 5 dc, ch 2, sc] in ea ch-3 sp around, sl st to 1st sc, do not turn—6 petals.

Rnd 4: Ch 1, *sc btw 2 sc, ch 5, sk petal; rep from * around, sl st to 1st sc, do not turn—6 ch-sps.

Rnd 5: [Sc, ch 2, 7 dc, ch 2, sc] in ea ch-5 sp around, sl st to 1st sc, do not turn—6 petals.

Rnd 6: Ch 1, *sc btw 2 sc, ch 6, sk petal; rep from * around, sl st to 1st sc, do not turn—6 ch-sps.

Rnd 7: [Sc, ch 2, 9 dc, ch 2, sc] in ea ch-6 sp around, sl st to 1st sc, do not turn—6 petals.

Rnd 8: Ch 1, *sc btw 2 sc, ch 8, sk petal; rep from * around, sl st to 1st sc, fasten off, do not turn—6 ch-sps.

Rnd 9: Join new color to ch-8 sp with sl st, ch 3 (counts as dc), [7 dc, ch 2, 4 dc] in next ch-8 sp, 7 dc in next ch-8 sp, [4 dc, ch 2, 8 dc] in next ch-8 sp, [7 dc, ch 2, 4 dc] in next ch-8 sp, 7 dc in next ch-8 sp, [4 dc, ch 2, 7 dc] in next ch-8 sp, sl st to top of t-ch, do not turn—60 dc.

Rnd 10: Ch 3 (counts as dc), *dc in ea dc to ch-2 sp, [2 dc, ch 2, 2 dc] in next ch-2 sp; rep from * around to last ch-sp, dc in ea dc to end, sl st to top of t-ch, fasten off, do not turn—76 dc.

Rnd 11: Join new color with sl st to next dc, *sc in next dc, ch 5, sk 3 dc, sc in next dc, ch 5, [sc, ch 5, sc] in ch-2 sp, [ch 5, sk 3 dc, sc in next dc] twice, ch 5; rep from * around to 1st sc, ch 2, dc in 1st sc, do not turn—24 ch-sps.

Rnd 12: Ch 1, sc around post of dc, *[ch 5, sc in next ch-5 sp] twice, ch 5, [sc, ch 5, sc] in next ch-5 sp, [ch 5, sc in next ch-5 sp] 3 times; rep from * around, sl st to 1st sc, fasten off—28 ch-sps.

Carnation Lace Motif

The allure of this motif is all in the flower. Crocheted all in one color, this sculptural flower seamlessly lies down in the background of the motif.

3 dtr-cl: *Yo 3 times, insert hk into st indicated, yo and pull up a lp, (yo and pull through 2 lps) 3 times; rep from * twice more in same st, yo and pull through remaining 4 lps on hk.

Ch 6, sl st to 1st ch to form a ring.

Rnd 1 (RS): Ch 5 (counts as dc, ch-2 sp), [dc, ch 2] 7 times in ring, sl st to 3rd ch on t-ch, do not turn—8 dc.

Rnd 2: [Sc, hdc, 3 dc, hdc, sc] in ea ch-2 sp around, sl st to 1st sc, do not turn—8 petals.

Rnd 3: Ch 1, *sc btw 2 sc on prev rnd, ch 4, sk petal; rep from * around, sl st to 1st sc, do not turn—8 ch-sps.

Rnd 4: [Sc, hdc, 5 dc, hdc, sc] in ea ch-4 sp around, sl st to 1st sc, do not turn—8 petals.

Rnd 5: Ch 1, *sc btw 2 sc on prev rnd, ch 5, sk petal; rep from * around, sl st to 1st sc, do not turn—8 ch-sps.

Rnd 6: [Sc, hdc, 7 dc, hdc, sc] in ea ch-5 sp around, sl st to 1st sc, fasten off, do not turn—8 petals.

Rnd 7: Join yarn with sl st to center dc on next petal, *ch 5, [(3 dtr-cl, ch 3) twice, 3 dtr-cl] in center dc of next petal, ch 5, sc in center dc of next petal; rep from * around, sl st to 1st sc, do not turn—16 ch-sps.

Rnd 8: Ch 3 (counts as dc), *7 dc in next ch-5 sp, 4 dc in next ch-3 sp, [2 dc, ch 3, 2 dc] in next 3 dtr-cl, 4 dc in next ch-3 sp, 7 dc in next ch-5 sp, dc in next sc; rep from * around, sl st to top of t-ch, fasten off—108 dc.

Vikna Lace Motif

This motif mimics Gothic stained glass when combined with a larger fabric.

Ch 8, sl st to 1st ch to form a ring.

Rnd 1 (RS): Ch 1, *sc in ring, ch 3, 2 tr-cl in ring, ch 3; rep from * around, sl st to 1st sc, do not turn.

Rnd 2: Ch 7 (counts as dtr, ch-2 sp), *[dc, ch 5, dc] in tr-cl, ch 2, dtr in next sc, ch 5, dc in center of prev dtr, ch 2; rep from * 3 times, [dc, ch 5, dc] in tr-cl, ch 2, dc in 3rd ch of t-ch, ch 2, dc in 5th ch of t-ch, do not turn—16 ch-sps.

Rnd 3: Ch 6 (counts as dc, ch-3 sp), *[(tr, ch 1) twice, tr, ch 3, (tr, ch 1) twice, tr] in ch-5 sp, ch 3, dc in next ch-5 sp, ch 3; rep from * to last ch-5 sp, *[(tr, ch 1) twice, tr, ch 3, (tr, ch 1) twice, tr] in last ch-5 sp, ch 3, sl st to 3rd ch of t-ch, do not turn—28 ch-sps.

Rnd 4: Ch 6 (count as dc, ch-3 sp), *dc in next tr, ch 4, [3 dc, ch 3, 3 dc] in ch-3 sp, ch 4, sk 2 tr, dc in next tr, ch 3, dc in dc; rep from * around, sl st to 3rd ch of t-ch, fasten off—20 ch-sps.

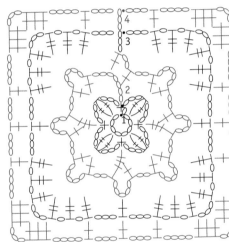

Maltese Lace Motif

The lacy fan in each corner of this motif creates a stunning, lacy design.

Picot: Ch 3, sl st to 1st ch.

Ch 6, sl st to 1st ch to form a ring.

Rnd 1 (RS): Ch 3 (counts as dc), 3 dc in ring, [ch 2, 4 dc] 3 times in ring, hdc in top of t-ch, do not turn—16 dc.

Rnd 2: Ch 3 (counts as dc), dc around post of hdc, *dc in next 2 dc, ch 7, dc in next 2 dc, [2 dc, ch 2, 2 dc] in ch-2 sp; rep from * around to last ch-2 sp, dc in next 2 dc, ch 7, dc in next 2 dc, 2 dc around post of hdc, hdc in top of t-ch, do not turn—32 dc.

Rnd 3: Ch 1, sc around post of hdc, *ch 4, 7 dc in ch-7 sp, ch 4, sc in ch-2 sp; rep from * around, sl st to 1st sc, do not turn—28 dc.

Rnd 4: Ch 1, *sc in sc, ch 6, [dc, ch 1] in next 6 dc, dc in next dc, ch 6; rep from * around to last sc, sc in last sc, ch 6, [dc, ch 1] in next 6 dc, dc in next dc, ch 3, dc in 1st sc, do not turn—28 dc.

Rnd 5: Ch 1, sc around post of dc, *ch 3, sc in next ch-6 sp, ch 3, [dc in next dc, picot, 2 dc in next ch-1 sp] 6 times, dc in next dc, picot, ch 3, sc in next ch-6 sp; rep from * around, sl st to 1st sc, fasten off—76 dc.

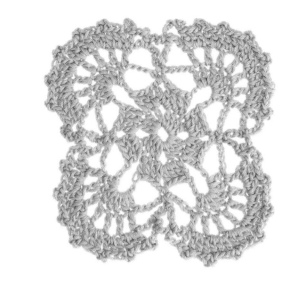

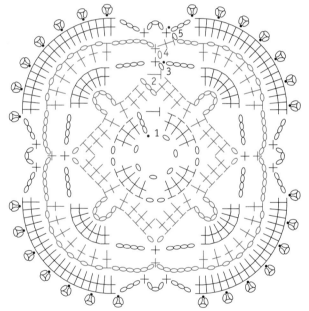

Kukka Lace Motif

The celestial design in this lacy motif makes for lovely shawls and tunics.

Ch 10, sl st to 1st ch to form a ring.

Rnd 1 (RS): Ch 3 (counts as dc), 2 dc in ring, [ch 9, 3 dc] 7 times in ring, ch 4, dtr in top of t-ch, do not turn—24 dc.

Rnd 2: Ch 1, sc around post of dtr, *ch 6, sk 1 dc, sc in next dc, ch 6, sc in ch-9 sp; rep from * around to last ch-9 sp, ch 6, sk 1 dc, sc in next dc, ch 4, hdc in 1st sc, do not turn—16 ch-sps.

Rnd 3: Ch 1, sc around post of hdc, *[ch 5, sc in next ch-6 sp] twice, ch 11, sc in next ch-6 sp, ch 5, sc in next ch-6 sp; rep from * around, sl st to 1st sc, do not turn—16 ch-sps.

Rnd 4: Sl st to ch-5 sp, ch 4 (counts as tr), 6 tr in same ch-5 sp, *ch 5, [2 dc, ch 2, 2 dc, ch 5, 2 dc, ch 2, 2 dc] in ch-11 sp, ch 5, sk ch-5 sp, 7 tr in next ch-5 sp; rep from * around, sl st to top of t-ch, do not turn—28 tr.

Rnd 5: Ch 5 (counts as tr, ch-1 sp), *[tr, ch 1] in ea tr to last tr, tr in last tr, ch 6, sk 1 ch-5 sp, [2 dc, ch 2, 2 dc, ch 5, 2 dc, ch 2, 2 dc] in next ch-5 sp, ch 6; rep from * around, sl st to 4th ch of t-ch, do not turn—44 ch-sps.

Rnd 6: Ch 1, *[sc, ch 3] in ea ch-1 sp across, ch 7, sk ch-6 sp, [2 dc, ch 2, 2 dc, ch 5, 2 dc, ch 2, 2 dc] in next ch-5 sp, ch 7; rep from * around, sl st to 1st sc, fasten off.

Sweetheart Lace Motif

This large motif has lovely lace that transforms from a circle to a square.

Ch 7, sl st to 1st ch to form a ring.

Rnd 1 (RS): Ch 4 (counts as dc, ch-1 sp), [dc, ch 1] 15 times in ring, sl st to 3rd ch of t-ch, do not turn—16 dc.

Rnd 2: Ch 1, [sc, ch 3] in ea ch-1 sp around to last ch-1 sp, sc in ch 1 sp, ch 1, hdc in 1st sc, do not turn—16 sc.

Rnd 3: Ch 1, sc around post of hdc, [ch 4, sc] in ea ch-3 sp around, ch 2, hdc in 1st sc, do not turn—16 ch-sps.

Rnd 4: Ch 1, sc around post of hdc, [ch 5, sc] in ea ch-4 sp around, ch 2, dc in 1st sc, do not turn—16 ch-sps.

Rnd 5: Ch 1, sc around post of dc, *[ch 1, dc in ch-5 sp] 8 times, ch 1, [sc in next ch-5 sp, ch 5] twice, sc in next ch-5 sp; rep from * around to last 3 ch-5 sps, [ch 1, dc in ch-5 sp] 8 times, ch 1, sc in next ch-5 sp, ch 5, sc in next ch-5 sp, ch 2, dc in 1st sc, do not turn—44 ch-sps.

Rnd 6: Ch 1, sc around post of dc, *[ch 2, dc in dc] 8 times total, ch 2, sc in next ch-5 sp, ch 5, sc in next ch-5 sp; rep from * around to last 2 ch-5 sps, [ch 2, dc in dc] 8 times total, ch 2, sc in next ch-5 sp, ch 2, dc in 1st sc, do not turn—40 ch-sps.

Rnd 7: Ch 1, sc around post of dc, *[ch 3, dc in dc] 3 times, ch 3, sk 1 ch-2 sp, [3 dc, ch 7, 3 dc] in next ch-2 sp, sk 1 ch-2 sp, [ch 3, dc in dc] 3 times, ch 3, sc in next ch-5 sp; rep from * around, sl st to 1st sc, fasten off—36 ch-sps.

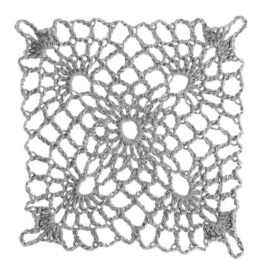

Gothic Lace Motif

You can transform this exquisite design into an amazing fabric when you connect motifs at the corner chain spaces.

Ch 4, sl st to 1st ch to form a ring.

Rnd 1 (RS): Ch 1, [sc, ch 3, tr, ch 3] into ring 4 times, sl st to 1st sc, do not turn—4 tr.

Rnd 2: Ch 7 (counts as dc and ch-4 sp), [sc in next tr, ch 4, dc in next sc, ch 4] 3 times, sc in last tr, ch 4, sl st to 3rd ch of t-ch, do not turn—8 ch-4 sps.

Rnd 3: Ch 3 (counts as dc), dc in same ch as sl st, *sc in next ch-4 sp, ch 1, [2 tr, ch 2, 2 tr] in next sc, ch 1, sc in next ch-4 sp, 3 dc in next dc; rep from * around to last dc, sc in next ch-4 sp, ch 1, [2 tr, ch 2, 2 tr] in next sc, ch 1, sc in next ch-4 sp, dc 3rd ch of t-ch on prev rnd, sl st to top of t-ch, do not turn—12 ch-sps.

Rnd 4: Ch 1, sc in t-ch, *sc in next dc, sc in next sc, sc in next ch-1 sp, sc in next 2 tr, 3 sc in next ch-2 sp, sc in next 2 tr, sc in next ch-1 sp, sc in next sc, sc in next 2 dc; rep from * around, sl st to 1st sc, do not turn—56 sc.

Rnd 5: Ch 5 (counts as dc, ch-2 sp), sk 1 sc, *dc in next sc, ch 2, sk 1 sc, hdc in next sc, ch 2, hdc in next sc, ch 1, sk 1 sc, sc in next sc, ch 1, sk 1 sc, hdc in next sc, ch 2, hdc in next sc, [sk 1 sc, ch 2, dc in next sc] twice, sk 1 sc, ch 2; rep from * around, sl st to 3rd ch of turning ch, do not turn—32 ch-sps.

Rnd 6: Ch 1, [sc, ch 5, sc, ch 7, sc, ch 5, sc] in 3rd ch of t-ch (trefoil made), *[2 sc in next ch-2 sp] twice, ch 3, 2 sc in next ch-2 sp, sc in next ch-1 sp, sc in next sc, sc in next ch-1 sp, 2 sc in next ch-2 sp, ch 3, [2 sc in next ch-2 sp] twice, [sc, ch 5, sc, ch 7, sc, ch 5, sc] in next dc; rep from * around, sl st in 1st sc, fasten off.

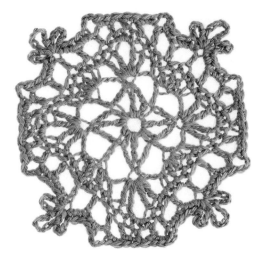

Sachem Blossom Motif

The picots in this motif draw the eye to the blossom in the center. When combined, the chain spaces on the last round look like railroad ties.

Picot: Ch 3, sl st to 1st ch.

Ch 10, sl st to 1st ch to form a ring.

Rnd 1 (RS): Ch 1, sc 24 times in ring, sl st to 1st sc, do not turn—24 sc.

Rnd 2: Ch 2, 2 dc-cl in 1st sc, *[ch 3, sk 1 sc, 3 dc-cl in next sc] twice, ch 5, sk 1 sc, 3 dc-cl in next sc; rep from * twice more, [ch 3, sk 1 sc, 3 dc-cl in next sc] twice, ch 2, dc in top of 2 dc-cl, do not turn—12 dc-cl.

Rnd 3: Ch 5 (counts as tr, ch-sp), [tr, picot, tr, ch 1, tr, picot, tr] around post of dc, *ch 2, sk 1 dc-cl, sc in next dc-cl, ch 2, [(tr, picot, tr, ch 1) 4 times, tr, picot, tr] in next ch-5 sp; rep from * twice, ch 2, sk 1 dc-cl, sc in next dc-cl, ch 2, [(tr, picot, tr, ch 1) twice, tr, picot] in next ch-2 sp, sl st to 4th ch of t-ch, do not turn—40 tr.

Rnd 4: Ch 1, sc in next ch, ch 5, sk (tr, picot, tr), sc in next ch-1 sp, *ch 5, sk (tr, picot, tr), dc2tog in next 2 ch-2 sps, [ch 5, sk (tr, picot, tr), sc in next ch-1 sp] 4 times; rep from * twice, ch 5, sk (tr, picot, tr), dc2tog in next 2 ch-2 sps, [ch 5, sk (tr, picot, tr) sc in next ch-1 sp] twice, ch 2, dc in 1st sc, do not turn—20 ch-sps.

Rnd 5: Ch 1, 3 sc around post of dc, [3 sc, ch 3, 3 sc] in ea ch-5 sp around, 3 sc in last ch-sp, ch 3, sl st in 1st sc, do not turn—120 sc.

Diamond Lasa Motif

Depending on your yarn choice, the fan- or X-shapes that the voids make will dominate the motif, and both will result in a unique design.

Make an adjustable ring.

Rnd 1 (RS): Ch 3 (counts as dc), 15 dc in ring, sl st to top of t-ch, do not turn, pull ring closed—16 dc.

Rnd 2: Ch 1, sc in top of t-ch, sc in next 3 dc, *ch 3, sc in next 4 dc; rep from * around, ch 1, hdc to 1st sc, do not turn—16 sc.

Rnd 3: Ch 5 (counts as dc, ch-2 sp), 2 dc around post of hdc, *ch 4, sk next sc, sc in next 2 sc, ch 4, sk next sc, [2 dc, ch 2, 2 dc] in next ch-3 sp; rep from * around to last ch-3 sp, ch 4, sk next sc, sc in next 2 sc, ch 4, sk next sc, dc in ch-1 sp, sl st to 3rd ch of t-ch, do not turn—8 sc.

Rnd 4: Ch 5 (counts as dc, ch-2 sp), 2 dc in ch-2 sp, *ch 3, sc in ch-4 sp, ch 5, sc in next ch-4 sp, ch 3, [2 dc, ch 2, 2 dc] in next ch-2 sp; rep from * twice, ch 3, sc in ch-4 sp, ch 5, sc in next ch-4 sp, ch 3, dc in ch-2 sp, sl st to 3rd ch of t-ch, do not turn—8 sc.

Rnd 5: Ch 5 (counts as dc, ch-2 sp), 2 dc in ch-2 sp, *ch 3, 11 dc in ch-5 sp, ch 3, [2 dc, ch 2, 2 dc] in next ch-2 sp; rep from * twice, ch 3, 11 dc in ch-5 sp, ch 3, dc in ch-2 sp, sl st to 3rd ch of t-ch, do not turn—60 dc.

Rnd 6: Ch 5 (counts as dc, ch-2 sp), 2 dc in ch-2 sp, *ch 3, [hdc, ch 1] in next dc and ea dc across to last dc, hdc in last dc, ch 3, [2 dc, ch 2, 2 dc] in next ch-2 sp; rep from * twice, ch 3, [hdc, ch 1] in next dc and ea dc across to last dc, hdc in last dc, ch 3, dc in ch-2 sp, sl st to 3rd ch of t-ch, do not turn—44 hdc.

Rnd 7: Ch 8 (counts as dc, ch-5 sp), 2 dc in ch-2 sp, *ch 4, [sc in next 2 ch-1 sps, ch 3] 4 times, sc in next 2 ch-1 sps, ch 4, [2 dc, ch 5, 2 dc] in next ch-2 sp; rep from * twice, ch 4, [sc in next 2 ch-1 sps, ch 3] 4 times, sc in next 2 ch-1 sps, ch 4, dc in ch-2 sp, sl st to 3rd ch of t-ch, fasten off—40 sc.

CHAPTER 8

Flower, Snowflake, and Joining Motifs

Kaihua Motif

This simple little flower makes a great appliqué around the neckline of a girl's top.

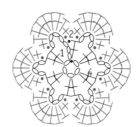

Ch 5, sl st to 1st ch to form a ring.

Rnd 1 (RS): Ch 7 (counts as dc, ch-4 sp), [2 dc in ring, ch 4] 5 times, dc in ring, sl st in 3rd ch of t-ch, do not turn—12 dc.

Rnd 2: [Sl st, sc, hdc, 5 dc, hdc, sc, sl st] in ea ch-sp around, fasten off—30 dc.

Daun Motif

The small flower makes for a great motif to fill in spaces between larger flower motifs.

Ch 5, sl st to 1st ch to form a ring.

Rnd 1 (RS): Ch 1, [sc, ch 7, sc] 4 times in ring, sl st to 1st sc, do not turn—8 sc.

Rnd 2: [Sc, 4 dc, ch 3, 4 dc, sc] in ea ch-sp around, sl st to 1st sc, fasten off—32 dc.

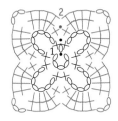

Bloei Motif

Classically simple in design, this motif makes a great accessory (scarf or headband) when combining multiple motifs together.

Ch 5, sl st to 1st ch to form a ring.

Rnd 1 (RS): Ch 3 (counts as 1st dc), 2 dc in ring, [ch 5, 3 dc] 4 times in ring, ch 5, sl st to top of t-ch, do not turn—15 dc.

Rnd 2: Ch 3 (counts as dc), [(dc, ch 1) 6 times, dc] in next 4 ch-5 sps, [(dc, ch 1) 6 times] in last ch-5 sp; sl st to top of t-ch, do not turn—35 dc.

Rnd 3: Ch 1, *[sc, ch 3] in next 5 ch-1 sps, sc in next ch-1 sp; rep from * around, sl st to 1st sc, fasten off—30 sc.

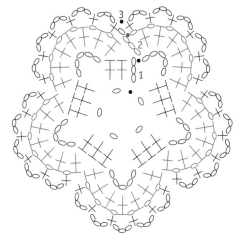

Nashi Motif

When made in thread and stiffened, this motif can be a fun earring.

Ch 8, sl st to 1st ch to form a ring.

Rnd 1 (RS): Ch 1, 16 sc in ring, sl st to 1st sc, do not turn.

Rnd 2: Ch 7 (counts as dc, ch-4 sp), *sk 1 sc, dc in next sc, ch 4; rep from * around, sl st to 3rd ch of t-ch, do not turn—8 dc.

Rnd 3: Ch 1, [sc, hdc, 2 dc, ch 3, 2 dc, hdc, sc] in ea ch-sp around, sl st to 1st sc, fasten off—32 dc.

Flor de Nieve Motif

The voids made by the chain spaces create a visible cross that you can use as a design feature when you combine them all together.

Trefoil: Ch 4, sl st in 4th ch, ch 6, sl st in 6th ch, ch 4, sl st in 4th ch.

Picot: Ch 4, sl st in 4th ch.

Make an adjustable ring.

Rnd 1 (RS): Ch 4 (counts as dc, ch 1), [(3 dc, trefoil, 3 dc, ch 1) 3 times, 3 dc, trefoil, 2 dc] in ring, sl st to 3rd ch of t-ch, pull adjustable ring closed, do not turn.

Rnd 2: Ch 3 (counts as dc), dc in ch-1 sp, *picot, ch 5, sc in ch-6 sp, ch 5, picot, 3 dc in ch-1 sp; rep from * around to last ch-1 sp, picot, ch 5, sc in next ch-6 sp, ch 5, picot, dc in last ch-1 sp, sl st to top of t-ch, fasten off.

Tusculum Motif

The back and forth of lace and solid rounds makes this flower great in a larger lace or solid project.

Ch 10, sl st to 1st ch to form a ring.

Rnd 1 (RS): Ch 3 (counts as dc), 23 dc in ring, sl st to top of t-ch, do not turn—24 dc.

Rnd 2: Ch 1, sc in top of t-ch, *ch 2, sk next dc, sc in next dc, ch 3, sk next dc, sc in next dc; rep from * around to last 3 dc, ch 2, sk next dc, sc in next dc, ch 1, hdc in 1st sc (counts as ch-3 sp), do not turn—12 ch-sps.

Rnd 3: Ch 4 (counts as dc, ch-1 sp), 3 dc around post of hdc, *sc in next ch-2 sp, [3 dc, ch 1, 3 dc] in next ch-3 sp; rep from * around, sc in last ch-2 sp, 2 dc in 1st ch-sp, sl st to 3rd ch of t-ch, do not turn—6 sc.

Rnd 4: Ch 1, *sc in ch-1 sp, ch 4, sk next dc, sc in next dc, ch 5, sk next [dc, sc, dc], sc in next dc, ch 4; rep from * around, sl st to 1st sc, fasten off—18 ch-sps.

Fuji Motif

The chain spaces on the last round make a perfect place to connect larger motifs together, while filling the fabric with adorable little flowers.

Ch 4, sl st to 1st ch to form a ring.

Rnd 1 (RS): Ch 1, [sc, ch 4, sc, ch 3] 4 times in ring, sl st to 1st sc, do not turn—8 ch-sps.

Rnd 2: Ch 1, *[sc, hdc, 2 dc, ch 3, 2 dc, hdc, sc] in next ch-4 sp, [sc, ch 5, hdc, ch 5, sc] in next ch-3 sp; rep from * around, sl st to 1st sc, fasten off—12 ch-sps.

Daisy Leaf Motif

This leafy motif can make a great base for a sculptural flower, or when combining motifs together, makes a great tablecloth fabric.

Ch 7, sl st to 1st ch to form a ring.

Rnd 1 (RS): Ch 2, 2 dc-cl in ring, ch 3, *3 dc-cl in ring, ch 5, 3 dc-cl in ring, ch 3; rep from * twice, 3 dc-cl in ring, ch 2, dc in top of 2 dc-cl, do not turn—seven 3 dc-cl.

Rnd 2: Ch 3, 2 tr-cl around post of prev rnd's dc, ch 4, 3 dc-cl around post of dc, ch 3, *sc in next ch-3 sp, ch 3, [3 dc-cl, ch 4, 3 tr-cl, ch 4, 3 dc-cl] in next ch-5 sp, ch 3; rep from * around, sc in last ch-3 sp, ch 3, 3 dc-cl in ch-2 sp, ch 4, sl st to top of 2 tr-cl, do not turn—eight 3 dc-cl.

Rnd 3: Ch 3 (counts as dc), *[dc, 3 hdc] in next ch-4 sp, 2 sc in next ch-3 sp, sl st to sc, 2 sc in next ch-3 sp, [3 hdc, dc] in next ch-4 sp, dc in 3 tr-cl; rep from * around, sl st to top of t-ch, do not turn—12 dc.

Rnd 4: [Sc, ch 3, sc, ch 5, sc, ch 3, sc] in top of t-ch, *ch 2, sc in next dc, [ch 2, sc in next hdc] 3 times, ch 2, sl st in next 2 sc, sk sl st, sl st in next 2 sc, [ch 2, sc in next hdc] 3 times, ch 2, sc in next dc, ch 2, [sc, ch 3, sc, ch 5, sc, ch 3, sc] in next dc; rep from * around, sl st to 1st sc, fasten off.

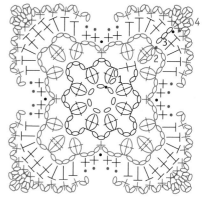

Windroos Motif

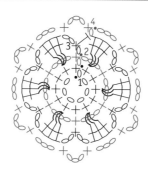

By slightly changing where you crochet the double crochet stitches on round 3, you can create a textured flower.

Ch 6, sl st to 1st ch to form a ring.

Rnd 1 (RS): Ch 1, 12 sc in ring, sl st to 1st sc, do not turn.

Rnd 2: Ch 1, *sc in next sc, ch 3, sk next sc; rep from * around, sl st to 1st sc, do not turn—6 sc.

Rnd 3: Ch 1, [sc in next sc, ch 2, 3 dc in next sc on rnd 1 behind ch-3 sp (push ch forward and work behind ch), ch 2] 5 times, sc in next sc, ch 2, 3 dc in next sc on rnd 1 behind ch-3 sp, hdc in 1st sc, do not turn—18 dc.

Rnd 4: Ch 1, sc around hdc post, *ch 3, sc in next ch-2 sp; rep from * around, ch 3, sl st to 1st sc, fasten off—12 ch-3 sps.

Tea Rose Motif

The three-dimensional nature of this motif is stunning on its own as a broach or ring.

Picot: Ch 3, sl st to 1st ch.

Ch 10, sl st to 1st ch to form a ring.

Rnd 1 (RS): Ch 1, 24 sc in ring, sl st to 1st sc, do not turn.

Rnd 2: Ch 1, *sc in next sc, ch 3, sk 2 sc; rep from * around, sl st to 1st sc, do not turn—8 ch-3 sps.

Rnd 3: [Sc, ch 2, 4 dc, ch 2, sc] in ea ch-3 sp around, sl st to 1st sc, do not turn—8 petals.

Rnd 4: Ch 1, *sc btw next 2 sc, ch 5; rep from * around, sl st to 1st sc, do not turn—8 ch-5 sps.

Rnd 5: [Sc, ch 2, 6 dc, ch 2, sc] in ea ch-5 sp around, sl st to 1st sc, do not turn—8 petals.

Rnd 6: Ch 1, *sc btw next 2 sc, ch 7; rep from * around, sl st to 1st sc, do not turn—8 ch-7 sps.

Rnd 7: [Sc, ch 2, 8 dc, ch 2, sc] in ea ch-7 sp around, sl st to 1st sc, do not turn—8 petals.

Rnd 8: Ch 1, *sc btw next 2 sc, ch 9; rep from * around, sl st to 1st sc, do not turn—8 ch-9 sps.

Rnd 9: [Sc, ch 2, (dc, picot) 5 times, dc, ch 2, sc] in ea ch-9 sp around, sl st to 1st sc, fasten off—8 petals.

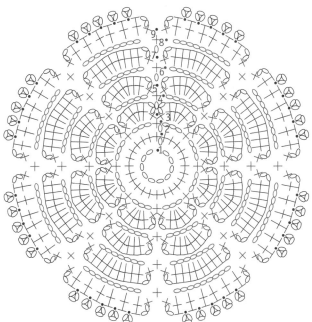

Tulipe Motif

Contrasting colors highlight the sculptural nature of this motif.

Ch 8, sl st to 1st ch to form a ring.

Rnd 1 (RS): Ch 3 (counts as dc), 23 dc in ring, sl st to top of t-ch, do not turn—24 dc.

Rnd 2: Ch 1, sc in top of t-ch, *ch 3, sk 1 dc, sc in next dc; rep from * around to last 2 dc, ch 1, hdc in 1st sc (counts as ch-3 sp), do not turn—12 ch-3 sps.

Rnd 3: Ch 1, sc around post of hdc, *7 dc in next ch-3 sp, sc in next ch-3 sp; rep from * around to last ch-3 sp, 7 dc in last ch-3 sp, sl st to 1st sc, fasten off—6 petals.

Rnd 4: Join new color to next sc on rnd 2, sc in same sc, *ch 5, sc in next sc on rnd 2 (push rnd 3 forward and work behind rnd), ch 3, sc in next sc on rnd 2; rep from * around to last 2 sc, ch 5, sc in next sc on rnd 2, ch 1, hdc in 1st sc, do not turn—12 sc.

Rnd 5: Ch 1, sc around post of hdc, *[6 dc, ch 2, 6 dc] in next ch-5 sp, sc in next ch-3 sp; rep from * around to last ch-3 sp, [6 dc, ch 2, 6 dc] in last ch-5 sp, sl st to 1st sc, fasten off—6 petals.

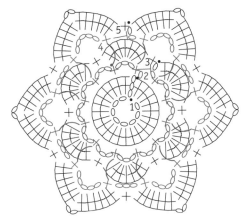

Amaryllis Motif

These simple flowers make great decorations to add to kids' projects.

Picot: Ch 4, sl st to 1st ch.

Ch 8, sl st to 1st ch to form a ring.

Rnd 1 (RS): Ch 3 (counts as dc), 17 dc in ring, sl st to top of t-ch, do not turn, fasten off color—18 dc.

Rnd 2: Join new color, *ch 6, 3 tr in next dc, picot, 3 tr in next dc, ch 6, sl st in next dc; rep from * around, sl st to top of t-ch, fasten off—36 tr.

Toets Motif

You can combine these realistic flowers for a brilliant purse or ottoman.

Popcorn (pop): 5 dc in st indicated, remove hk, insert hk into 1st dc, place free lp on hk and pull through dc.

Beginning Popcorn (beg pop): 4 dc in st indicated, remove hk, insert hk into 1st dc, place free lp on hk and pull through dc.

Make an adjustable ring.

Rnd 1 (RS): Ch 1, 6 sc in ring, pull ring closed, do not turn.

Rnd 2: Ch 3, beg pop in 1st sc, [ch 3, pop in next sc] 5 times, ch 3, sl st to beg pop, fasten off—6 pop.

Rnd 3: Join new color to beg pop, [sc, hdc, 3 dc, hdc, sc] in ea ch-3 sp around, sl st to 1st sc, do not turn—6 petals.

Rnd 4: Ch 1, sc in same st, ch 5, *sc btw next 2 sc, ch 5; rep from * around, sl st to 1st sc, fasten off—6 ch-5 sps.

Rnd 5: Join new color, [sc, hdc, 5 dc, hdc, sc] in ea ch-5 sp around, sl st to 1st sc, fasten off—6 petals.

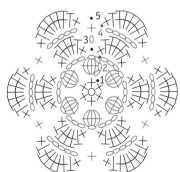

Protea Motif

The simple chain spaces create a unique texture that mimics sunflowers.

Ch 5, sl st to 1st ch to form a ring.

Rnd 1 (RS): Ch 1, [sc, ch 5] 7 times in ring, sc in ring, ch 2, dc in 1st sc, do not turn—8 sc.

Rnd 2: Ch 1, sc around post of dc, *ch 5, sc in next sc, ch 5, sc in next ch-5 sp; rep from * around to last ch-5 sp, ch 5, sc in next sc, ch 5, sl st to 1st sc, do not turn—16 ch-5 sps.

Rnd 3: Ch 7 (counts as hdc, ch-5 sp), *sk next 2 ch-5 sps, hdc in next sc, ch 5; rep from * around, sl st to 2nd ch of t-ch, do not turn—8 hdc.

Rnd 4: Ch 1, sc in t-ch, *[(ch 4, sc) 4 times, ch 4] in ch-5 sp, sc in next hdc; rep from * around, sl st to 1st sc, do not turn—40 ch-4 sps.

Rnd 5: Ch 1, sc in 1st sc, *ch 6, sk 5 ch-4 sps, sc in next sc (push ch-sps forward, sc behind them); rep from * around to last 5 sc, ch 6, sl st to 1st sc, do not turn—8 ch-6 sps.

Rnd 6: Ch 1, sc in 1st sc, *[(ch 5, sc) 5 times, ch 5] in ch-6 sp, sc in next sc; rep from * around, sl st to 1st sc, do not turn, fasten off—48 ch-5 sps.

Rnd 7: Join new color, ch 1, sc in 1st sc, *ch 7, sk 6 ch-5 sps, sc in next sc (push ch-sps forward, sc behind them); rep from * around to last 6 sc, ch 7, sl st to 1st sc, do not turn—8 ch-7 sps.

Rnd 8: Ch 1, [sc, hdc, 2 dc, 5 tr, 2 dc, hdc, sc] in ea ch-7 sp around, sl st to 1st sc, fasten off—8 petals.

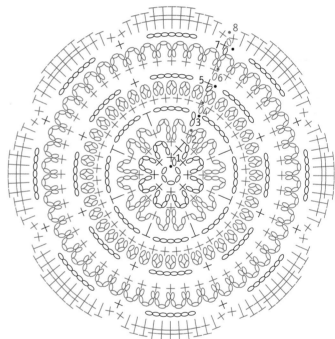

Gallica Motif

The popcorns burst from this motif to make eye-catching flowers that you can use as fun dish scrubbies.

Popcorn (pop): 5 dc in st indicated, remove hk, insert hk into 1st dc, place free lp on hk and pull through dc.

Beginning Popcorn (beg pop): 4 dc in st indicated, remove hk, insert hk into 1st dc, place free lp on hk and pull through dc.

Make an adjustable ring.

Rnd 1 (RS): Ch 1, 6 sc in ring, pull ring closed, do not turn.

Rnd 2: Ch 3, beg pop in 1st sc, [ch 3, pop in next sc] 5 times, ch 3, sl st to beg pop, do not turn—6 pop.

Rnd 3: Ch 3, beg pop in prev ch-sp, [(ch 3, pop) twice] in ea ch-3 sp around to last ch-sp, ch 3, pop in last ch-sp, ch 3, sl st in beg pop, do not turn—12 pop.

Rnd 4: Ch 3, beg pop in prev ch-sp, [(ch 3, pop) twice] in ea ch-3 sp around to last ch-sp, ch 3, pop in last ch-sp, ch 1, hdc in beg pop, do not turn—24 pop.

Rnd 5: Ch 3 (counts as dc), [dc, hdc, sc] around post of hdc, [sc, hdc, 3 dc, hdc, sc] in ea ch-3 sp around, [sc, hdc, dc] in 1st ch-1 sp, sl st to top of t-ch, fasten off.

Carnation

Bursting with joy, this flower looks equally lovely in a large bouquet or as a simple cummerbund.

Ch 32.

Row 1 (RS): Sc in 2nd ch from hk, [ch 4, sk 2 ch, sc in next ch] 6 times, *ch 3, sk 1 ch, sc in next ch; rep from * to end, turn—12 ch-sps.

Row 2: Ch 1, [sc, ch 2, 4 hdc, ch 2, sc] in ea ch-3 sp, [sc, ch 3, 6 dc, ch 3, sc] in ea ch-4 sp across, turn.

Row 3: *Sl st in sc, ch 6, sc btw 3rd and 4th dc, ch 3, sl st in same sc, ch 6, sl st in next sc; rep from * in over all large petals, **sl st in next sc, ch 4, sc btw 2nd and 3rd hdc, ch 3, sl st in same sc, ch 4, sl st in next sc; rep from ** over all small petals, fasten off with long tail.

Twist the flower into a rose by wrapping the large petals around the smaller petals, and securing them in the center.

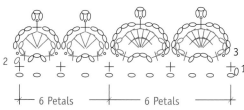

Chrysanthemum

Mums are one of the most unique flowers. The mums in this pattern work best with stiff acrylic or single-pile wool to let the petals curl. If your petals do not curl enough, try dropping down a few hook sizes before changing your yarn choice.

Make an adjustable ring.

Rnd 1 (RS): Ch 2 (counts as hdc), 11 hdc in ring, pull ring closed, sl st to t-ch, do not turn—12 hdc.

Rnd 2: *Ch 6, hdc in 3rd ch from hk and ea ch across (petal formed), sl st blp in next hdc; rep from * around, do not turn—12 large petals.

Rnd 3: Sl st flp to t-ch on rnd 1, *ch 4, sc in 2nd ch from hk and ea ch across (petal formed), sl st flp in next hdc on rnd 1; rep from * around, fasten off—12 small petals.

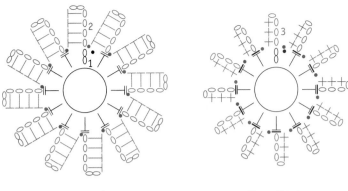

Outer Petals   Inner Petals

Spiral Motif

Crocheted one petal at a time, the motif spirals around itself into a Ferris wheel of a flower.

Ch 8, sl st to 1st ch to form a ring.

Rnd 1 (RS): Ch 1, 16 sc in ring, sl st to 1st sc, do not turn.

Petal 1: Ch 15, sl st in next sc, ch 3 (counts as dc), turn to work in ch-sp, 5 dc in ch-15 sp, ch 3 (counts as dc), sl st in 4th ch from rnd 1, sl st in next 5 ch, ch 3 (counts as dc); turn to work in ch-sp from the opp direction, 8 dc in ch-15 sp (around sl sts), sl st to top of ch 3, do not turn—16 dc.

Petal 2: Ch 9, sk next sc on rnd 1, sl st in next sc on rnd 1, ch 3 (counts as dc), turn to work in ch-sp, 5 dc in ch-9 sp, ch 3 (counts as dc), sl st in 4th ch from rnd 1, sl st in next 5 ch, ch 3 (counts as dc), turn, 8 dc in ch-9 sp, sl st to top of ch 3, do not turn—16 dc.

Petals 3–8: Rep petal 2, sl st to petal 1, fasten off.

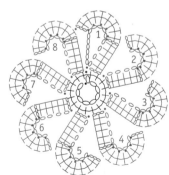

Anjer Motif

When left unblocked, this flower curls into a pretty daisy.

Ch 5, sl st to 1st ch to form a ring.

Rnd 1 (RS): Ch 1, [sc in ring, ch 6] 6 times, sl st to 1st sc, do not turn—6 sc.

Rnd 2: [Sc, hdc, 5 dc, hdc, sc] in ea ch-6 sp around, do not turn—6 petals.

Rnd 3: *Sl st to next sc, sc in next hdc, ch 1, hdc in next dc, [ch 1, dc in next dc] 3 times, ch 1, hdc in next dc, ch 1, sc in next hdc, sl st in next sc; rep from * around, do not turn—6 petals.

Rnd 4: *Sl st to next sc, sc in next ch-1 sp, [sc, ch 3, sl st] in next 4 ch-1 sps, sc in next ch-1 sp, sl st to next sc; rep from * around, fasten off—24 ch-sps.

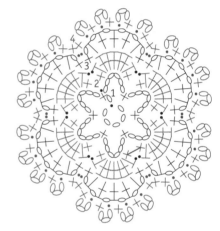

Nelke Motif

This can be both a flower motif and a tiny doily. Stretch out and stiffen for a snowflake, or crochet tightly with a thick yarn to let the yarn curl the petals.

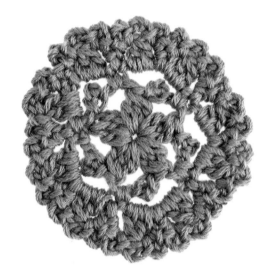

Picot: Ch 3, sl st to 1st ch.

Ch 4, sl st to 1st ch to form a ring.

Rnd 1 (RS): Ch 2, 2 dc-cl in ring, [ch 3, picot, 3 dc-cl in ring] 4 times, ch 3, picot, sl st to dc-cl, do not turn—5 dc-cl.

Rnd 2: Sl st in ch-3 sp, ch 1, sc in same ch-3 sp, *ch 5, sc in next ch-5 sp; rep from * to last ch-5 sp, ch 2, dc in 1st sc, do not turn—5 ch-sps.

Rnd 3: Sl st around post of dc, ch 2, 2 dc-cl around post of dc, ch 2, sl st to next sc, *[ch 2, 2 dc-cl, ch 2, sl st, ch 2, 2 dc-cl, ch 2] in next ch-5 sp, sl st in next sc; rep from * around, ch 2, 2 dc-cl in 1st ch-2 sp, hdc in 1st sl st, do not turn—10 dc-cl.

Rnd 4: Ch 3, sl st to hdc, *sl st to next ch-2 sp, ch 3, [sl st, ch 3, sl st] in next dc-cl, ch 3, sl st to next ch-2 sp; rep from * around to last ch-2 sp, sl st to last ch-2 sp, ch 3, [sl st, ch 3, sl st] in next dc-cl, fasten off—30 ch-3 sps.

Victoria Motif

Easy repeating rounds make this doily burst from your hook with lightning speed.

Picot: Ch 3, sl st to 1st sc.

Ch 12, sl st to 1st ch to form a ring.

Rnd 1 (RS): Ch 3 (counts as dc), 39 dc in ring, sl st to top of t-ch, do not turn—40 dc.

Rnd 2: Ch 3 (counts as dc), dc in next dc, *ch 3, dc in next 4 dc; rep from * around to last 2 dc, ch 3, dc in next 2 dc, sl st to top of t-ch, do not turn—10 ch-3 sps.

Rnd 3: Ch 3 (counts as dc), dc in next dc, *ch 4, dc in next 4 dc; rep from * around to last 2 dc, ch 4, dc in next 2 dc, sl st to top of t-ch, do not turn—10 ch-4 sps.

Rnd 4: Ch 3 (counts as dc), dc in next dc, *ch 5, dc in next 4 dc; rep from * around to last 2 dc, ch 5, dc in next 2 dc, sl st to top of t-ch, do not turn—10 ch-5 sps.

Rnd 5: Ch 3 (counts as dc), dc in next dc, *ch 7, dc in next 4 dc; rep from * around to last 2 dc, ch 7, dc in next 2 dc, sl st to top of t-ch, do not turn—10 ch-7 sps.

Rnd 6: Ch 1, sc in top of t-ch, *[2 dc, (picot, 3 dc) twice, picot, 2 dc] in next ch-7 sp, sk next dc, sc in next 2 dc; rep from * around, sl st to 1st sc, fasten off—30 picots.

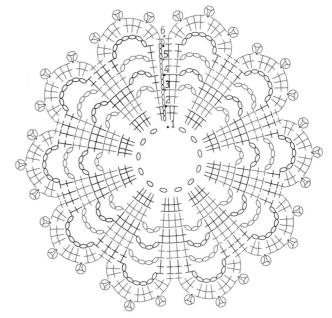

TIP

Doily Ideas

Ever fall in love with a doily, but think, "what will I do with it after I am done?" Sure, you can use it as a centerpiece on the dining room table, but do you really want it to get dirty, even by accident? Here are some ways I have used my doily love around the house: made them with bulky yarn and a big hook for a cozy afghan; dipped them in stiffening solution and laid them on top of a plastic bowl to dry (making a doily bowl, great for collecting keys); spray mounted them onto fabric and framed them for funky artwork; appliquéd them on to kids' clothes and afghans; used tiny sewing thread to make beautiful earrings; and even encased them in plastic to make spill-proof coasters. Never let your doily love go to waste; there are always ways to show off crochet in any style house.

Letitia Motif

The tiny groups of chains on the final round of the doily make it ruffle ever so slightly for a feminine look.

Ch 10, sl st to 1st ch to form a ring.

Rnd 1 (RS): Ch 1, 16 sc in ring, sl st to 1st sc, do not turn—16 sc.

Rnd 2: Ch 5 (counts as tr, ch-1 sp), *tr in next sc, ch 1; rep from * around, sl st in 4th ch of t-ch, do not turn—16 tr.

Rnd 3: Ch 1, *2 sc in ch-1 sp, ch 1, sk next tr; rep from * around to t-ch, sl st to 1st sc, do not turn—32 sc.

Rnd 4: Ch 3 (counts as dc), dc in next sc, ch 1, sk next ch-1 sp, *dc in next 2 sc, ch 1, sk next ch-1 sp; rep from * around, sl st to top of t-ch, do not turn—32 dc.

Rnd 5: Ch 7 (counts as dc, ch-4 sp), sk next ch-1 sp, dc in next ch-1 sp, ch 3, dc in skipped ch-1 sp (by inserting hk behind prev dc made), *ch 4, dc in next ch-1 sp, ch 3, dc in prev ch-1 sp (by inserting hk behind prev dc made); rep from * around, ch 4, dc in 1st ch-1 sp, ch 3, sl st in 3rd ch of t-ch, do not turn—32 ch-sps.

Rnd 6: Ch 1, *[(sc, ch 3) 3 times, sc] in next ch-4 sp, 2 sc in next ch-3 sp; rep from * around, sl st to 1st sc, fasten off—96 sc.

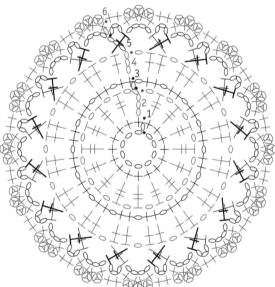

Eudora Motif

If you have not tried crocheting into the post of a stitch to see the cool shapes it makes, this doily will give you all the practice you need to master the technique.

Ch 10, sl st to 1st ch to form a ring.

Rnd 1 (RS): Ch 1, 24 sc in ring, sl st to 1st sc, do not turn—24 sc.

Rnd 2: Ch 6, *sk next sc, dtr in next sc, ch 4, dc in middle of dtr post; rep from * around, dc in 3rd ch of t-ch, ch 2, hdc in 6th ch of t-ch (counts as ch-sp), do not turn—12 ch-4 sps.

Rnd 3: Ch 1, 3 sc around post of hdc, *ch 3, 5 sc in next ch-4 sp; rep from * around, ch 3, 2 sc in ch-2 sp, sl st to 1st sc, do not turn—60 sc.

Rnd 4: Ch 6, *dtr in next ch-3 sp, ch 4, dc in middle of dtr post, sk 2 sc, dtr in next sc, ch 4, dc in middle of dtr post; rep from * around, dtr in next ch-3 sp, ch 4, dc in middle of dtr post, dc in 3rd ch of t-ch, ch 2, hdc in 6th ch of t-ch, do not turn—23 ch-4 sps.

Rnd 5: Ch 1, 3 sc around post of hdc, *[sc, 4 hdc, sc] in next ch-4 sp, [3 sc, ch 2, 3 sc] in next ch-4 sp; rep from * around, [sc, 4 hdc, sc] in last ch-4 sp, 3 sc in ch-2 sp, ch 2, sl st to 1st sc, fasten off—96 sc.

Julia Motif

Simple and classic, this motif can be used to fill in spaces between larger, more intricate ones.

Ch 8, sl st to 1st ch to form a ring.

Rnd 1 (RS): Ch 3 (counts as dc), 17 dc in ring, sl st to top of t-ch, do not turn—18 dc.

Rnd 2: Ch 4 (counts as dc, ch-1 sp), [dc, ch 1] in ea dc around, sl st to 3rd ch of t-ch, do not turn—18 dc.

Rnd 3: [Sc, ch 4, sc] in ea ch-1 sp around, sl st to 1st sc, fasten off—18 ch-4 sps.

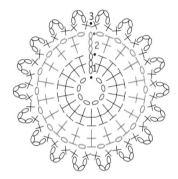

Zylphia Motif

Ruffles and popcorn—what is not to love about this textured crazy motif? Use it alone in fun coasters or connected together in a shawl.

Popcorn (pop): 5 dc in sp indicated and remove hk. Insert hk into top of 1st dc from front to back. Place free lp on hk and pull through 1st dc. Ch 1.

Ch 5, sl st to 1st ch to form ring.

Rnd 1 (RS): Ch 4 (counts as dc, ch-1 sp), [dc, ch 1] in ring 11 times, sl st to 3rd ch of t-ch, do not turn—12 dc.

Rnd 2: Ch 5 (counts as dc, ch-2 sp), [dc, ch 2] in ea dc around, sl st to 3rd ch of t-ch, do not turn—12 dc.

Rnd 3: Ch 1, sc in 3rd ch of t-ch, *ch 2, pop in next ch-2 sp, ch 2, sc to next dc; rep from * around to last dc, ch 2, pop in last ch-2 sp, ch 2, sl st to 1st sc, do not turn—12 pop.

Rnd 4: *Ch 7, sk pop, sl st to next sc; rep from * around to beg sl st, sl st in sl st, do not turn—12 ch-7 sps.

Rnd 5: Ch 1, [2 sc, 2 hdc, 6 dc, 2 hdc, 2 sc] in ea ch-7 sp around, sl st to 1st sc, fasten off—12 petals.

Lorena Motif

The delicate picots are highlighted in the final solid round of this motif.

Picot: Ch 4, sl st to 1st ch.

Ch 4, sl st to 1st ch to form ring.

Rnd 1 (RS): Ch 5 (counts as dc, ch-2 sp), [dc, ch 2] 6 times in ring, dc in ring, hdc to 3rd ch of t-ch, do not turn—8 dc.

Rnd 2: Ch 3 (counts as dc), *[ch 1, picot] twice, ch 1, dc in next ch-2 sp; rep from * around to last ch-2 sp, [ch 1, picot] twice, ch 1, sl st to 3rd ch of t-ch, fasten off—8 ch-sps.

Rnd 3: Join yarn to ch-sp btw picots with sl st, sc in same sp, *ch 7, sc to next ch-sp btw picot; rep from * around, ending ch 7, sl st to 1st sc, do not turn—8 sc.

Rnd 4: [Sc, hdc, 9 dc, hdc, sc] in ea ch-7 sp around, sl st to 1st sc, fasten off—8 petals.

Constance Motif

Depending on your blocking technique, this motif can look very smooth and circular or spiky and ridged.

Ch 10, sl st to 1st ch to form a ring.

Rnd 1 (RS): Ch 1, 24 sc in ring, sl st to 1st sc, do not turn—24 sc.

Rnd 2: Ch 6, *sk next sc, dtr in next sc, ch 3, dc in middle of dtr post; rep from * around, dc in 3rd ch of t-ch, ch 1, hdc in 6th ch of t-ch, do not turn—11 ch-3 sps.

Rnd 3: Ch 1, sc around post of hdc, *ch 4, sc in next ch-3 sp; rep from * around, ch 4, sl st to 1st sc, do not turn—12 sc.

Rnd 4: Ch 1, *6 sc in ch-4 sp, ch 3; rep from * around, sl st to 1st sc, fasten off—72 sc.

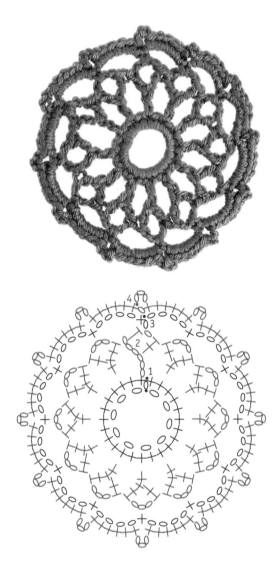

Orpha Motif

Bursting with chain-space petals, this motif makes for stunning jewelry when combined with simple beads.

Ch 5, sl st to 1st ch to form a ring.

Rnd 1 (RS): Ch 4 (counts as dc, ch-1 sp), [dc, ch 1] in ring 11 times, ch 1, sl st to 3rd ch of t-ch, do not turn—12 dc.

Rnd 2: Ch 1, [sc, ch 2, sc] in ea ch-1 sp around, sl st to 1st sc, do not turn—24 sc.

Rnd 3: Ch 9 (counts as dc, ch-6 sp), sk sc and ch-2 sp, *dc btw next 2 sc, ch 6, sk ch-2 sp; rep from * around to last 3 sc, dc btw next 2 sc, ch 6, sl st to 3rd ch of t-ch, do not turn—12 dc.

Rnd 4: Ch 1, [3 sc, ch 3, sc, ch 4, sc, ch 3, 3 sc] in ea ch-6 sp around, sl st to 1st sc, fasten off.

Hasu Flower Motif

This unassuming motif can make the most incredible fabric when you combine it multiple times in a sweater.

Picot: Ch 3, sl st to 1st ch.

Ch 6, sl st to 1st ch to form a ring.

Rnd 1 (RS): Ch 4 (counts as dc, ch-1), [3 dc, ch 1] into ring 7 times, 2 dc in ring, sl st to 3rd ch of t-ch, do not turn—24 dc.

Rnd 2: Ch 2, [dc, ch 2, 2 dc-cl] in ch-1 sp, ch 5, *[2 dc-cl, ch 2, 2 dc-cl] in next ch-1 sp, ch 5; rep from * around to last ch-1 sp, [2 dc-cl, ch 2, 2 dc-cl] in last ch-1 sp, ch 2, dc to top of dc, do not turn—15 dc-cl.

Rnd 3: Ch 3 (counts as dc), [2 dc, picot, 2 dc] around post of dc, *sc in next ch-2 sp, [2 dc, picot, 3 dc, ch 5, 3 dc, picot, 2 dc] in next ch-5 sp; rep from * around 6 more times, sc in next ch-2 sp, [2 dc, picot, 3 dc] in last ch-2 sp, ch 5, sl st to top of t-ch, fasten off—80 dc.

Riverbed Flower Motif

Earthy in look, this motif works equally well in vests and tunics as it does in coasters and jewelry.

Double Crochet Three Together (dc3tog): *Yo, insert hk into st indicated, yo, draw up lp, yo, draw through 2 lps on hk; rep from * twice in next st, yo, draw through last lps on hk.

Double Crochet Four Together (dc4tog): *Yo, insert hk into st indicated, yo, draw up lp, yo, draw through 2 lps on hk; rep from * once in same st; rep from * twice in next st, yo, draw through last lps on hk.

Ch 4, sl st to 1st ch to form a ring.

Rnd 1 (RS): Ch 1, 8 sc in ring, sl st to sc, do not turn.

Rnd 2: Ch 2, dc3tog working 1st leg in 1st sc and next two legs in next sc, ch 4, [dc4tog in prev sc and next sc, ch 4] 7 times, sl st to top of dc3tog, do not turn—8 ch-sps.

Rnd 3: Ch 1, *[3 sc, ch 4, 3 sc] in next ch-4 sp; rep from * around, sl st to 1st sc, do not turn—8 ch-sps.

Rnd 4: Ch 1, sc between 1st and last sc from last rnd, ch 3, sc in next ch-4 sp, ch 3, *sk 2 sc, sc between next 2 sc, ch 3, sc in next ch-4 sp, ch 3; rep from * around, sl st to 1st sc, do not turn.

Rnd 5: Ch 1, *4 sc in next ch-3 sp, ch 3, 4 sc in next ch-3 sp; rep from * around, sl st to 1st sc, do not turn.

Zimni Snowflake

If you are looking for a snowflake to mimic actual ones, this is for you. All the trefoils in the snowflake fan out to create a stunning motif.

Ch 9, sl st to 1st ch to form a ring.

Rnd 1 (RS): Ch 4 (counts as tr), 4 tr in ring, [ch 4, 5 tr in ring] 5 times, ch 4, sl st in top of t-ch, do not turn—30 tr.

Rnd 2: Sl st in next 4 tr, *[sl st, ch 2, hdc, (ch 5, sl st to 1st ch) 3 times, sl st to prev hdc, hdc, ch 7, sl st in 3rd ch from hk, [ch 5, sl st to 1st ch] twice, sc in next 2 ch, hdc, [ch 5, sl st to 1st ch] 3 times, sl st to prev hdc, hdc, ch 2, sl st] in next ch-sp, sl st in next 5 tr; rep from * around, fasten off—6 petals.

TIP

Snowflake motifs do not have to be stiffened to be enjoyed, but when they are, the world opens up to what you can do with them. You can add a hook and make a quick ornament, or add beads and make a quick necklace. The key to stiffening is not in the solution you use, but in the pins. Whether you use a fabric stiffener or a cornstarch solution, be sure to dip your motif fully in the mixture, pat it dry, and then place it on wax or parchment paper. Make sure to pin down each and every picot and chain exactly where you want it to go. They do take a while to pin and you will go through a ton of pins, but the results are so worth the effort.

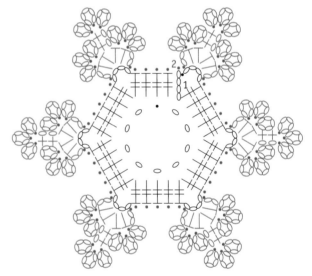

Daisy Snowflake

This flowery snowflake looks equally cute whether blocked and stiffened or unblocked and curly; try it each way to find your favorite look.

Single Crochet Spike Stitch (spike st): Insert hk in next st 2 rnds below, yo, draw up a lp to height of current rnd, yo, pull through both lps on hk.

Picot: Ch 3, sl st to prev sc.

Ch 10, sl st to 1st ch to form a ring.

Rnd 1 (RS): Ch 1, 24 sc into ring, sl st to 1st sc, do not turn.

Rnd 2: Ch 1, *sc in next 2 sc, [sc, ch 7, sc] in next sc, sc in next sc; rep from * around, sl st to 1st sc, do not turn—30 sc.

Rnd 3: Ch 1, sc in 1st sc, *[2 hdc, 13 dc, 2 hdc] in next ch-7 sp, sk 2 sc, sc in next sc; rep from * around to last ch-7 sp, sl st to 1st sc, do not turn, fasten off color— 6 petals.

Rnd 4: Join new color, ch 1, *spike st in next sc on rnd 1, ch 3, sk 2 hdc and 2 dc, sc in next dc, picot, ch 3, sk 3 dc, sc in next dc, picot, ch 3, sk 3 dc, sc in next dc, picot, ch 3, sk 2 dc and 2 hdc; rep from * around, sl st to 1st spike st, fasten off.

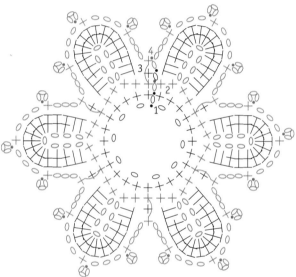

Uriah Snowflake

Like a star that fell from heaven, this snowflake shines with the beauty of clusters and arches.

Ch 7, sl st to 1st ch to form a ring.

Rnd 1 (RS): Ch 1, [sc, ch 4] into ring 11 times, sc in ring, ch 2, hdc to 1st sc, do not turn—12 sc.

Rnd 2: Ch 2, 2 dc-cl around post of hdc, *ch 3, 3 dc-cl in next ch-4 sp; rep from * around, ch 3, sl st to 2 dc-cl, do not turn—12 ch-sps.

Rnd 3: Ch 1, [3 sc, ch 3, 3 sc] in ea ch-3 sp around, sl st to 1st sc, do not turn—12 ch-sps.

Rnd 4: Sl st in next 2 sc, sl st in ch-3 sp, ch 2, [2 dc-cl, ch 7, 3 dc-cl] in same ch 3-sp, *[3 dc-cl, ch 6, 3 dc-cl] in next ch-3 sp, [3 dc-cl, ch 7, 3 dc-cl] in next ch-3 sp; rep from * around, [3 dc-cl, ch 6, 3 dc-cl] in last ch-3 sp, sl st to 2 dc-cl, do not turn—24 dc-cl.

Rnd 5: *[6 sc, ch 3, 6 sc] in next ch-7 sp, 11 sc in next ch-6 sp; rep from * around, sl st to 1st sc, fasten off—138 sc.

Ambrose Snowflake

Delicate and lacy, this snowflake combines easily with itself to make a beautiful fabric that almost looks like lattice.

X-Stitch (X-st): Yo 3 times, insert hk in next dc, yo and draw up lp, [yo, pull through 2 lps on hk] twice, sk 2 dc, yo, insert hk in next dc, yo and draw up lp, [yo, pull through 2 lps on hk] twice (dc made), [yo and pull through 2 lps] twice, ch 3, dc in top of dc just made.

Ch 6, sl st to 1st ch to form a ring.

Rnd 1 (RS): Ch 3 (counts as dc), dc in ring, ch 3, [2 dc, ch 3] into ring 5 times, sl st to top of t-ch, do not turn—12 dc.

Rnd 2: Ch 3, dc in t-ch, 2 dc in next dc, ch 4, sl st to 2nd ch, ch 1, *2 dc in next 2 dc, ch 4, sl st to 2nd ch, ch 1; rep from * around, sl st to top of t-ch, do not turn—24 dc.

Rnd 3: Ch 3, sk 2 dc, dc in next dc, ch 6, dc in prev dc, ch 6, sl st to 4th ch, ch 3, *sk ch-sp, X-st over next 4 dc, ch 6, sl st to 4th ch, ch 3; rep from * around, sl st to 3rd ch of 1st ch-6 sp, do not turn.

Rnd 4: Ch 2, [2 dc-cl, ch 3, 3 dc-cl, ch 5, 3 dc-cl, ch 3, 3 dc-cl] in ch-3 sp, ch 6, sl st to 4th ch, ch 3, *sk ch-6 sp, [3 dc-cl, ch 3, 3 dc-cl, ch 5, 3 dc-cl, ch 3, 3 dc-cl] in next ch-3 sp of X-st, ch 6, sl st to 4th ch, ch 3; rep from * around, sl st to 2 dc-cl, fasten off.

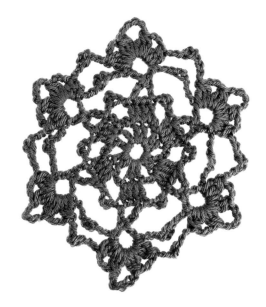

Leander Snowflake

Part flower, part snowflake—this motif can stand in as either in your next crochet project.

Trefoil: Ch 7, sl st in 7th ch, ch 9, sl st in 9th ch, ch 7, sl st in 7th ch.

Small Picot (sm picot): Ch 3, sl st in 3rd ch.

Large Picot (lg picot): Ch 5, sl st in 5th ch.

Ch 11, sl st to 1st ch to form ring.

Rnd 1 (RS): Ch 3 (counts as dc), 23 dc in ring, sl st to top of t-ch, do not turn—24 dc.

Rnd 2: *[Sl st, ch 1, sm picot, ch 1, lg picot, 2 tr, trefoil, 2 tr, lg picot, ch 1, sm picot, ch 1, sl st] in next st, sl st to next 3 dc; rep from * around, fasten off—6 petals.

Mudan Snowflake

The numerous chain spaces on the last round of this snowflake give you multiple chances to connect it with other motifs or places to thread it onto an earring hook.

Shell (sh): [Sc, hdc, 2 dc, ch 2, 2 dc, hdc, sc] in st indicated.

Ch 6, sl st to 1st ch to form ring.

Rnd 1 (RS): Ch 1, 12 sc in ring, sl st to 1st sc, do not turn—12 sc.

Rnd 2: Ch 7 (counts as dc and ch 4), sk next sc, [dc in next sc, ch 4, sk 1 sc] 4 times, sk 1 sc, dc in next sc, ch 1, dc in 3rd ch of beg ch-7, do not turn—6 ch-sps.

Rnd 3: Ch 5 (counts as dc and ch 2), [2 dc, hdc, sc] around post of dc, [sh in next 4-ch sp] 5 times, [sc, hdc, dc] in the next ch-1 sp, join with a sl st to 3rd ch of beg ch-5, do not turn—6 sh.

Rnd 4: Ch 4 (counts as tr), 4 tr in 1st ch-2 sp, [9 tr in next ch-2 sp] 5 times, 4 tr in 1st ch-2 sp, join with a sl st to 4th ch of beg ch-4, do not turn—54 tr.

Rnd 5: Ch 8 (counts as dc, ch-5 sp), 2 dc in top of t-ch, *ch 2, sk 2 tr, sc in next tr, ch 2, sk 1 tr, [dc, ch 3, dc] in sp btw 9 tr of prev rnd, ch 2, sk 1 tr, sc in next tr, ch 2, sk 2 tr, [2 dc, ch 5, 2 dc] in next tr; rep from * 4 times more, ch 2, sk 2 tr, sc in next tr, ch 2, sk 1 tr, [dc, ch 3, dc] in sp btw 9 tr of prev rnd, ch 2, sk 1 tr, sc in next tr, ch 2, dc in top of t-ch, sl st to 3rd ch of beg ch-8, fasten off—36 ch-sps.

Lujoso Snowflake

This star-like snowflake will seem far out after crocheting the first two rounds. You will have to stick with the directions to watch it transform into the beautiful motif it truly is.

Trefoil: [Ch 7, sl st to 7th ch, ch 11, sl st to 11th ch, ch 7, sl st to 7th ch] in st indicated.

Ch 9, sl st to 1st ch to form a ring.

Rnd 1 (RS): Ch 1, 18 sc in ring, sl st to 1st sc, do not turn—18 sc.

Rnd 2: Ch 6, sl st to same sc, *sl st to next sc, ch 6, [2 dc, ch 3, sl st] in 3rd ch, sc in next 2 ch, sl st in prev sc, [sl st, ch 3, dc] in next sc, [dc, ch 3, sl st] in next sc; rep from * around to last 2 sc, sl st to next sc, ch 6, [2 dc, ch 3, sl st] in 3rd ch, sc in next 2 ch, sl st in prev sc, [sl st, ch 3, dc] in last sc, sl st to 3rd ch of t-ch—6 petals.

Rnd 3: *Ch 6, [sl st, trefoil, sl st] btw next 2 dc, ch 6, sl st btw next 2 dc; rep from * around, fasten off—6 trefoils.

Bernard Snowflake

The lacy chain spaces of this snowflake's center set up the final round for the dramatic set of double crochet. Be sure to block to get the snowflake to lay flat.

Picot: Ch 4, sl st to prev sc.

Ch 6, sl st to 1st ch to form a ring.

Rnd 1 (RS): Ch 2, 2 dc-cl in ring, [ch 4, 3 dc-cl] in ring 5 times, ch 2, hdc in top of 2 dc-cl, do not turn—6 dc-cl.

Rnd 2: Ch 1, sc around post of hdc, *ch 5, sc in dc-cl, ch 5, sc in ch-4 sp; rep from * around to last ch-4 sp, ch 5, sc in dc-cl, ch 2, dc in 1st sc (counts as ch-sp), do not turn—12 ch-sps.

Rnd 3: Ch 1, sc around post of dc, *ch 7, sc in next ch-5 sp; rep from * around to last ch-5 sp, ch 3, tr in 1st sc, do not turn—12 ch-sps.

Rnd 4: Ch 3 (counts as dc), 6 dc around post of dc, *sc in next ch-7 sp, picot, 13 dc in next ch-7 sp; rep from * around to last ch-7 sp, sc in last ch-7 sp, picot, 6 dc in ch-3 sp, sl st to top of t-ch, fasten off.

Magairlin Snowflake

Moroccan inspired, this snowflake highlights trefoils on two rounds to draw the eye to their beauty.

Trefoil: [Ch 3, sl st to 1st ch] 3 times.

Ch 10, sl st to 1st ch to form a ring.

Rnd 1 (RS): Ch 4 (counts as tr), 23 tr in ring, sl st to top of t-ch, do not turn—24 tr.

Rnd 2: Ch 1, sc in top of t-ch, *ch 4, sk 2 tr, sc in next tr; rep from * around, sl st to 1st sc, do not turn—8 ch-sps.

Rnd 3: [Sc, hdc, 2 dc, trefoil, sl st to prev dc, 2 dc, hdc, sc] in ea ch-4 sp around, sl st to 1st sc, do not turn—8 petals.

Rnd 4: Ch 1, sc in sl st, *ch 6, sk 1 ch-3 sp, sc in next ch-3 sp, ch 6, sc btw next 2 sc; rep from * around, sl st to 1st sc, do not turn—16 ch-sps.

Rnd 5: Ch 1, *7 sc in next ch-6 sp, trefoil, sl st to prev sc, 7 sc in next ch-6 sp; rep from * around, sl st to 1st sc, fasten off—8 trefoils.

Surrey Snowflake

The crossed double crochets in the snowflake add just a touch of texture to this classical design.

Crossed Double Crochet (crossed dc): Sk next 2 sc, dc in next sc, ch 3, dc in prev 3rd sc (sk same 2 sc backward).

Ch 7, sl st to 1st ch to form a ring.

Rnd 1 (RS): Ch 1, 12 sc in ring, sl st to 1st sc, do not turn.

Rnd 2: Ch 5 (counts as dc, ch-2 sp), *dc in next sc, ch 2; rep from * around, sl st to 3rd ch of t-ch, do not turn—12 dc.

Rnd 3: Ch 1, sc on top of t-ch, *2 sc in ch-2 sp, sc in next dc; rep from * around, sl st to 1st sc, do not turn—36 sc.

Rnd 4: Ch 6 (counts as dc, ch-3 sp), dc in prev 3rd sc (sk prev 2 sc), [ch 2, crossed dc] 11 times, ch 2, sl st to 3rd ch of t-ch, do not turn—12 crossed dc.

Rnd 5: Ch 1, *[2 sc, ch 2, 2 sc] in ch-3 sp, 2 sc in next ch-2 sp, [sc, (ch 3, hdc) 3 times, ch 3, sc] in next ch-3 sp, 2 sc in next ch-2 sp; rep from * around, sl st to 1st sc, fasten off—18 hdc.

Clinton Snowflake

This chunky snowflake is made more delicate with the tiny picots on the last rounds. The picots also make a great location to join other motifs to this one.

Ch 7, sl st to 1st ch to form a ring.

Rnd 1 (RS): Ch 2, 2 dc-cl in ring, [ch 3, 3 dc-cl] in ring 7 times, ch 1, hdc in top of 2 dc-cl, do not turn—8 dc-cl.

Rnd 2: Ch 2 (counts as hdc), 2 hdc around post of hdc, *ch 5, 4 hdc in next ch-3 sp; rep from * around, ch 5, hdc in ch-1 sp, sl st to top of t-ch, do not turn—32 hdc.

Rnd 3: Sl st in next hdc, *[3 hdc, ch 3, sl st in prev hdc, 2 hdc, ch 3, 3 hdc, ch 3, sl st in prev hdc, 2 hdc] in next ch-5 sp, sl st btw next 2nd and 3rd hdc; rep from * around, sl st to 1st sl st, fasten off—80 hdc.

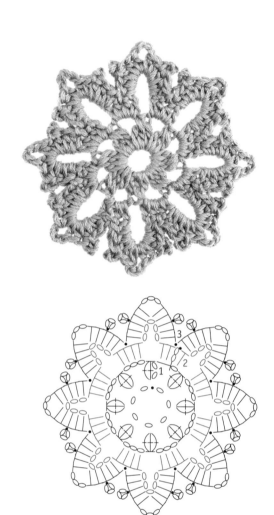

Wilfred Snowflake

The star shape to this simple snowflake makes it a standout in any project from shawl to scarf.

Ch 7, sl st to 1st ch to form a ring.

Rnd 1 (RS): Ch 1, 12 sc into ring, sl st to 1st sc, do not turn.

Rnd 2: Ch 2, 2 dc-cl in 1st sc, ch 3, *3 dc-cl in next sc, ch 5, 3 dc-cl in next sc, ch 3; rep from * around to last sc, 3 dc-cl in last sc, ch 2, dc in top of 2 dc-cl, do not turn—12 dc-cl.

Rnd 3: Ch 3 (counts as dc), 4 dc around post of dc, *sc in next ch-3 sp, [5 dc, ch 3, 5 dc] in next ch-5 sp; rep from * around to last ch-3 sp, sc in last ch-3 sp, 5 dc in ch-2 sp, ch 3, sl st to top of t-ch, fasten off—60 dc.

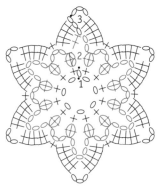

Slip Stitch Seam

This simple seam creates a little pucker that you can use as a design feature, or turn it upside down and make it invisible.

Pin motifs together with wrong sides together for a ridge seam, or right sides together for a hidden seam.

Join the yarn to the edge, slip stitch across each stitch in both motifs (inserting the hook through both motifs at the same time), and fasten off.

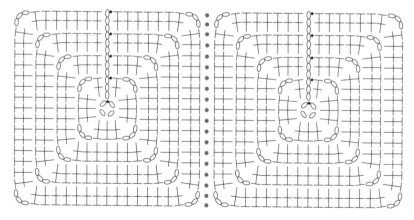

Reverse Single Crochet Seam

This seam uses the ridge to add a gentle wave between each motif.

Reverse Single Crochet (rev sc): Insert hk back into prev st (to the right in the clockwise direction), yo, pull up lp twisting hk around to face upwards, yo, pull through sts on hk.

Pin the motifs together with wrong sides together.

Join the yarn to the left edge, and reverse single crochet across each stitch in both motifs at the same time (inserting the hook through the back loop of the motif closest to you and the front loop of the motif farthest from you); working across to the right edge, fasten off.

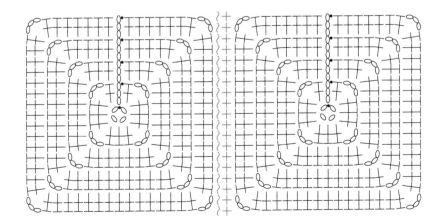

Double Crochet Track Seam

This incredibly simple seam looks more complex, which makes the beauty of it sing. This motif looks great on motifs with solid final rounds or ones with a regular spacing of tall stitches, like granny squares.

Hold the motifs together with wrong sides facing.

Join the yarn to the edge of the motif closest to you. Ch 3 (counts as dc), dc in next st of motif closest to you, *sk 2 sts in motif farthest from you, dc in next 2 sts of far motif, sk 2 sts in near motif, dc in next 2 sts of near motif; rep from * across, fasten off.

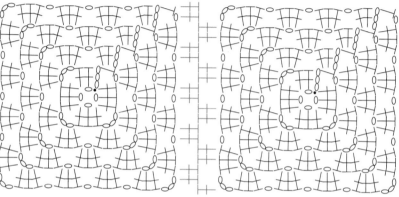

Chain Space Seam

This is one of the most common ways to join two lacy motifs. The chain spaces become invisible in the larger fabric.

Align the edges of the motifs side-by-side, and join the yarn to the motif on the right.

Ch 1, sc in same sp as join, *ch 3, sc in next ch-sp on motif on left, ch 3, sc in next ch-sp on motif on right; rep from * across, fasten off.

Slip Stitch Motifs Together

Less of a seam and more of a way just to join two motifs, you can crochet motifs together as you go, by replacing a chain with a slip stitch and literally crocheting one motif onto another.

Crochet the next motif to the last round.

Follow the directions for the last round of the motif. When you get to a chain space, remove the middle chain and replace it with a slip stitch to the same space on an adjoining motif. In the example, you would chain 2, slip stitch to the adjoining motif, chain 2, and then continue crocheting the working motif.

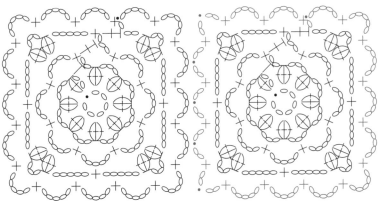

TIP

You will notice that none of the joining techniques listed ever mention sewing. Hand sewing motifs together is fine if you like sewing. Whipstitching motifs can create a smooth fabric, and when the motif is nearly solid, almost an invisible seam. The one thing to watch is how well you weave in your ends. When you crochet motifs together instead of sewing, it is almost impossible for them to unravel. Nothing is more upsetting than when only days after you sew together your afghan, it starts to come apart at the seam. All seams here are shown in a contrasting color to highlight the seaming; when seaming your project, you can decide whether to spotlight the seam or to hide it by choosing a contrasting or matching color yarn, respectively.

Small Motif Join

When motifs are connected and have a void, you can use small motifs to fill in the space and make the resulting fabric sturdier.

This can work with any motif. Just replace a chain for a slip stitch join as in the previous joining.

In the example shown, ch 7, sl st to 1st ch to make a ring. Ch 2, 2 dc-cl in ring, *ch 1, sl st to adjoining motif's picot, ch 1, 3 dc-cl in ring, ch 1, sl st to adjoining motif's next picot, ch 1, 3 dc-cl in ring; rep from * for each additional motif around, sl st to 2 dc-cl, fasten off.

Cluster Chain Seam

This fancy seam adds a little vine of clusters between motifs. It looks quite impressive on both solid and lacy motifs.

Align the edges of the motifs side-by-side, and join the yarn to the edge of the motif on the right.

Ch 1, sc in same sp as join, *ch 3, 2 dc-cl in 1st ch, sc in next ch-sp (or sk 3 sts and sc in next st) on motif on left, ch 3, 2 dc-cl in 1st ch, sc in next ch-sp (or sk 3 sts and sc in next st) on motif on right; rep from * across, fasten off.

V-Stitch Seam

This technique to join two motifs is very commonly used in Belgium lace crochet. Here it adds a bit of lace to solid motifs to transform them into a completely different fabric.

V-Stitch (v-st): [2 dc, ch 1, 2 dc] in same st or sp.

Align the edges of the motifs side-by-side, and join the yarn to the motif on the left; chain 7.

Row 1 (RS): Sl st to corner of motif on right, sk 3 ch, v-st in next ch, ch 1, sl st to motif on left (about the same height as row 1), turn.

Row 2: Ch 1, v-st in ch-1 sp on v-st, ch 1, sk 3 sts on right motif, sl st to next st of motif on right, turn.

Row 3: Ch 1, v-st in ch-1 sp on v-st, ch 1, sl st to motif on the left, turn.

Rep rows 2 and 3 up the motifs to the end, fasten off.

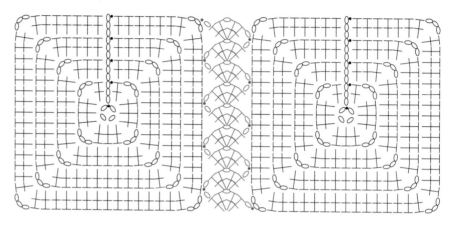

CHAPTER 9

Edgings

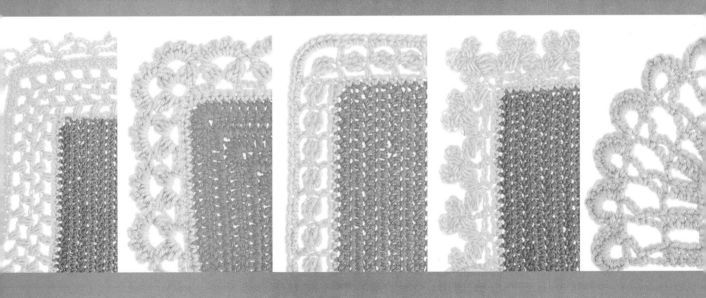

Reverse Single Crochet Edging

This is the simplest of all edgings, but is quite effective for finishing off a project.

Reverse Single Crochet (rev sc): Insert hk back into prev st (to the right in the clockwise direction), yo, pull up lp twisting hk around to face upward, yo, pull through sts on hk.

This stitch pattern is any number of stitches. Join the yarn to the edge with a sl st, and ch 1.

Rnd 1 (RS): *Sc across edge, 3 sc in corner; rep from * around, sl st to 1st sc, do not turn.

Rnd 2: Ch 1, rev sc in ea sc around, sl st to 1st sc, fasten off.

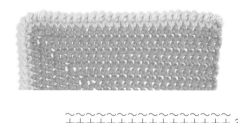

> ## TIP
> Following edging patterns can be really simple until you get to the corner, and then—uh oh!—what do you do next? The edgings here all assume that you are crocheting around a rectangular shape, whether it's a blanket or a shawl. If you are crocheting just a single edge, then add one to each multiple number to chain and follow the directions as written, ignoring the corner directions.

Double Arch Edging

When you change the colors and slightly shift the last round, the edging almost looks corded or braided.

The stitch pattern is a multiple of 3 plus 1 on the sides. Join the yarn to the edge with a sl st, and ch 1.

Rnd 1 (RS): *Sc across edge in a multiple of 3 plus 1 st, 3 sc in corner; rep from * around, sl st to 1st sc, do not turn.

Rnd 2: Ch 1, sc in 1st sc, *ch 5, sk 2 sc, sc in next sc; rep from * to corner, ch 5, turn project 90 degrees, sc in next sc, cont around sl st to 1st sc, fasten off color, turn.

Rnd 3: Join new color to rnd 1 with sl st next to a skipped sc on row 2. Rep rnd 2 directions around, fasten off.

Picot Edging

This edging comes in handy when you need something simple and delicate.

Picot: Ch 3, sl st in 1st ch.

The stitch pattern is a multiple of 3 on the sides. Join the yarn to the edge with a sl st, and ch 1.

Rnd 1 (RS): *Sc across edge in a multiple of 3, 3 sc in corner; rep from * around, sl st to 1st sc, do not turn.

Rnd 2: Ch 1, *[sc in next 2 sc, picot, sc in next sc] across to corner, [sc, picot, sc, picot, sc] in corner sc; rep from * around, sl st to 1st sc, fasten off.

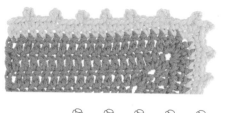

Spike Cluster Edging

This wide edging adds a whole new dramatic finish to blankets or towels.

Single Crochet Spike (sc spike): Insert hk into st indicated 2 rows below, yo, pull up a lp, insert hk into st indicated 4 rows below, yo, pull up a lp, insert hk into st indicated 2 rows below, yo, pull up a lp, yo, pull through all lps on hk.

The stitch pattern is a multiple of 6 plus 3 on the sides. Join the yarn to the edge with a sl st, and ch 1.

Rnd 1 (RS): *Sc across edge in a multiple of 6 plus 3, 3 sc in corner; rep from * around, sl st to 1st sc, turn.

Rnd 2: Ch 1, *sc in ea sc to corner, 3 sc in corner; rep from * around, sl st to 1st sc, turn.

Rnds 3 and 4: Rep rnd 2 twice more, fasten off, turn.

Rnd 5: Join contrasting color, ch 1, sc in 1st sc, *[sc spike over (prev sc 2 sts away, next sc, sc 2 sts away), sc in next 5 sc] across to corner, [sc, sc spike over (prev sc 2 sts away, corner sc, sc 2 sts away), sc] in corner; rep from * around, sl st to 1st sc, fasten off.

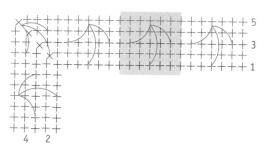

Chain Lace Edging

This simple edging is easy to memorize, making for a super-quick option.

The stitch pattern is a multiple of 4 plus 3 on the sides. Join the yarn to the edge with a sl st, and ch 2 (this counts as a half double crochet).

Rnd 1 (RS): *Hdc across edge in a multiple of 4 plus 3, 3 hdc in corner; rep from * around, sl st to top of t-ch, do not turn.

Rnd 2: Ch 1, sc in top of t-ch, *(ch 4, sk 3 hdc, sc in next hdc) across to corner hdc, ch 4, sk corner hdc, sc in next hdc; rep from * around, sl st to 1st sc, do not turn.

Rnd 3: Ch 1, sc in 1st sc, *ch 6, sk ch-4 sp, sc in next sc; rep from * around, sl st to 1st sc, do not turn.

Rnd 4: Ch 1, sc in 1st sc, *ch 8, sk ch-6 sp, sc in next sc; rep from * around, sl st to 1st sc, do not turn.

Rnd 5: Ch 1, sc in 1st sc, *ch 9, sk ch-8 sp, sc in next sc; rep from * around, sl st to 1st sc, fasten off.

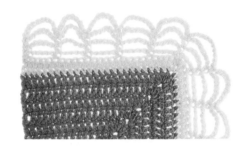

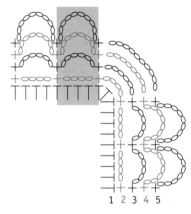

Picot Curls Edging

This adorable edging adds a bit of whimsy to any project.

Picot: Ch 3, sl st in 1st ch.

The stitch pattern is a multiple of 3 on the sides. Join the yarn to the edge with a sl st, and ch 1.

Rnd 1 (RS): *Sc across edge in a multiple of 3, 3 sc in corner; rep from * around, sl st to 1st sc, do not turn.

Rnd 2: Ch 2 (counts as hdc), hdc in next 2 sc, *[picot, hdc in next 3 sc] across to 1 sc before corner sc, picot, hdc in sc before corner, [2 hdc, picot, 2 hdc] in corner sc, hdc in next sc; rep from * around, sl st to top of t-ch, do not turn.

Rnd 3: Sl st to next 2 hdc, ch 1, sc in same hdc, *ch 5, sk 2 hdc, sc in next hdc; rep from * to corner, ch 7 sk 2 corner hdc, sc in next hdc; rep from * around, sl st to 1st sc, fasten off.

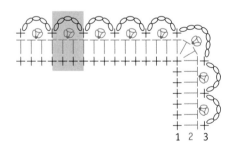

Net Cluster Edging

Even though this edging has a number of rounds, they are easily repeatable. When you stack these repeatable rounds, the product is quite stunning as an edging or entire pattern.

Picot: Ch 3, sl st in 1st ch.

The stitch pattern is a multiple of 6 plus 3 on the sides. Join the yarn to the edge with a sl st, and ch 1.

Rnd 1 (RS): *Sc across edge in a multiple of 6 plus 3, 3 sc in corner; rep from * around, sl st to 1st sc, turn.

Rnd 2: Sl st in next sc, ch 2, 2 hdc-cl in same sc, *[ch 2, sk 2 sc, 3 hdc-cl in next sc] across to corner, ch 2, [3 hdc-cl, ch 3, 3 hdc-cl] in corner sc; rep from * around, sl st to 1st 2 hdc-cl, turn.

Rnd 3: Sl st in next ch-2 sp, ch 2, 2 hdc-cl in same ch-2 sp, *[ch 2, 3 hdc-cl in next ch-2 sp] across to corner, ch 2, [3 hdc-cl, ch 3, 3 hdc-cl] in corner ch-3 sp; rep from * around, sl st to 1st 2 hdc-cl, turn.

Rnds 4 and 5: Rep rnd 3 twice.

Rnd 6: Ch 1, *3 sc in ea ch-2 sp to corner, 5 sc in ch-3 sp at corner; rep from * around, sl st to 1st sc, turn.

Rnd 7: Ch 1, *sc in ea sc to corner sc, 3 sc in corner sc; rep from * around, sl st to 1st sc, turn.

Rnd 8: Sl st in next 4 sc, sc in next sc, *[ch 3, picot, ch 3, sk 5 sc, sc in next sc] across to sc 2 sts from corner sc, ch 3, picot, ch 3, sk 3 sc at corner, sc in next sc; rep from * around, sl st to 1st sc, turn.

Rnd 9: Ch 1, sc in 1st sc, *ch 4, picot, ch 4, sc in next sc; rep from * across to corner ch-sp, ch 5, picot, ch 5, sc in next sc; rep from * around, fasten off.

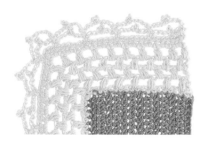

Cluster Picot Edging

This lacy edging is a simple chain lace with just a bit of fancy clusters on the final round.

Picot: Ch 3, sl st in 1st ch.

Cluster: *Yo, insert hk into st indicated, yo, pull up lp, yo, pull through 2 lps on hk, yo, insert hk into same st, yo, pull up lp, yo, pull through 2 lps on hk; rep from * in next st indicated, yo, pull through all lps on hk.

The stitch pattern is a multiple of 3 plus 2 on the sides. Join the yarn to the edge with a sl st, and ch 1.

Rnd 1 (RS): *Sc across edge in a multiple of 3 plus 2, 3 sc in corner; rep from * around, sl st to 1st sc, turn.

Rnd 2: Ch 1, sc in next sc, *ch 5, sk corner sc, sc in next sc, [ch 4, sk 2 sc, sc in next sc] across to sc before corner; rep from * around to 1st corner ch-sp, ch 2, hdc in 1st sc, turn.

Rnd 3: Ch 1, sc in hdc, *[ch 4, sc in next ch-4 sp] across corner ch-sp, ch 4, [sc, ch 7, sc] in ch-5 sp; rep from * around to 1st sc, ch 2, hdc in 1st sc, turn.

Rnd 4: Ch 1, sc in hdc, ch 4, *[sc, ch 9, sc] in corner ch-sp, [ch 4, sc in next ch-4 sp] across to corner ch-sp; rep from * around to 1st sc, ch 2, hdc in 1st sc, turn.

Rnd 5: Ch 2, cluster in 1st and next ch-sp, *ch 2, picot, ch 2, cluster in prev and next ch-sp; rep from * to corner ch-sp, ch 2, picot, ch 2, cluster in prev and corner ch-sp, ch 2, picot, ch 2, [4 dc-cl, ch 2, picot, ch 2, 4 dc-cl] in corner ch-sp, ch 2, picot, ch 2, cluster in corner ch-sp and next ch-4 sp; rep from * around, ch 2, picot, ch 2, sl st to 1st cluster, turn.

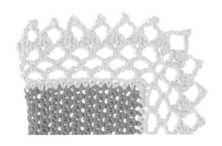

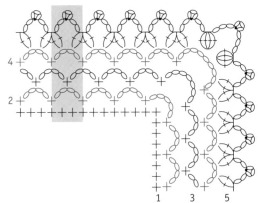

Mission Edging

The shells on the final round of this edging are highlighted not only in color but also by being separated by the simple rounds.

Shell (sh): [(Dc, ch 1) 3 times, dc] in st indicated.

The stitch pattern is a multiple of 8 plus 5 on the sides. Join the yarn to the edge with a sl st, and ch 1.

Rnd 1 (RS): *Sc across edge in a multiple of 8 plus 5 to corner, 3 sc in corner; rep from * around, sl st to 1st sc, turn.

Rnd 2: Ch 3 (counts as dc), dc in next dc, *5 dc in corner sc, dc in ea sc to corner; rep from * around, sl st to top of t-ch, turn.

Rnd 3: Sl st in next dc, sc in next 2 dc, *[ch 2, sk 2 dc, sc in next 2 dc] across to sc 2 away from corner, ch 2, sk 1 dc, sc in corner dc, ch 2, sk 1 dc, sc in next 2 dc; rep from * around, sl st to 1st sc, turn.

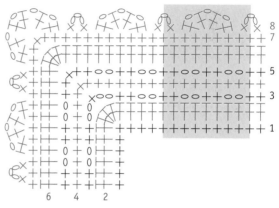

Rnd 4: Ch 1, *[2 sc in next ch-2 sp, sc in next 2 sc] across to corner, 2 sc in next ch-2 sp, 3 sc in corner sc; rep from * around, sl st to 1st sc, turn.

Rnd 5: Ch 1, sc in next 2 sc, *[ch 2, sk 2 sc, sc in next 2 sc] across to sc 3 away from corner, ch 2, sk 2 sc, sc in next sc, 3 sc in corner sc, sc in next sc; rep from * around, sl st to 1st sc, turn.

Rnd 6: Ch 3 (counts as dc), dc in ch-2 sp, *[dc in next 2 sc, 2 dc in next ch-2 sp] cross to corner, dc in next 2 sc, 5 dc in corner sc; rep from * around, sl st to top of t-ch, fasten off, turn.

Rnd 7: With RS facing, join contrasting color to dc 3 sts after a corner st, *sc in ea dc across to corner, 3 sc in corner dc; rep from * around, sl st to 1st sc, do not turn.

Rnd 8: Ch 1, [sc, ch 3, sc] in same sc, *[sk 3 sc, sh in next sc, sk 3 sc, (sc, ch 3, sc) in next sc] across to corner, [(dc, ch 1) 5 times, dc] in corner sc, sk 3 sc, [sc, ch 3, sc] in next sc; rep from * around, omitting last [sc, ch 3, sc], sl st to 1st sc, fasten off.

TIP

As with lace patterns, blocking makes edgings come alive. Pinning out each shell may take a while, but the effort is well worth it when the final project goes from crumpled to stunning.

Mystic Edging

You can completely block this fancy edging to its last round for a classic look. If you leave its last round unblocked, it will ruffle slightly.

The stitch pattern is a multiple of 8 plus 1 on the sides. Join the yarn to the edge with a sl st, and ch 1.

Rnd 1 (RS): *Sc across edge in a multiple of 8 plus 1 st, 3 sc in corner; rep from * around, sl st to 1st sc, turn.

Rnd 2: Ch 3 (counts as dc), dc in next sc, *[dc, ch 7, dc] in corner sc, dc in next 4 sc, [ch 5, sk 3 sc, dc in next 5 sc] rep to corner; rep from * around, sl st to top of t-ch, turn.

Rnd 3: Ch 1, sc in top of t-ch, *[4 dc, ch 2, 4 dc] in next ch-5 sp, sk 2 dc, sc in next dc, sk 2 dc; rep from * to corner, [(4 dc, ch 2) twice, 4 dc] in corner ch-sp, sk 2 dc, sc in next dc, sk 2 dc; rep from * around, sl st to 1st sc, do not turn.

Rnd 4: Sl st in next dc, turn, ch 2, dc in next dc (sk sc), ch 1, *sk next dc, dc in next dc, ch 1, sk next dc, [dc, ch 2, dc] in next ch-2 sp, ch 1, sk next dc, dc in next dc, ch 1, dc btw next 2 dc, ch 1, dc in next dc, ch 1, [dc, ch 2, dc] in next ch-2 sp, ch 1, sk next dc, dc in next dc, ch 1, sk next dc, dc2tog in next 2 dc (sk sc), ch 1, **sk next dc, dc in next dc, ch 1, sk next dc, [dc, ch 2, dc] in next ch-2 sp, ch 1, sk next dc, dc in next dc, ch 1, sk next dc, dc2tog in next 2 dc (sk sc), ch 1; rep from ** to corner; rep from * around to beg, sl st in 1st dc, turn.

Rnd 5: Ch 1, *[sc in next ch-1 sp, ch 2] twice, [sc, ch 4, sc] in next ch-2 sp, [ch 2, sc in next ch-1 sp] twice, ch 2; rep from * to corner, [sc in next ch-1 sp, ch 2] twice, [sc, ch 4, sc] in next ch-2 sp, [ch 2, sc in next ch-1 sp] twice, ch 4; rep from * around, sl st to 1st sc, fasten off.

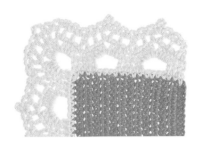

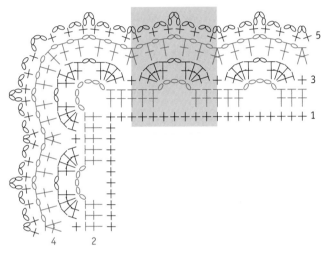

Belle Edging

This sweet little edging adds a touch of cluster charm to any project.

The stitch pattern is a multiple of 6 on the sides. Join the yarn 3 sts before the corner to the edge with a sl st, and ch 1.

Rnd 1 (RS): *Sc across edge in a multiple of 6, 3 sc in corner; rep from * around, sl st to 1st sc, do not turn.

Rnd 2: Sl st to next sc, ch 1, sc in same sc, *ch 2, sk 2 sc, [sc, ch 5, sc] in corner sc, **ch 2, sk 2 sc, sc in next sc, ch 3, sk 2 sc, sc in next sc; rep from ** to sc 2 sts away from corner; rep from * around, sl st to 1st sc, turn.

Rnd 3: Sl st in next ch-3 sp, ch 3, [2 dc-cl, ch 3, 3 dc-cl] in same ch-3 sp, *[3 dc-cl, ch 3, 3 dc-cl] in ea ch-3 sp to corner ch-5 sp, [(3 dc-cl, ch 3) twice 3 dc-cl] in corner ch-5 sp; rep from * around, sl st to 1st 2 dc-cl, turn.

Rnd 4: Sl st to next 3 dc-cl, sl st to next ch-3 sp, [(sc, ch 2) 4 times, sc] in ea ch-3 sp around, sl st to 1st sc, fasten off.

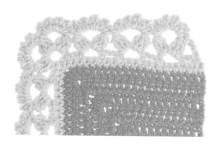

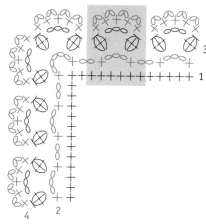

Kika Shell Edging

This exotic edging mixes solid shells with large chain spaces twice for a stacked and dramatic effect.

Picot: Ch 3, sl st in 1st ch.

The stitch pattern is a multiple of 9 plus 3 on the sides. Join the yarn to the edge with a sl st, and ch 1.

Rnd 1 (RS): *Sc across edge in a multiple of 9 plus 3, 3 sc in corner; rep from * around, sl st to 1st sc, turn.

Rnd 2: Ch 7 (counts as dc, ch-4 sp), sk 2 sc, *[dc, ch 6, dc] in corner sc, **ch 4, sk 2 sc, dc in next sc; rep from ** to 2 st from corner sc, ch 4, sk 2 sc; rep from * around to t-ch, ch 2, hdc in 3rd ch of t-ch (counts as ch-4 sp), turn.

Rnd 3: Ch 1, sc around post of hdc, *[3 dc, ch 2, 3 dc] in next ch-4 sp, sc in next ch-4 sp, ch 4, sc in next ch-4 sp; rep from * to corner ch-5 sp, [3 dc, ch 2, 6 dc, ch 2, 3 dc] in ch-5 sp, sc in next ch-4 sp, ch 4, sc in next ch-4 sp; rep from * around to 1st sc, ch 2, hdc in 1st sc (counts as ch-4 sp), turn.

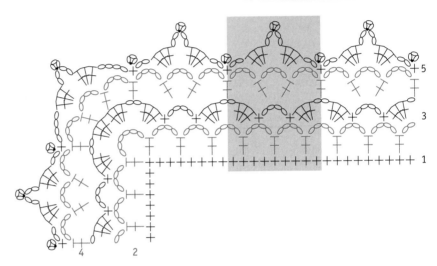

Rnd 4: Ch 7 (counts as dc, ch-4 sp), *dc in ch-2 sp, ch 4, [dc, ch 4, dc] in btw 3rd and 4th dc, ch 4, dc in ch-2 sp, **ch 4, [dc, ch 4, dc] in next ch-4 sp, ch 4, dc in next ch-2 sp; rep from ** to corner; rep from * around to last ch-2 sp, ch 4, dc in last ch-4 sp, ch 4, sl st to 3rd ch of t-ch, turn.

Rnd 5: Sl st in ch-4 sp, ch 3 (counts as dc), [2 dc, ch 2, picot, ch 2, 3 dc] in same ch-4 sp, ch 2, *sc in next dc, picot, ch 2, sk next ch-4 sp, [3 dc, ch 2, picot, ch 2, 3 dc] in next ch-4 sp, ch 2, sk next ch-4 sp; rep from * across to corner ch-4 sps, sc in next dc, picot, ch 4, sk next ch-4 sp, [3 dc, ch 2, picot, ch 2, 3 dc] in next ch-4 sp, ch 4, sk next ch-4 sp; rep from * around, sc in next dc, picot, ch 2, sl st to top of t-ch, fasten off.

Maria Shell Edging

The picots the shells on this edging are reminiscent of time gone by.

Picot: Ch 3, sl st to 1st ch.

Shell (sh): [(2 dc, picot) twice, dc, (picot, 2 dc) twice] in st indicated.

The stitch pattern is a multiple of 7 plus 5 on the sides. Join the yarn to the edge with a sl st, and ch 1.

Rnd 1 (RS): *Sc across edge in a multiple of 7 plus 5, 3 sc in corner; rep from * around, sl st to 1st sc, turn.

Rnd 2: Ch 1, sc in 1st sc, *3 sc in corner sc, sc in ea sc across to corner; rep from * around, sl st to 1st sc, turn.

Rnd 3: Ch 3 (counts as dc), dc in next 4 sc, *ch 4, sk 2 sc, dc in next 5 sc; rep from * across to corner, ch 4, sk 2 sc, [dc, ch 4, dc] in corner sc; rep from * around, ch 2, hdc in top of t-ch, turn.

Rnd 4: Ch 4 (counts as tr), 2 tr in 1st ch-sp, *ch 5, sk corner ch-4 sp, [3 tr, ch 5, 3 tr] in next ch-4 sp and ea ch-sp across to corner ch-sp; rep from * around to 1st ch-sp, 3 tr in 1st ch-sp, ch 5, sl st to top of t-ch, turn.

Rnd 5: Sl st in 1st ch-5 sp, ch 3 (counts as dc), [dc, picot, 2 dc, picot, dc, (picot, 2 dc) twice] in same ch-5 sp, sh in ea ch-5 sp around, sl st to top of t-ch, fasten off.

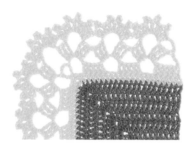

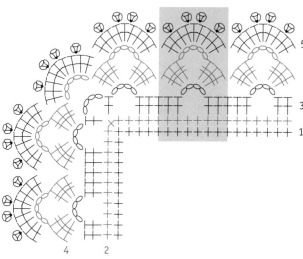

Sorbet Shell Edging

This delicate edging looks much more complex and adds a dramatic ending to any project.

Picot: Ch 3, sl st in 1st ch.

The stitch pattern is a multiple of 3 on the sides. Join the yarn to the edge with a sl st, and ch 1.

Rnd 1 (RS): *Sc across edge in a multiple of 3, 3 sc in corner; rep from * around, sl st to 1st sc, turn.

Rnd 2: Sl st in next sc, ch 1, *[sc, ch 5, sc] in corner sc, **ch 5, sk 3 sc, sc in next sc; rep from ** across to corner, ch 5, sk 3 sc; rep from * around ch 2, dc in 1st sc, turn.

Rnd 3: Ch 1, sc in dc, *[ch 5, sc in next ch-5 sp] twice, 7 dc in next ch-5 sp, sc in next ch-5 sp; rep from * across to last 3 ch-5 sps before corner, [sc in next ch-5 sp, ch 5] twice, sc in next ch-5 sp, 9 dc in corner ch-5 sp, sc in next ch-5 sp; rep from * around, sl st to 1st sc, turn.

Rnd 4: Sl st to 1st dc, ch 4 (counts as dc, ch-1 sp), *[dc, ch 1] in ea dc to last dc, dc in last dc, sc in next ch-5 sp, ch 5, sc in next ch-5 sp; rep from * around, sl st to 3rd ch of t-ch, turn.

Rnd 5: Ch 1, *[(sc, ch 2) 4 times, sc] in next ch-5 sp, [2 sc, ch 2] in ea ch-1 sp to last, 2 sc in last ch-1 sp; rep from * around, sl st to 1st sc, fasten off.

Gemma Edging

The layered edging adds a sweet-as-can-be touch to afghans or skirts.

The stitch pattern is a multiple of 4 plus 2 on the sides. Join the yarn to the edge with a sl st, and ch 1.

Large Outside Edging

Rnd 1 (RS): *Sc across edge in a multiple of 4 plus 2, 3 sc in corner; rep from * around, sl st to 1st sc, do not turn.

Rnd 2: Sl st in next 2 sc, ch 3 (counts as dc), dc-blp in next sc, *ch 3, sk 2 sc, dc-blp in next 2 sc; rep from * across to 3rd st from corner sc, ch 3, sk 2 sc, dc-blp in next sc, [dc-blp, ch 3, dc-blp] in corner sc, dc-blp in next sc; rep from * around, ch 1, hdc to top of t-ch, do not turn.

Rnd 3: Ch 1, sc around hdc, *ch 5, sc in next ch-3 sp; rep from * across to corner ch-sp, ch 5, [sc, ch 5, sc] in corner ch-sp; rep from * around to 1st sc, ch 2, dc in 1st sc, do not turn.

Rnd 4: Ch 3 (counts as dc), dc around dc post, *ch 3, 2 dc in next ch-5 sp; rep from * across to corner ch-sp, ch 3, [2 dc, ch 3, 2 dc] in corner ch-sp; rep from * around to t-ch, ch 1, hdc in top of t-ch, do not turn.

Rnd 5: Ch 1, sc around hdc post, *ch 5, sc in ch-3 sp; rep from * across to corner ch-sp, ch 5, [sc, ch 5, sc] in corner ch-sp; rep from * around, ch 5, sl st to 1st sc, do not turn.

Rnd 6: Ch 1, *4 sc in next ch-5 sp, [(ch 3, dc, ch 3, sl st) 3 times] in 4th sc, 3 sc in same ch-5 sp; rep from * around, sl st to 1st sc, fasten off.

Small Inside Edging

Rnd 2 (RS): Join yarn 4th st after corner sc on rnd 1, ch 3 (counts as dc), dc-flp in next sc (going in the unused lp), *ch 3, sk 2 sc, dc-flp in next 2 sc; rep from * across to 3rd st from corner sc, ch 3, sk 2 sc, dc-flp in next sc, [dc-flp, ch 3, dc-flp] in corner sc, dc-flp in next sc; rep from * around, ch 1, hdc to top of t-ch, do not turn.

Rnd 3: Ch 1, sc around hdc, *ch 5, sc in next ch-3 sp; rep from * across to corner ch-sp, ch 5, [sc, ch 7, sc] in corner ch-sp; rep from * around to 1st sc, ch 5, sl st to 1st sc, do not turn.

Rnd 4: Ch 1, *4 sc in next ch-5 sp, [(ch 4, sl st) 3 times] in 4th sc, 3 sc in same ch-5 sp; rep from * around, sl st to 1st sc, fasten off.

Clover Edging

The clovers on the last round of this fabric join together for an incredibly unique edging.

Clover: Ch 7, sl st in prev clover last dc, dc in 5th ch, ch 4, sl st in same ch, [ch 4, dc in same ch, ch 4, sl st in same ch] twice, ch 3.

The stitch pattern is a multiple of 6 on the sides. Join the yarn to the edge with a sl st, and ch 1.

Rnd 1 (RS): *Sc across edge in a multiple of 6, 3 sc in corner; rep from * around, sl st to 1st sc, do not turn.

Rnd 2: Sl st in next sc, turn, ch 1, sc in same sc, *ch 2, sk 2 sc, [sc, ch 5, sc] in corner sc, **ch 2, sk 2 sc, sc in next sc, ch 3, sk 2 sc, sc in next sc; rep from ** across to 2 sts before corner sc; rep from * around, sl st to 1st sc, turn.

Rnd 3: Ch 2, 4 dc-cl in next ch-3 sp, ch 8, dc in 5th ch, ch 4, sl st in same ch, [ch 4, dc in same ch, ch 4, sl st in same ch] twice (clover made), ch 3, 4 dc-cl in same ch-3 sp, sk ch-2 sp, *4 dc-cl in next ch-3 sp, clover, ch 3, 4 dc-cl in same ch-3 sp; rep from * across to corner ch-5 sp, [(4 dc-cl twice, 4 dc-cl in corners ch-5 sp, sl st to 1st 4 dc-cl, fasten off.

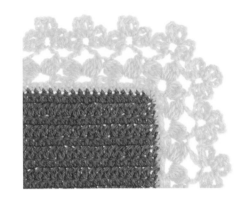

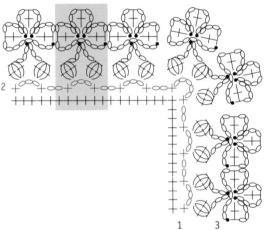

Mari Cluster Edging

The sweet little clusters look like peas in a pod nestled between the half double crochet borders for this geometric edging.

The stitch pattern is a multiple of 3 plus 2 on the sides. Join the yarn to the edge with a sl st, and ch 1.

Rnd 1 (RS): *Sc across edge in a multiple of 3 plus 2 to corner, 3 sc in corner; rep from * around, sl st to 1st sc, turn, sl st back to last sc, turn.

Rnd 2: Ch 5 (counts as hdc, ch 3), 2 dc-cl in 3rd ch from hk, sk next 2 sc, hdc in next sc, *ch 3, 2 dc-cl in 3rd ch from hk, sk 2 sc, hdc in next sc, rep from * across to corner, ch 3, 2 dc-cl in 3rd ch from hk, sk 1 sc, hdc in next sc; rep from * around, sl st to 2nd ch of t-ch, do not turn.

Rnd 3: Ch 4 (counts as hdc, ch-2 sp), hdc in next hdc, *ch 2, hdc in next hdc; rep from * to corner, ch 7, hdc in next hdc at corner; rep from * around, sl st to 2nd ch of t-ch, do not turn.

Rnd 4: Ch 1, sc in same ch of t-ch, 2 sc in all ch-2 sps across, sc in all hdc, 9 sc in all ch-7 sps, sl st to 1st sc, fasten off.

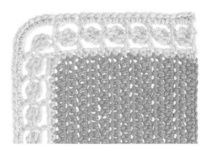

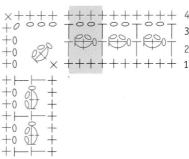

Aragon Crossed Edging

X-, Y-, and P-stitches are so different to crochet yet leave a classic-looking stitch. This edging will look like a lattice on the end of your next project with some shells on the edge.

X-Stitch (X-st): Yo 3 times, insert hk into next st indicated, yo, pull up a lp, yo, draw though 2 lps on the hk, yo, sk next st, insert hk into next st, yo, pull up a lp, yo, draw through 2 lps, yo, draw through 3 lps, yo, draw through 2 lps, yo, draw though last 2 lps, ch 1, dc into middle horiz bar of st just made (at the intersection of the bottom legs of the st).

Y-Stitch (Y-st): Dtr in st indicated, [ch 1, dc into middle horiz bar of st just made] 3 times.

P-Stitch (P-st): Dtr in st indicated, ch 1, dc into middle horiz bar of st just made.

Picot: Ch 3, sl st to 1st ch.

Shell (sh): [Dc, ch 1, (dc, picot) twice, dc, ch 1, dc] in st indicated.

Corner Shell (corner sh): [Dc, ch 1, (dc, picot) 5 times, dc, ch 1, dc] in st indicated.

The stitch pattern is a multiple of 6 plus 5 on the sides. Join the yarn to the edge with a sl st, and ch 1.

Rnd 1 (RS): *Sc across edge in a multiple of 6 plus 5 sts, 3 sc in corner; rep from * around, sl st to 1st sc, turn.

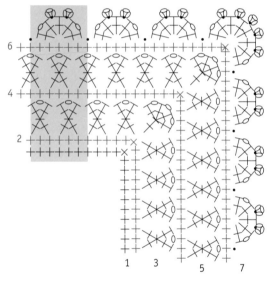

Rnd 2: Ch 1, sc in 1st 2 sc, *3 sc in corner sc, sc in ea sc across to corner; rep from * around, sl st to 1st sc, turn.

Rnd 3: Sl st in 1st sc, ch 2, sk 1 sc, P-st in next sc, *X-st over next 3 sc and ea group of 3 sc across to corner sc, Y-st in corner sc, X-st in corner sc and 2 sts away; rep from * around, sl st to top of P-st, turn.

Rnd 4: Ch 1, 3 sc in ea ch-1 sp around, sl st to 1st sc, turn.

Rnd 5: Sl st in next 2 sc, ch 2, sk 1 sc, P-st in next sc, *X-st over next 3 sc and ea group of 3 sc across to corner sc, Y-st in corner sc, X-st in corner sc and 2 sts away; rep from * around, sl st to top of P-st, turn.

Rnd 6: Rep rnd 4.

Rnd 7: Sl st in next 2 sc, *sk 2 sc, sh in next sc, sk 2 sc, sl st in next sc; rep from * across to corner sc, corner sh in corner sc, sk 2 sc, sl st in next sc; rep from * around, fasten off.

Chrysler Edging

The unique construction on this ending adds an architectural touch to any project.

Picot: Ch 3, sl st to 1st ch.

Shell (sh): [(Dc, ch 1) twice, dc, picot, dc, (ch 1, dc) twice] in st indicated.

Corner Shell (corner sh): [(Dc, ch 1) 3 times, dc, picot, dc, (ch 1, dc) 3 times] in st indicated.

Petal: [(Ch 1, dc) 4 times, picot, (dc, ch 1) 4 times] in st indicated.

The stitch pattern is a multiple of 8 plus 5 on the sides. Join the yarn to the edge with a sl st, and ch 1.

Rnd 1 (RS): *Sc across edge in a multiple of 8 plus 5, 3 sc in corner; rep from * around, sl st to 1st sc, do not turn.

Rnd 2: Sl st to next 2 sc, ch 1, sc in same sc, *ch 2, sk 3 sc, [2 dc, ch 2, 2 dc] in next sc, sk 3 sc, ch 2, sc in next sc; rep from * across to 3 sts from corner sc, ch 2, [(2 dc, ch 2) twice, 2 dc] in corner sc, ch 2, sk 3 sc, sc in next sc; rep from * around, sl st in 1st sc, do not turn.

Rnd 3: Ch 9, sl st in 6th ch from hk, ch 2, *sk next ch-2 sp, [sc, ch 2, sc] in next ch-2 sp, ch 2, sk next ch-2 sp, dc in sc, ch 6, sl st-flp in prev dc, ch 2; rep from * across to corner, sk next ch-2 sp, [sc, ch 2, sc] in next ch-2 sp, ch 2, dc in btw next 2 dc, ch 6, sl st-flp in prev dc, ch 2, [sc, ch 2, sc] in next ch-2 sp, ch 2, sk next ch-2 sp, dc in next sc, ch 6, sl st-flp in prev dc, ch 2; rep from * around, sl st to 3rd ch of t-ch, do not turn.

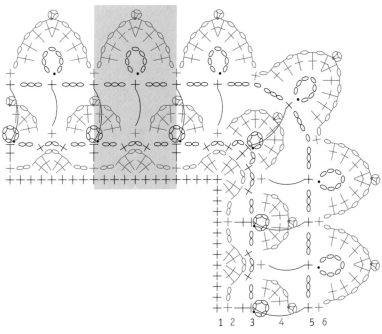

1 2   3   4   5 6

Rnd 4: Sl st in ch-6 sp, ch 4, [dc, ch 1, dc, picot, dc, (ch 1, dc) twice] in same ch-6 sp, *sk next ch-2 sp, sc in next ch-2 sp, sh in next ch-6 sp; rep from * across to corner, sk next ch-2 sp, sc in next ch-2 sp, corner sh in corner ch-6 sp; rep from * around, sl st to 3rd ch of t-ch, fasten off.

Rnd 5: Join yarn to dc on rnd 3 close to corner (behind shells), sc-blp in same dc, *ch 3, sc in sc on rnd 4, ch 7, sl st in prev sc, ch 3, sc-blp in next dc on rnd 3 (working behind shells); rep from * across to corner, ch 3, sc in sc on rnd 4, ch 7, sl st to prev sc, ch 7, sc-blp in corner dc on rnd 3, ch 7, sl st in prev sc, ch 7, sc in next sc on rnd 4, ch 7, sl st to prev sc, ch 3, sc-blp in next dc on rnd 3; rep from * around, sl st to 1st sc, do not turn.

Rnd 6: Ch 1, sc in 1st sc, *petal in next ch-7 sp, sc in next sc; rep from * around to corner, petal in next ch-7 sp, sc in next ch-7 sp, petal in next ch-7 sp, sc in next ch-7 sp; rep from * around, sl st to 1st sc, fasten off.

Lucky Clover Edging

The clover flowers on this edging make it a perfect ending for any garden-themed project.

The stitch pattern is a multiple of 6 plus 3 on the sides. Join the yarn to the edge with a sl st, and ch 1.

Rnd 1 (RS): *Sc across edge in a multiple of 6 plus 3, 3 sc in corner; rep from * around, sl st to 1st sc, turn.

Rnd 2: Sl st to corner sc, *[sc, ch 3, sc] in corner sc, **ch 3, sk 2 sc, sc in next sc; rep from ** across to corner; rep from * around, sl st to 1st sc, turn.

Rnd 3: Ch 1, sc in 1st sc, *ch 3, 3 dc-cl in prev sc, tr in next sc, [ch 3, 2 dc-cl, ch 3, sl st to prev tr] twice, [ch 3, 3 dc-cl] in same tr, sc in next sc; rep from * to corner, ch 3, 3 dc-cl in prev sc, tr in next ch-3 sp, [ch 3, 2 dc-cl, ch 3, sl st to prev tr] twice, [ch 3, 3 dc-cl] in same tr, sc in next sc; rep from * around, sl st to 1st sc, fasten off.

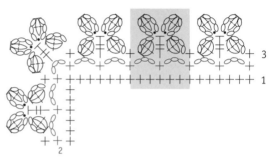

St. Basil Edging

Just as the roof of St. Basil's Cathedral is so distinct, this extraordinary edging will turn heads on your next project.

Picot: Ch 3, sl st to 1st ch.

The stitch pattern is a multiple of 12 plus 7 on the sides. Join the yarn to the edge with a sl st, and ch 1.

Rnd 1 (RS): *Sc across edge in a multiple of 12 plus 7, 3 sc in corner; rep from * around, sl st to 1st sc, turn.

Rnd 2: Sl st to corner sc, ch 1, sc in corner sc, *ch 4, sk 2 sc, sc in next sc, **ch 4, sk 3 sc, sc in next sc; rep from ** across to 2 sts from corner sc, ch 4, sk 2 sc, sc in corner sc; rep from * around, sl st to 1st sc, turn.

Row 3: Ch 1, 9 sc in next 2 ch-4 sps, 5 sc in next ch-4 sp, turn.

Row 4: Ch 7, sk 9 sc, sc in next sc, ch 6, sk 9 sc, sc in next sc, turn.

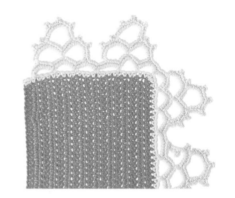

Row 5: Ch 1, [(3 sc, picot) twice, 6 sc] in next ch-6 sp, 5 sc in next ch-7 sp, turn.

Row 6: Ch 9, sk 9 sc, sc in next sc, turn.

Row 7: Ch 1, [(3 sc, picot) 3 times, 3 sc] in ch-9 sp, sc in last sc on row 5, [sc, (picot, 3 sc) twice] in ch-7 sp on row 4, sc in last sc on row 3, 4 sc in ch-4 sp on rnd 2, do not turn.

Rep rows 3–7 around, sl st to 1st sc on row 3, fasten off.

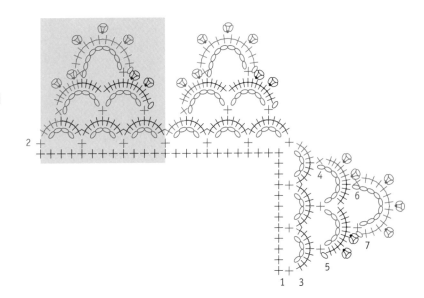

Anderlecht Edging

This classic Belgium lace crochet goes from classic to exceptional with the shell and picots on the last round that ruffle slightly.

Picot: Ch 3, sl st in 1st ch.

The stitch pattern can conform to any number of stitches on each side of the project. Ch 8.

Row 1 (RS): Dc in 6th ch from hk and next 2 ch, do not turn.

Row 2: Ch 2, sl st to edge of project, ch 2, turn, dc in ea dc across, turn.

Row 3: Ch 5, dc in ea dc across, do not turn.

Rep rows 2 and 3 across edge, evenly spacing the sl sts, at the corner; work rows 2 and 3 halfway between last sl st and corner, work a "rows 2–3" set at corner, place another set halfway from typical edge sets; rep around ending with a row 2, fasten off with long tail. Weave tail through 1st and last rows, seaming them tog.

Last row: Join yarn to a ch-5 sp, ch 1, [3 sc, picot, 3 sc] in same ch-5 sp, *[2 sc, dc, picot, tr, picot, dtr, picot, tr, picot, dc, 2 sc] in next ch-5 sp, [3 sc, picot, 3 sc] in next ch-5 sp; rep from * around, sl st to 1st sc, fasten off.

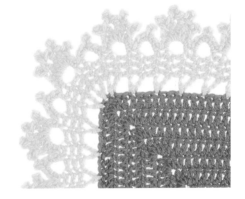

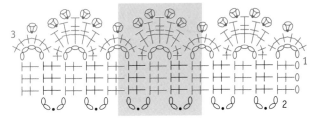

Flapper Edging

This edging is partially filet crochet and partially Belgium lace crochet, producing a lacy special ending to your project.

The stitch pattern can conform to any number of stitches on each side of the project. Ch 11, sl st to the edge, ch 2, sl st to the edge, and turn.

Row 1 (WS): Dc in next 5 ch, ch 3, sk 2 ch, sc in next ch, ch 3, dc in last ch, ch 5, sl st to 1st ch, turn.

Row 2: [Sc, 2 hdc, 5 dc] in ch-5 sp, dc in dc, ch 5, dc in next dc, ch 4, dc in sl st, sl st to edge, do not turn.

Row 3: Ch 2, sl st to edge, turn, 4 dc in ch-4 sp, dc in next dc, ch 3, sc in ch-5 sp, ch 3, dc in next dc, ch 5, sl st in same dc, turn.

Rep rows 2 and 3 across edge, evenly spacing the sl sts, at the corner: work rows 2 and 3 halfway between last sl st and corner, work rows 2 and 3 at corner, place another set halfway from typical edge sets; rep around ending with a row 2, fasten off with long tail. Weave tail through 1st and last rows, seaming them together.

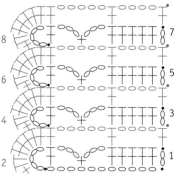

Ruffle Edging

This Victorian edging is actually a Belgium lace modified with shells. The heavy double crochet shells on the last round curl to ruffle around your project.

Shell (sh): [(Dc, ch 2) 3 times, dc] in st indicated.

The stitch pattern can conform to any number of stitches on each side of the project. Join the yarn to the edge with a sl st.

Row 1 (RS): Ch 9, sh in 6th ch, ch 2, sl st to edge, turn, ch 2.

Row 2: Sk 1st ch-2 sp on sh, sh in next ch-2 sp, ch 5, turn.

Row 3: Sk 1st ch-2 sp on sh, sh in next ch-2 sp, ch 2, sl st to edge, turn, ch 2.

Rep rows 2 and 3 across edge evenly spacing the sl sts, at the corner; work rows 2 and 3 halfway between last sl st and corner, work rows 2 and 3 at corner, place another set halfway from typical edge sets; rep around ending with a row 2, do not fasten off.

Last row: Sk 1st ch-2 sp on sh, 6 dc in next ch-2 sp, dc in next ch-2 sp, 9 dc in next and ea ch-5 sp around, 9 dc in t-ch sp, ch 2, sl st to 1st ch, fasten off.

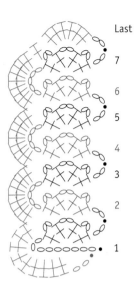

Bubble Edging

You can use this unusual pattern as an edging, or it can stand alone as a scarf or bracelet.

The stitch pattern can conform to any number of stitches on each side of the project.

Beginning Circle: Ch 9, sl st to 1st ch to form ring, ch 3, 18 dc in ring, sl st to edge, 5 dc in ring, sl st to top of t-ch, do not turn, cont to circle A.

Circle A: Ch 7, sl st to 4th ch to form ring, ch 2, sl st to 1st ch, 3 dc in ring, sl st to edge, 3 dc in ring, do not turn, cont to circle B.

Circle B: Ch 13, sl st to 9th ch to form ring, ch 2, sl st to 1st ch, 6 dc in ring, sl st to edge, 6 dc in ring, do not turn, cont to next circle.

Rep circle B, circle A, circle B around, ending with a circle A.

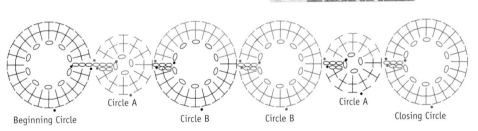

Beginning Circle   Circle A   Circle B   Circle B   Circle A   Closing Circle

Closing Circle: Ch 13, sl st to 9th ch to form ring, ch 2, sl st to 1st ch, 6 dc in ring, sl st to edge, 17 dc in ring, sl st to t-ch, cont to circle A.

Circle A: 5 dc in ring, sl st to t-ch, cont to circle B.

Circle B: 11 dc in ring, sl st to t-ch, cont to next circle.

Rep circles A and B to end. Fasten off.

Glossary

Abbreviations

BPsc	back post single crochet
BPdc	back post double crochet
BPtr	back post treble crochet
blp	through back loop(s) only
btw	between
ch	chain
ch-sp	chain space
cont	continue
dc	double crochet
dc-cl	double crochet cluster
dtr	double treble crochet
ea	each
esc	extended single crochet
eesc	extra extended single crochet
esk	edge Solomon's knot
est	established
fdc	foundation double crochet
flp	through front loop(s) only
foll	follow/follows/following
FPsc	front post single crochet
FPhdc	front post half double crochet
FPdc	front post double crochet
FPtr	front post treble crochet
fsc	foundation single crochet
fwd	forward pass
hdc	half double crochet
hdc-cl	half double crochet cluster
lp(s)	loop(s)
msk	main Solomon's knot

opp	opposite
patt	pattern
pop	popcorn
prev	previous
rem	remain/remaining
rep	repeat(s)
rev sc	reverse single crochet
rnd	round
RS	right side
rtn	return pass
sc	single crochet
sh	shell
sk	skip
sl st	slip stitch
st(s)	stitch(es)
t-ch	turning chain
tog	together
tr	treble crochet
tr-cl	treble crochet cluster
Tss	Tunisian simple stitch
Tks	Tunisian knit stitch
Tps	Tunisian purl stitch
Tdc	Tunisian double crochet
WS	wrong side
yo	yarn over
*	repeat instructions following asterisk as directed
**	repeat all instructions between asterisks as directed
( )	alternate instructions
[ ]	work bracketed instructions specified number of times

Symbols

Basic Stitches
○ ch
• sl st
+ sc
T hdc
⊤ dc
‡ tr
⧧ dtr
⧻ triple tr
⧼ quad tr

Cluster Stitches
⋂ 2hdc-cl
⋔ 3hdc-cl
⨎ 2dc-cl
⨸ 3dc-cl
⨁ 4dc-cl
⨁ pop
⟨⟩ 2tr-cl
⨁ 3tr-cl

Special Stitches
⋏ sc2tog
⸸ esc
⸸ fsc
⸸ sc spike
⸸ linked dc
⸌ BPdc
⸸ FPdc
⋏ dc2tog
⸸ esk
⸸ msk

Tunisian Stitches
⌐ Tss
⌐ Tps
⌐ Tks
⌐ Tdc
⌐ Tes
⌐ twisted st
⌐ Tss bet sts
⌐ Tss in top bar
⌐ chain
⌐ slipped st
⌐ dc cluster
⌐ Tss dec
⌐ Tss shell

Crochet Techniques

Adjustable Ring   Make a large loop with the yarn crossing the end of the yarn over the working strand. Holding the loop with your fingers, insert the hook into the loop and pull the working strand through. Chain 1 to lock the loop. Continue to work the indicated number of stitches into the loop. Pull on the strand's end to close the loop.

Stitch Pattern Repeat   The stitches highlighted in gray in the charts, are duplicated on the same row to create the stitch pattern.

Turning Chain (t-ch)   The turning chain is the beginning of every row or round, whether it is one or five chains. The turning chain always counts as a stitch in the row or round, unless it is before a single crochet.

Crochet Stitches

Crochet Chain (ch)   Make a slipknot and place it on the hook. Yarn over and draw through the loop on the hook.

Slip Stitch (sl st)   Insert the hook into the stitch, yarn over and draw a loop through the stitch and loop on the hook.

Single Crochet (sc)   Insert the hook into the stitch, yarn over and draw up a loop, yarn over and draw through both loops on the hook.

Single Crochet Together (sc#tog)   *Insert the hook into the next indicated stitch, yarn over and draw up a loop; repeat from * # times total, yarn over and draw through the remaining loops on the hook.

Half Double Crochet (hdc)   Yarn over, insert the hook into the stitch, yarn over and draw up a loop (3 loops on hook), yarn over and draw through all loops on the hook.

Half Double Crochet Cluster (#hdc-cl)   [Yarn over, insert the hook into the indicated stitch, yarn over and draw up a loop] # times total in the same stitch, yarn over and draw through the remaining loops on the hook.

Double Crochet (dc)   Yarn over, insert the hook into the stitch, yarn over and draw up a loop (3 loops on hook), yarn over and draw through 2 loops, yarn over and draw through the remaining 2 loops.

Double Crochet Together (dc#tog)   *Yarn over, insert the hook into the next indicated stitch, yarn over and draw up a loop, yarn over and draw the yarn through 2 loops on the hook; repeat from * # times total, yarn over and draw through the remaining loops on the hook.

Double Crochet Cluster (#dc-cl)   [Yarn over, insert the hook into the indicated stitch, yarn over and draw up a loop, yarn over and draw through 2 loops on the hook] # times total in the same stitch, yarn over and draw through the remaining loops on the hook.

Treble Crochet (tr)   Yarn over twice, insert the hook into the stitch, yarn over and draw up a loop (4 loops on hook), yarn over and draw through 2 loops, yarn over and draw through the next 2 loops, yarn over and draw through the remaining 2 loops on the hook.

Treble Crochet Cluster (#tr-cl)   [Yarn over twice, insert the hook into the indicated stitch, yarn over and draw up a loop,(yarn over and draw through 2 loops on the hook) twice] # times total in same stitch, yarn over and draw through the remaining loops on the hook.

Double Treble Crochet (dtr)   Yarn over 3 times, insert the hook into the stitch, yarn over and draw up a loop (5 loops on hook), (yarn over and draw through 2 loops on the hook) 4 times.

Front Post (FP)   Complete the stitch around the post of the next indicated stitch by inserting the hook from front to back to front around the post.

Back Post (BP)   Complete the stitch around the post of the next indicated stitch by inserting the hook from back to front to back around the post.

Tunisian Crochet Stitches

Tunisian Simple Stitch (Tss)   **Forward:** (Loop on hook counts as first stitch), insert the hook into the vertical bar of the next stitch and pull up a loop, repeat across the row to the last stitch, insert the hook under 2 loops of the last stitch and pull up a loop. **Return:** Yarn over and pull through 1 loop on the hook, *yarn over and pull through 2 loops on the hook, repeat from * to end.

Tunisian Purl Stitch (Tps)   **Forward:** (Loop on hook counts as first stitch), *move the yarn to the front of the work, insert the hook into the vertical bar of the next stitch, yarn over and pull up a loop, repeat from * across the row to the last stitch, insert the hook under 2 loops of the last stitch and pull up a loop. **Return:** Yarn over and pull through 1 loop on the hook, *yarn over and pull through 2 loops on the hook, repeat from * to end.

Tunisan Knit Stitch (Tks)   **Forward:** (Loop on hook counts as first stitch), *insert the hook from front to back between the front and back vertical bars and under all horizontal bars of the next stitch, yarn over and pull up a loop, repeat from * across to the last stitch, insert the hook under 2 loops of the last stitch and pull up a loop. **Return:** Yarn over and pull through 1 loop on the hook, *yarn over and pull through 2 loops on the hook, repeat from * to end.

Tunisian Double Crochet (Tdc)   **Forward:** Ch 1 (counts as first st), *yarn over, insert the hook behind the vertical bar of the stitch as for Tunisian simple stitch, yarn over and pull a loop through the stitch, yarn over and draw through 2 loops, leaving the last loop on the hook; repeat from * across to the last stitch, yarn over, insert the hook under 2 loops of the last stitch and pull up a loop, yarn over and draw through 2 loops on the hook. **Return:** Yarn over and pull through 1 loop on the hook, *yarn over and pull through 2 loops on the hook, repeat from * to end.

Work off Loops as Normal   **Return:** Yarn over, pull through 1 loop on the hook, *yarn over and pull through 2 loops on the hook, repeat from * to end.